SUNY Series in
Chinese Philosophy and Culture

David L. Hall and Roger T. Ames, Editors

The Tao Encounters the West

Explorations in Comparative Philosophy

Chenyang Li

State University of New York Press

Cover illustration: Chinese, *The Three Religions* (San-chiao t'u)
Ming Dynasty (1368–1644)
Hanging scroll, ink and color on silk
57-3/4″ × 29″ (146.7 × 73.7 cm.)
(Original screened by the publisher for design
purposes)

Courtesy The Nelson-Atkins Museum of Art, Kansas City, Missouri
(Gift of Bronson Trevor in honor of his father, John B. Trevor)

Production by Ruth Fisher
Marketing by Nancy Farrell

Published by
State University of New York Press, Albany

For information, address the State University of New York Press,
State University Plaza, Albany, NY 12246

Library of Congress Cataloging-in-Publication Data
Li, Chenyang 李晨阳, 1956–
   The Tao encounters the West : explorations in comparative
philosophy / Chenyang Li.
      p.   cm. — (SUNY series in Chinese philosophy and culture)
   Includes bibliographical references and index.
   ISBN 0-7914-4135-0 (alk. paper). — ISBN 0-7914-4136-9 (pbk. :
alk. paper)
   1. Philosophy, Confucian. 2. Philosophy. 3. Philosophy,
Comparative. 4. East and West. 5. Democracy—China. I. Title.
II. Series.
B127.C65L495   1999
181'.11—dc21
                                                            98–31714
                                                               CIP

10 9 8 7 6 5 4 3 2 1

To the memory of

my mother, Wang Shu-ying 王淑英 (1932–1980)
and my father, Li Ren-jie 李仁杰 (1927–1994)

Contents

Acknowledgments

The conception of this book started more than eight years ago when I first began doing comparative philosophy. During these years I have benefited from more people than I can name here. Professor Joel J. Kupperman, my mentor at the University of Connecticut, has given me continuous moral and professional support. At various times he read drafts of individual chapters and provided me with invaluable comments and suggestions. Without his encouragement and help, this book would never have been written. My deepest gratitude goes to him.

I was fortunate to become friends with Professor Walter Benesch of the University of Alaska Fairbanks, chair of the Department of Philosophy and Humanities when I taught there 1992–93. Walter's expertise in Asian and comparative philosophy, his sense of humor, and his resounding laughter, have inspired me ever since. He was kind enough on two occasions to read the whole manuscript, offered numerous critiques and suggestions, and edited English expressions. To him, I am forever in debt.

I owe many thanks to Roger Ames, coeditor of this series. In the summer of 1994 when we were both visiting Beijing (Peking) University, I had a chance to bring up this book project to him. His support and encouragement have made the publication possible.

Thanks also to Acquiring Editor Nancy Ellegate, Production Editor Ruth Fisher, and Copy Editor David Hopkins at the State University of New York Press, for their patience and help throughout the process of producing this book. I would also like to thank my friends Qingjie (James) Wang and Xiaosi Yang for their comments and suggestions on various chapters and for their friendship; and the students in my Asian philosophy and religion class fall 1997 at

Monmouth College, with whom I shared chapters, particularly Thomas Siegel, who read the whole manuscript. Their comments helped me make the work more accessible to nonspecialist readers.

My wife Hong Xiao has given me persistent support. She not only undertook the primary responsibilities in raising our daughter and son, Fay and Hansen, who were born during the years I was writing this book, but also has served as an important intellectual resource for me.

I would also like to take this opportunity to acknowledge the Center for East Asian Studies and Midwest Faculty Seminar, both of the University of Chicago, the Center for Chinese Studies of the University of Michigan, and Monmouth College, for their generous support of this project.

All errors that may exist in this book are, of course, my sole responsibility.

While I used Chinese literature in Chinese and made most of the translations myself, I consulted numerous existing English versions. Some of my translations are based on these versions. I hereby gratefully acknowledge my debt to them. Works that I consulted most are: Wing-tsit Chan, *A Source Book in Chinese Philosophy* (Princeton, New Jersey: Princeton University Press, 1963); A. C. Graham, trans., *Chuang Tzu: The Inner Chapters* (London: George Allen & Unwin Ltd., 1981); D.C. Lau, *The Analects: Translated with an Introduction* (New York: Penguin Classics, 1979); D. C. Lau, *Mencius: Translated with an Introduction* (New York: Penguin Classics, 1970); Victor H. Mair, trans., *Wandering on the Way: Early Taoist Tales and Parables of Chuang Tzu* (New York: Bantam Books, 1994); Tu Wei-ming, *Centrality and Commonality: An Essay on Confucian Religiousness* (Albany: State University of New York Press, 1989).

An earlier version of several parts of this book have appeared in various journals. Chapter 1 was developed from my article "What-Being: Chuang Tzu versus Aristotle," *International Philosophical Quarterly* 33.3 (1993). The second half of chapter 3 was based on my article "Natural Kinds: Direct Reference, Realism, and the Impossibility of Necessary *A Posteriori* Truth," *Review of Metaphysics* 47.2 (1993). An early version of chapter 4 was published as "The Confucian Concept of *Jen* and the Feminist Ethics of Care: A Comparative

Study," in *Hypatia: A Journal of Feminist Philosophy* 9.1 (1994). Chapter 5 is an expansion of my article "Shifting Perspectives: Filial Morality Revisited," *Philosophy East and West* 47.2 (1997). An ancestor of chapter 6 has appeared as "How Can One Be a Taoist-Buddhist-Confucian?—A Chinese Illustration of Multiple Religious Participation," *International Review of Chinese Religion and Philosophy* 1 (1996). A brief version of chapter 7 appeared as "Confucian Value and Democratic Value," *Journal of Value Inquiry* 31.2 (1997). I appreciate the editors and publishers for giving me permission to use them in this book.

Introduction

The Problematic and Approach

For people who are interested in Chinese culture, contemporary times can be perplexing. On the one hand, scholars such as Joseph Levenson lament over what they see as the inevitable failing of Confucianism in the modern world.[1] Some think that with Confucianism and other major world traditions eventually becoming irrelevant in similar ways, we may have come to "the end of history," that is, humankind will have finally exhausted all viable systematic alternatives to Western liberal ideology.[2] On the other hand, one hears about the "third epoch" of Confucianism.[3] This ancient tradition is said to be approaching another high tide after its first two glorious appearances in history (i.e., classical Confucianism and Neo-Confucianism), and that having endured in Hong Kong, Taipei, Kyoto, and Seoul, it is being revived in mainland China, and will make its presence felt in New York, Paris, Cairo, and Madras.[4] What, then, will be the role of Confucianism, and indeed the Chinese cultural tradition as a whole, in today and tomorrow's world?

It is not the philosopher's job to predict the future, of course. Sometimes historic accidents will determine more than anything else what the future will be. The task of the philosopher is to look for the desirable (i.e., "oughtness") within the confines of the possible, and it is in this sense that my main concern in this book is with what should be the relation between tradition and modernization in China. More specifically, it is about Confucianism and democracy in

1

China. I shall argue for a future for China where both can coexist as independent value systems, and I shall advance this thesis with a comparative study of Chinese and Western ideas and philosophies of "being," "truth," "language," "ethics," "religion," and "values."

The book may be seen as a study of Chinese and Western versions of Tao. "Tao 道," as the word is used in Chinese, is not limited to Taoism; in all major Chinese systems it refers to the right way (the Way) or cosmic order even though different schools have different interpretations.[5] Chinese philosophy, therefore, may be seen as studies of various aspects of the Tao. Neither Chinese nor Western philosophy is homogeneous. There are, however, certain philosophies and philosophers who have had a defining influence within their own cultures and traditions, and I believe that a comparative study of these philosophies and philosophers can be used to demonstrate different thought patterns of the two cultures. Such a study illuminates the Chinese harmony model of life, which serves as a cornerstone of my argument for the coexistence of Confucianism and democracy.

This book serves a dual purpose. While each chapter contributes directly or indirectly to the main thesis, each also stands on its own as a comparative study of a specific dimension of Western and Chinese philosophical and ethicoreligious traditions.

Chapter 1, "Being: Perspective versus Substance," investigates the differences between Chinese ontology and Aristotelian ontology, which is the most influential in the West. Aristotle's view of being is a substance ontology, according to which the world is composed of various individual substances. The Chinese philosopher Zhuang Zi's 庄子 ontology, which reflects on the background of Chinese thinking in general, is a perspective ontology. According to this ontology, the being or identity of an entity is always contextually situated and perspective-dependent. These ontological differences occur at a fundamental level and thus underlie many other philosophical positions that distinguish Chinese from Western views. Communication and mutual understanding can be enhanced with a clear understanding of these differences. For example, the Chinese "contextual perspective" ontology has profound implications for people's attitudes toward many other significant aspects of life, including truth, morality, and religious practice. Because of the significance of Chinese ontology for Chinese philosophy in general, this first chapter not only provides the basis for chapter 2, on truth, it also has direct relevance to chapters 4 and 5 as the foundation of the Confucian understanding of "personhood."

Chapter 2, "Truth: Confucius and Heidegger," investigates various concepts of truth, which is a central value in the West and in China. In the West, truth is usually understood semantically; it is a relation between language and reality. The Chinese understand it primarily as a matter of being a good person, as a way of life; being true is the way to realize one's potential for becoming fully human. Different understandings of truth in Western and Chinese philosophies affect value judgments in significant ways. Heidegger is chosen here not because he represents a typical Western understanding of truth (he does not), but because he presents a root metaphor of truth that is shared by both the Chinese and the Westerner. Through exploring Heidegger's view on truth, this chapter demonstrates how the Chinese and Western notions of truth, although sharing the same common metaphor of "unveiling (*aletheia*)," lead in different directions. This understanding of Chinese truth as a way of life and self-realization provides further ground for discussion in chapters 4, 5, 6, and 7.

Chapter 3, "Language: Pragmatic versus Semantic," relates understandings of truth, as discussed in chapter 2, to language. This chapter treats various interpretations of the functions of language, the first and most important of which is the Confucian doctrine of the "rectification of names." The chapter then examines a contemporary Western theory of naming as found in Saul Kripke's account of the rigid designation of names, which presupposes an Aristotelian ontology. These two positions are based on different, yet perhaps equally strong intuitions about the nature of language. The Confucian account stresses its social function, but appears short on semantic theory. Kripke's account is solely semantic and logical, but seems to have left out language's social and pragmatic dimensions. While attempting to make the Confucian account of language more intelligible, this chapter provides a critique of Kripke's account within his own theoretical framework. In the discussion of the Chinese understanding of language, the reader is presented with another dimension of Chinese philosophy that reflects points raised in the preceding chapters.

Chapter 4, "Ethics: Confucian *Jen* and Feminist Care," is a study of Confucian ethics and feminist ethics that explores important similarities between these two value systems. The chapter attempts to treat the apparent opposition between feminism and Confucianism, between a philosophy that proposes a philosophical foundation for women's rights and a philosophy that has a notorious reputation for oppressing women. As David Hall and Roger Ames pointed out, "What from our [Western] perspective might appear radically novel may be found within an alternative cultural mainstream."[6] The text proposes that some "new" concepts in feminism also have their counterparts in Confucianism and that these counterparts were formed long before feminist movements in the West. Therefore, feminism may find in Confucianism an ally in the struggle with Western patriarchical traditions and, at the same time, under Confucian influence, countries like China may embrace feminism more readily than initially expected.

The relationship between "care" and "justice" has been a major issue for Western feminism.[7] Hopefully the study of the connection between Confucian *jen* and the feminist care undertaken in this chapter coupled with the conclusion drawn in chapter 7 will clarify from a Chinese perspective the relationship of "care" and "justice."

If one were to pinpoint one area that divides the Chinese and the West most clearly, in my opinion, it would be filial morality. Chapter 5, "Family: Duty versus Rights," examines the fundamental differences between the two sides on this issue. It presents various unsuccessful attempts by Western philosophers to justify or reject filial morality within their own conceptual frameworks, and then formulates the concept of filial morality as a fundamental human value in Confucianism. This chapter shows how basic problems in one tradition may not be problems at all in another; however, understanding this requires a holistic gestalt shift across traditions. This chapter operates both as an argument for, and an illustration of the conclusion to be drawn in chapter 7.

Chapter 6, "Religion: Multiple Participation versus Exclusionism," serves as a direct prelude to the concluding argument in chapter 7 that Confucianism and democracy are or can be two independent value systems in China. Chapter 6 shows that the Chinese attitude toward life is very different from that expressed in Western orthodox monotheisms. Chinese multiple religious practice is both a manifestation and a consequence of the Chinese "perspective ontology" and "epistemic-metaphysical" concepts of truth. With chapters 1 and 2 in mind, readers will see how this inclusive attitude toward multiple religious practice, seemingly impossible and unintelligible in Western traditions, makes perfect sense to the Chinese. In a way, this chapter provides a premodern solution to a postmodern problem, the problem of living with fragmented and contradictory values in today's world.

Chapter 7, "Justice: Confucian Values and Democratic Values," is a critical exposition of issues that are urgent for China today as it goes through modernization and democratization. This section discusses democracy within a philosophical context as a "value system" and considers its incompatibility with Confucianism. Unlike many New-Confucians 新儒家 today who advocate democratization of Confucianism as the solution to the problem of China's future, I argue in this chapter that the two are not compatible within a single value system and therefore a democratic Confucianism is impossible. However, based on some Chinese characteristics investigated in previous chapters, particularly chapters 4, 5, and 6, I propose to explore the possibility of the existence of democracy as an independent value system in China. Confucianism and democracy may well be seen to complement one another, as has been the case with the coexistence of Confucianism, Taoism, and Buddhism.

Comparative Philosophy as Bridge-Building

The methodology employed in this book is that of comparative philosophy. In a very loose sense, almost any kind of philosophy can be said to be comparative. Aristotle, for example, early in the Greek tradition already compared numerous philosophies. Most philosophers, however, tend to philosophize within one culture or tradition. A tradition provides a set of limited premises and one or a very limited number of acceptable methodologies. Thus, philosophers within one tradition usually work within a rather limited horizon. Comparative philosophy across traditions can broaden our horizons. Drawing from different philosophies gives us different perspectives and sheds new light on issues in any particular tradition, and it can help open our minds and generate new and creative insights. This is perhaps the greatest value of comparative philosophy.

I do not believe that the primary goal of comparative philosophy is to prove one view right and others wrong. As we do comparative philosophy, we compare doctrines and beliefs in major traditions that may have survived for hundreds, even thousands of years, and have proved themselves within their own contexts in time. An idea or doctrine may be criticized from other points of view; the final judgment, however, can only be made either within the idea's own cultural and philosophical context or by showing that the cultural tradition in which it is situated is entirely wrong. The latter in most cases seems highly unlikely if not impossible. If in comparative philosophy the emphasis is upon philosophizing as the processing of ideas and beliefs, not in philosophies as a collection of static end products, then criticizing views as "right" or "wrong" may not be as important or as interesting as explaining both their evolutionary development and their implications for the future.

In this book I try to build bridges across a cultural gap. The Chinese and the West are like two green lands separated by a river. The best way to connect them is to build bridges. While bridges do not eliminate the gap, they make it easier for people on both sides to communicate with and learn from each other; they make it possible for explorers from one side to reach the other side. After crossing the river over a bridge, one can extend one's explorations further on the other side. "Bridging" in this context does not only mean to look for similarities on both sides, but also to recognize differences, especially fundamental differences. While seeing similarities will bring us closer, seeing differences will enhance mutual understanding and tolerance. Crossing the bridge, a mindful person will want to find out how and why some things are similar and others are dissimilar. Either way, one can deepen understanding not only of one's own culture and values but also of the culture and values of others.

Cross-Cultural Translation as Metaphor

Doing comparative philosophy, one cannot avoid the problem of cross-cultural translation. In order to compare different philosophies on the same issue, we need to determine whether philosophers of different cultures and languages are discussing the same issue, despite their use of different terminology. One must determine whether one concept in one culture or language has a counterpart in another culture or language. This can be quite difficult.

Is cross-cultural translation possible? The answer to this question, I believe, depends on what one means by translation. Translation understood as a one-to-one correspondence between two languages, whether at the level of individual words or individual sentences, is usually impossible in philosophy. Most terms and sentences across two languages, particularly two as different as Chinese and English, simply do not match well. Yet, if one sees translation as a working process that provides a contextual direction in figuring out meanings in another language, then effective translation is definitely possible.

Perhaps languages such as Chinese and English do not match well because different peoples evolved in different environments, had different needs for language, and thereby developed different language patterns (words, expressions, ideas, and ideals, etc.). If one takes translation as a matching game, then one is likely to be led astray. For example, words like "Tao 道" and "*jen* 仁" probably cannot be matched in English. Even words for concrete objects do not always relate well. For instance, the Chinese use two distinct words "*e* 鵝" (pronounced like "er") and "*yan* 雁" for geese; *yan* fly whereas *e* are nonflying domestic geese.

In translation, one understandably looks for close correspondence between two languages. This can be misleading. Take the example of two triangles of similar size, one isosceles and the other not. When we try to match them together, they will overlap for the most part but some parts will not coincide. Now, suppose the only triangle someone knows is the isosceles triangle, how can we communicate the shape of the other triangle without long descriptions of it? Since the isosceles triangle is the closest thing that this person knows to the other triangle, we must take advantage of his knowledge of the isosceles triangle while at the same time being careful not to leave him with the impression that the other shape is also an *isosceles* triangle. Unable to see the other shape, he would tend to assume the other also has two equal sides—in translation this would be equivalent to an additional meaning that the reader inadvertently and innocently adds to the original meaning in the other language if he can know the word only through translation. In this process, he will inevitably miss some meaning of the original word that cannot be conveyed through a simple translation. As with the triangles, if the second triangle has a right angle, this feature may get lost entirely in translation.

Personally as a philosopher and speaker of both English and Chinese, I like to think of cross-cultural translation as metaphors. As metaphor, translation is always context-dependent. Whether a metaphor is apt depends on the purpose for which the metaphor is used, and without context or purpose, one cannot ask whether a metaphor is apt or not. With metaphors, we make sense of one thing in terms of a different thing. Clearly a metaphor is never a perfect match between two terms, ideas, or things. The two entities involved in a metaphor have similarities and differences. In order for the metaphor to work, that is, to communicate an idea, we need to focus on the similarities and ignore the differences. The listener or reader does not get the point until he grasps these similarities. However, as soon as he overinterprets the similarities as the only characteristics present, he has pushed the metaphor too far. This often happens in translation. As in the example cited above, the Chinese word "*e*" is usually rendered in English as "goose." This translation works well until one thinks that some "*e*" fly (wild geese) and some do not (domestic geese). The fact is that in Chinese "*e*" only designates nonflying domestic geese. That "*e*" means "goose" is metaphorical in that it only highlights part of the meaning of "*e*" by "goose."

Readers of a foreign language through translation must be cautious in the use of translations, and remember that any metaphor is always used in a partial sense. There is always some aspect in the metaphor that is excluded. For example, when we say "time is money," we mean that time is something that can be used, wasted, saved, even "borrowed," or converted into money. We do not mean time is something that one can deposit in a time bank and withdraw from the ATM when needed as is the case with money.

In cross-cultural translation, we have a similar discrepancy. When we say that "Tao is *logos*," this means that there are many similarities in the use of the two words in the Chinese and Greek traditions and thus there is a partial overlapping in their meanings. However, they also have many meanings that do not overlap. Thus we must be careful not to stretch the translation too far. When we say that the Confucian concept of "*jen*" means humanity, benevolence, kindness, humaneness, and so on, this is like telling someone who has not seen a zebra that it is partly like a horse, a donkey, and so forth. This kind of translation is useful and often indispensable, but can also be misleading. In philosophy when we think about *A* in terms of *B* as we do in a metaphor, we must remind ourselves that it is not exactly so. Scholars sometimes dispute over whether a translation is correct. For example, while one person says that Tao is *logos*, another says that it is not. Based on our understanding of translation as metaphor, it is possible that both are right. The real question is in what aspect or sense Tao is *logos* and in what aspect or sense it is not. Without these specifications, such disputes are often superficial.

Another important aspect of translation in comparative philosophy is that translation can at the same time shed new light on the concept being translated. In their book *Metaphors We Live By*, George Lakoff and Mark Johnson tell a story about understanding the expression "the solution of my problems." It may be taken metaphorically to mean "a large volume of liquid, bubbling and smoking, containing all of your problems, either dissolved or in the form of precipitates, with catalysts constantly dissolving some problems (for the time being) and precipitating out others."[8] From this understanding one may gain the insight that problems are part of the natural order of things rather than disorders to be cured, and they are never solved once and for all. We have to live with problems and transform them. In a similar way, in translating philosophical terminologies, we may discover or work out new meanings. Should "*jen*" be translated as "humanity" or "benevolence"? In Confucianism there is a close connection between humanity and benevolence, and in *jen* these terms are two aspects of the same idea. Therefore, difficulties in translation may also be the key to better understandings of philosophical concepts.

Finally, in speaking of cross-cultural translation as metaphor, I do not mean to imply that translation is not a serious undertaking. Metaphor is serious and as in literature, using metaphor is an art form that requires expertise and skill. When metaphor is used appropriately, it often conveys ideas more effectively than nonmetaphorical elaborations. However one must remember that in translation, as in metaphor, everything is context-dependent.

Being

Perspective versus Substance

The question of being may be understood as the question of the nature of things and of how they are in the world; our understanding of being has profound implications for the way we understand the world as a whole. Therefore it is appropriate to begin this study with the question of being.

Being as Identity

This question may be investigated in at least two ways. One is to ask generally what it means to exist; this is the question about the nature of existence. Such was the approach of Martin Heidegger when he asked and addressed the question "What is being?" Another way to investigate being is to ask specifically what an existent is; it is the question of identity, the question about the nature of the basic elements of the world. For example, according to Sir Arthur Eddington, the entity I am observing can be viewed in two ways: on the one hand a commonsensical table that has extension, occupies a chunk of space, and is substantial, and on the other a table that is actually a mass of electrons with ample empty space between them.[1] Presumably there is only one thing here. Now, which one is the thing? Some people say that there is only one thing that is self-identical and it has attributes or properties. Then the question is, what is it? In the above case, is the table a property of the mass of electrons or is the mass of electrons a property of the table? Others may insist that there are actually two things, which coincide in space. Then, are there just two of them or are there more? What is the relationship between them in addition to their spatial coincidence?

The question of being is one of extreme importance, because, whether we are aware of it or not, many of our views on other aspects of the world are dependent on our views on this issue. As a matter of fact, every person, philosopher or nonphilosopher alike, has some view on it, even though most people hold their views tacitly. People who hold different perspectives on this issue hold fundamentally different worldviews. Their worldviews can be so radically different that they hardly share enough common ground to convey to each other their positions on related issues.

My focus in this chapter is on the issue of being as identity, that is, the question of what an existent can be said to be. I believe the dominant views on this issue in the East and the West are quite different, and that many other disparate views are consequences of this fundamental difference. For this reason it is crucial that we recognize their dissimilarities if we wish to understand both sides and their perspectives on many other issues.

Roughly speaking, the dominant view in the West has tended to see the world as consisting of basic elements or "bricks" (e.g., atoms) that are extended in space and make up the world largely through spatial organization. From this perspective, change is merely in appearances, and the world is static at a fundamental level. The philosophical focus within this assumption is usually on identifying the basic elements or fundamental bricks, and then explaining how change is possible in a world of these mostly static elements (e.g., in Descartes's view). In contrast, many Eastern philosophers believe that the fundamental element or elements in the world are more subtle and formless. For these philosophers the fundamental nature of the world is change. The static is found merely in the appearance of a world that is essentially dynamic. One of their challenges here is to account for apparent constancy amid change.

In the Chinese tradition, the so-called "five-elements (*wu xing* 五行)," namely, metal, wood, water, fire, and earth, are not understood as five static "bricks," but as dynamic principles that are agents themselves. The five elements may be reminiscent of the ancient Greek philosopher Empedocles' "four elements," namely, water, air, fire, and earth. They are, however, in fact very different in that the Chinese "five elements" are not inertial matter that has to be activated from without by some external principles as Empedocles' "four elements" are. The Han Confucian Dong Zhongshu 董仲舒 (179–104 B.C.E.) said *"xing zhe xing ye* 行者行也," that is, *"xing"* means "acting" or "behaving."[2] Therefore, *"wu xing"* can be better translated as "five agents" or "five operations."

The "five elements" are believed to be five types of *qi* 气 (*chi*).[3] The Chinese believe that the fundamental element or material of the world is *qi*, which has been appropriately translated into English as "energy-force." Unlike atoms, in Chinese philosophy *qi* is intangible, dynamic, and yet forms the myriad of things in the world. This concept of something intangible as the foundation of reality may appear to many Westerners incomprehensible. Fortunately, modern physics has provided a useful instrument for making sense of this concept. *Qi* is not exactly energy in modern physics, but if one can comprehend how, at the fundamental level of the world, energy, which is intangible and dynamic, is equivalent or convertible to matter, one has a good analogy to work with in comprehending the Chinese *qi*.[4]

While *"qi"* denotes reality at the fundamental level, our everyday life, however, deals mostly with the so-called "midsized" entities, such as chairs, horses, and trees. Most people in both the West and the East seem to agree that there are indeed these entities. It does not mean, however, that they agree on the way the world is constituted at this level. The dominant Chinese understanding of the world at its fundamental level as fluid, *qi*-like extends to various levels of the world, including the level of "midsized" objects. In this chapter I will compare the view of Zhuang Zi 庄子 (Chuang Tzu, b. 369 B.C.E.), a Chinese Taoist philosopher, on what an entity is with a highly influential Western view that derives from Aristotle. I will show not only that they are different but also how Zhuang Zi's ontology is a viable alternative to Aristotelian ontology.

The Being of the Ox

A common view of being in the West goes like this: an entity falls into a certain substance category *S* and is an *s*; there are other things that can be said of the *s*, but those are merely qualities or properties; being *s* is its primary being and it determines the entity's identity. For example, the entity is an *ox*, which falls into the substance category "ox." Being that individual ox determines the entity's identity; its being brown, seven feet long, composed of the mass *m*, and so on, are its properties. This is a view held, explicitly or implicitly, by many Western philosophers.

The origin of this view may be traced back to Aristotle's doctrine of *ousia*, that is, primary being or substance,[5] as it is usually interpreted. Aristotle discusses the problem of *ousia* in *Metaphysics*, mainly in the "central books." His discussions are lengthy, meticulous, and sometimes inconsistent. Commentators are often widely divided with regard to what is really Aristotle's position on the issues. Here I present Aristotle in a standard interpretation.

Aristotle maintains that philosophy is the science of Being *qua* Being:

> The term "being" is used in several senses, as we pointed out previously in our account of the various senses of terms. In one sense, it signifies whatness and a *this*; in another, it signifies a quality or a quantity or one of the others which are predicated in this way. Although "being" is used in so many senses, it is evident that of these the primary sense is whatness, and used in this sense it signifies a substance. For when we state that this has some quality, we say it is good or bad but not that it is three cubits long or a man; but when we state what it is, we say that it is a man or a god but not white or hot or three cubits long.[6]

Accordingly, there are many ways in which one can speak of an individual entity's whatness, but only one way refers to primary substance ("a what" or "a something"), the others are predicates (or properties). It is to this primary being that the "what-it-is-to-be" or essence (*to ti en einai*) belongs.[7] Thus, Aristotle reduces the question "what is being?" to the question "what is substance?"[8] The way in which Aristotle speaks about essence and primary being clearly indicates that he believes that, for each individual entity (or at least a natural entity), there is only one essence and one primary being.[9] Because the essence of an entity is (determined by) its form, and presumably one entity has only one form, one entity can have only one essence.[10] An entity may have secondary being, but only one primary being.

From this follow several interrelated Aristotelian claims in regard to an entity's whatness. First of all, viewing an entity as a collection of its constituent parts does not reveal the entity's reality. The essence belongs to the entity as a whole, not to its constituent parts. Since the primary being of an entity is determined by its essence, which its constituent parts do not possess, the primary being of an entity cannot be revealed by an analysis into its parts. In other words, an entity is a particular *this*, but not only a *this*; it is also a definite *such*, that is, a *this-such*. It cannot be a *this* without being also a *such*.[11] Second, for Aristotle, because there is only one essence in an entity, there is only one primary being in it, and therefore there is a single objectively right answer to the question of what an entity is primarily. The right answer is one that reveals the entity's essence and primary substance. Third, Aristotle maintains that the essence of an entity is linked to its species, and the species to which an entity belongs has a hold on the entity's primary being. Hence, a withdrawal of its membership from the species means losing the entity's primary being and hence its destruction. These views represent a substantial part of the Aristotelian metaphysics; further philosophical observations are based on them.

The metaphysics of Zhuang Zi, a near contemporary of Aristotle, may be viewed at two levels. At the fundamental level, every thing belongs to the Tao, or the Way. The Tao is the ultimate truth of the universe. Every thing in the world has its root in the Tao. In this sense, all are One; the differences between things are negligible from the viewpoint of the Tao. At the entity level, each individual entity can be both a "this" and a "that." An entity's being a "this" does not exclude its also being a "that." The two levels are linked: an individual's being a "this" and being a "that" are ways of the Tao's presenting itself. In the following I will focus on the second level, on the issue of an entity's whatness.

For Aristotle, to be a primary substance is to be a member of its lowest-level substance-kind;[12] for example, being an ox is a primary being.[13] Accordingly, ceasing to be an ox means losing its primary being, and our recognizing the entity as the individual ox is the only right way for us to recognize its primary being. Interestingly, Zhuang Zi also used the ox to make his point. But he has a different account of what an ox is. In his story about Cook Ding 庖丁, the cook says:

> When I first began to cut oxen, what I saw was nothing but whole oxen. After three years, I no longer saw whole oxen. . . . In accord with the natural grain, I slice at the great crevices, lead the blade through the great cavities. Following its inherent structure, I never encounter the slightest obstacle even where the veins and arteries come together or where the ligaments and tendons join, much less from obvious big bones. A good cook changes his cleaver once a year because he chops. An ordinary cook changes his cleaver once a month because he hacks. Now I've been using my cleaver for nineteen years and have cut up thousands of oxen with it, but the blade is still as fresh as though it had just come from the grindstone. Between the joints there are spaces, but the edge of the blade has no thickness. Since I am inserting something without any thickness into an empty space, there will certainly be lots of room for the blade to play around in. That's why the blade is still as fresh as though it had just come from the grindstone.[14]

The main purpose of Zhuang Zi's story is to tell us how to find our way in the world. He suggests that it can be done by properly recognizing and using things in the world. After three years of fine training, Cook Ding saw an ox no longer as a whole thing but as a pack of flesh and bones.

For Zhuang Zi, Cook Ding was not mistaken. What the cook saw was real. The entity was certainly also an ox. What this shows is that an ox can be recognized not only as an individual ox, but also as a pack of flesh and bones. Thus, in telling the story Zhuang Zi suggests that, as a being, the entity is both an ox and a pack of flesh and bones.

This differs from Aristotle who writes:

> Of the composite of statue the bronze is a part, but not a part of that which is called "the form" of the statue. For what should be stated is the form, or the thing qua having the form, but the material part should never be stated by itself.[15]

In a sense, the bronze is a part of the statue as an entity, and flesh and bones are parts of an ox.[16] But these parts are not the elements of the entity's form. Since Aristotle sometimes seems to believe that an entity's primary being is its form, in a sense these parts are not constituent parts of the entity's primary being. An ox as a whole has the essence of being an ox, while the parts do not possess this essence. Aristotle treats the relation between a pack of flesh and bones on the one hand and an ox on the other as the relation between potentiality and actuality. The pack of flesh and bones is matter that has the potential to be an ox. It is the form that gives the entity actuality and makes it an actual ox.[17] The primary being of the substance is exclusively the ox.

Zhuang Zi, however, believes that the analysis into its constituent parts is a legitimate approach to an entity's reality. On the one hand, its being an ox does not exhaust its entire being. It is an ox, but it is also a pack of flesh and bones. The entity's being a pack of flesh and bones is not merely a potentiality. The pack of flesh and bones is as real as the ox. In Cook Ding's eyes, it is not the case that the pack of flesh and bones are actualized in being an ox, nor is the entity potentially a pack of flesh and bones that will be actualized after the ox is killed. In his eyes, the entity *is* a pack of flesh and bones. On the other hand, Zhuang Zi recognizes no essence or primary being. He does not believe there is such a thing as essence that exclusively determines the entity's being. Therefore, the entity's being an aggregate of parts is no less real than its being an ox.

Thus, conceptually, Zhuang Zi views the entity at a level different from its being an ox or a pack of flesh and bones. While being an ox and being a pack of flesh and bones are not the same way of being, they are the same entity that has both ways of being. Contrary to the Aristotelian view that every particular is a *this-such*, Zhuang Zi states:

> Every thing is a "that," and every thing is a "this." You cannot see it as a "this" if you are from the viewpoint of "that"; you see it as a "this" when you are from the viewpoint of "this." "That" comes from "this" and "this" comes from "that." ... Thus, the sage does not bother with these distinctions but sees all things in the ways they are. "This" is also "that," and "that" is also "this." ... When there is no more separation between "this" and "that," it is called the pivot of the Tao. At the pivot in the center of the circle one can see the infinite in all things.[18]

For Zhuang Zi, we always look at things from a certain point of view. If I begin from where I am and see a thing as I see it, as a "this," then it may also become possible for me to see it as another sees it, as a "that." Therefore, seeing it as a "this" and seeing it as a "that" depend on each other and complement each other. It means that, in addition to being a "this" (i.e., an ox), the entity is also a "that" (i.e., a pack of flesh and bones). Although the entity's being is not confined to being an ox and being a pack of flesh and bones (it is also an aggregate of molecules, etc.), these are ways for it to be a *this* and a *that*.[19] Because being an ox and being a pack of flesh and bones are two ways of the same entity's being, an individual ox is a pack of flesh and bones, and a particular aggregate of parts is an ox. Only when we see it not merely as an ox, but also as an entity that is both a "this" and a "that," can we get to the pivot of the Tao.

In Zhuang Zi's eyes, the fact that the ox lasts longer than the pack of flesh and bones does not necessarily make the entity more of an ox. For him, quantitative measures are always relative. It can be said that the tip of a downy hair is heavy, Mount Tai is small, a child who dies at infancy has a long life, and (the long-lived) Progenitor Peng 彭祖 dies young.[20] It all depends on the context. Even though the pack of flesh and bones does not last as long as the ox, it lasts long enough to make it an entity. If we call the ox a "this," then the pack of flesh and bones is a "that." The entity can be both a "this" and a "that."

One may want to object: perhaps instead of one entity, what we have here are really two entities, one ox and one pack of flesh and bones; although they spatially coincide, they are not the same entity. Aristotle, however, does not seem to favor this view. He strives for the unity of an entity. When he speaks of the statue and the bronze, he seems to have treated the bronze merely as matter. Instead of suggesting that there are two entities, one statue and one mass of bronze, he treats it as one entity:

> But, as we have stated, the last matter and the form are one and the same, the one exists potentially, the other as actuality. Thus, it is like asking what the cause of unity is and what causes something to be one; for each thing is a kind of unity, and potentiality and actuality taken together exist somehow as one.[21]

He explicitly rejects the suggestion that one individual can be two. He believes that the matter and the form are the same unity; it is not the case that there is a statue *and* a mass of bronze:

> In some cases, after the thing has been generated, it is called, when referred to the matter out of which it was generated, not "that" but "that-y" (or "that-en"); for example, the statue is called not "stone" but "stony." . . . So, just as we do not say of a healthy man, who became so from being sick, that he is a sick man, so of the statue we say not that it is wood but (by varying the word) that it is wooden, not bronze but brazen, not stone but stony, and of the house not bricks but brick-en; for if we look at the situation very carefully, we would not say without qualification that the wood becomes a statue, or the bricks a house, since that which becomes must change and not remain. It is because of this fact that we speak in this manner.[22]

Thus, after the bricks become a house, the bricks (as bricks) are no more; after the bronze becomes a statue, the bronze (as bronze) is no more. After they become a house or a statue, they only exist as the properties of something else. So, when one points to the statue and asks, "How many entities are there?" the answer for Aristotle is definitively "one."

One reason for me to agree with Aristotle in this regard is that the two-entities account inflates the number of entities in the world. It is not the case that there is an ox *plus* a pack of flesh and bones; there is only *one* thing that is both an ox and an aggregate of parts. Suppose two persons dispute over whether the entity is an ox or a pack of flesh and bones. If there were two entities, there would be no dispute at all because they would be talking about two different entities, one ox and one aggregate of parts: while one would hold that an ox is an ox, the other would hold that a pack of flesh and bones is a pack of flesh and bones. But we know the dispute is over the same entity. We may want to say to the disputants that "yes, it is an ox, but it is also a pack of flesh and bones." Here the two "it's" must refer to the same entity or the sentence would make no sense. In the story of Cook Ding, the cook sees an aggregate of parts in the same entity in which others see an ox. The entity can only be that which is both an ox and a pack of flesh and bones. At a certain time t, the ox o and the pack of flesh and bones p are one and the same entity.

Some contemporary philosophers want to update Aristotle by saying that an entity is "a four-dimensional spatiotemporal worm."[23] Accordingly, an entity can only exist over time and it is extended in space and time as a worm is extended in space; only a part of it can exist at a time. Two entities are identical only if they have the same history in time and space. Here again only one story can be told about the entity. Two observations can be made on Zhuang Zi's behalf. First, it is questionable that an entity has to be a spatiotemporal worm. It appears that our ordinary idea of an entity is something that exists at a certain time. If an entity is a four-dimensional thing, it would itself extend over time; "Johnny" for instance would refer to not the boy playing a computer game now, but his whole four-dimensional movement from birth to death; then it would only make sense to say that a part of him exists now, not the whole Johnny. That does not sound right. Also, if an entity is a four-dimensional worm, one that takes a very different route in space and time would not be the same four-dimensional worm and therefore not the same entity. I think that our ordinary notion is that the same entity might have been at a spatiotemporal spot different from where it actually is. Furthermore, if an entity is a four-dimensional whole, a half of it would be a half entity. Since it is true that if an entity's "life span" is cut short, the entity is still a whole entity, not a broken one, what we mean by "an entity" is not a "four-dimensional worm," but something that endures in time.

Second, even if we grant that an entity is a spatiotemporal worm, that will only change the terminology, not the issue at stake. In that case, what we have been calling an entity would be a time stage of an entity. Then the question of whether the time stage is substantially and primarily a time stage of an ox or a time stage of a pack of flesh and bones (which presumably lasts longer than an instant in time) still remains for the Aristotelians. Following Zhuang Zi's way of thinking one could still say that the same time stage is both the time stage of the ox and the time stage of the aggregate of parts, without one being primary and the other secondary.[24]

Knowing What There Is

Because Aristotle believes that an entity only has one essence and one primary being, it follows that, for Aristotle, there is a single objectively right answer to the question of what an entity primarily is. He holds that the question of what a thing is refers essentially to primary being.[25] In other words, the "what-it-is" of an entity belongs to primary being, and to other categories merely potentially and derivatively, merely as a quality or a quantity. For example, an entity *o* is a member of the kind *ox*, and that it is an ox is the right answer to the question "what is *o*?" Zhuang Zi denies that there is primary being and that there is a single objectively right answer to the question of what an entity is. He believes that saying the entity is an ox is not the only right way to answer the question of what the entity is; that the entity is a pack of flesh and bones is also an appropriate response.

Zhuang Zi does not think, as Aristotle apparently does, there is an "objective" way of knowing:

> Knowing what Heaven does and what humans do would be the utmost in knowledge. . . . However, there is a problem. Knowing depends on conditions that are only matched later. And these conditions are not fixed. How can we ever know what is due to Heaven but not due to humans, or vice versa?[26]

The Chinese word for "Heaven," "*tian* 天," can also be rendered as "nature" in this context. It is not difficult to figure out Zhuang Zi's meaning here. For Zhuang Zi, knowing is not like mirroring an objective reality (i.e., what Heaven or nature makes). It is always inevitably situated under some circumstances. These circumstances are not fixed and cannot be separated from the entity ("what is due to Heaven") and the knower ("what is due to humans"). The way of the Tao, for Zhuang Zi, is not to put the two in opposition, but to see them in unity.

This way of thinking may be called "interactive thinking." Things are always relational and situational, and should be seen as such. To see things within relations and situations is to see things in a network of various factors that interact with one another, is to see things in context, in perspective.

Then, how is it that the entity is an ox and that the entity is a pack of flesh and bones are both right? In Zhuang Zi's view, "a way comes into being through walking upon it; a thing is so because people say that it is."[27] Originally there were no ways in the world. A way emerges only after we walk it. "Say" (谓 "*wei*"), which may also be translated as "naming" here, can be understood as recognizing.[28] A thing is so because we recognize it this way. The individual entity is an ox when we recognize it so; it is a pack of flesh and bones when we recognize it so. This may sound rather subjectivistic. But it should not be taken as meaning that we can view an entity arbitrarily. Zhuang Zi continues the remark by saying, "Why so? By being so. Why not so? By not being so. It is inherent in a thing that from somewhere that's so of it, from somewhere that's allowable of it." Gia-Fu Feng and Jane English translated the last sentence as "Everything has its own nature and its own function."[29] It is not arbitrary for one to recognize an entity as "a something" because an entity has its own nature and its own function. From this it may be said that a thing's being a *such* is not a pure invention of ours. The Tao has its ways. We have the view that an ox is more an ox than a pack of flesh and bones, or vice versa, because we come to recognize it that way. We can do this because of its "being so." It is, however, not true that there is only one right way to recognize things.

Zhuang Zi's view appears even more appealing as we look at artificial entities. In analogy to Aristotle's bronze statue example, I can ask a similar question: Is my ring a primary substance that has a property of being gold, or is this piece of gold a primary substance that has a property of being a ring? On the one hand, this piece of gold is a primary substance if anything is a primary substance in the Aristotelian sense; on the other hand, there is no reason why my ring should not be a primary substance when other individual entities, such as bricks and statues, are primary substances. If there is only one primary substance in this entity, which is it? Zhuang Zi would have no problem saying that it is both, with neither being more primary than the other without a context. At this point an Aristotelian may want to retreat and hold that only natural entities are substances. If so, at least Zhuang Zi's ontology would have the advantage of covering both natural entities and artificial entities.

Zhuang Zi opposes dogmatic thinking:

The Tao has never had borders; saying has never had constants. It is by a "That's it" demarcations are made. Let me say something about demarcations. Left and right, order and propriety, dividing up and discriminating between alternatives, competing over and fighting over: these I call our Eight Powers. . . . To "divide," then, is to leave something undivided;

to "discriminate between alternatives" is to leave something which is neither alternative. "How can that be?" you may ask. The sage keeps it in his breast, common men argue over alternatives to show it to each other. Hence I say: To "discriminate between alternatives" is to fail to see something.[30]

The Eight Powers are ways to define the boundaries of things in the world. Some people use the first four powers to delimit the "That's it" and "That's not it" in human relations; some others use the last four powers to delimit the "That's it" and "That's not it" in our general knowledge of the world.[31] For Zhuang Zi, they are all fundamentally mistaken. He holds that the Tao has no borders and that the being of an entity has alternatives. When common people ask the question "What is it?" they use the Eight Powers to draw borders, divide things, and discriminate between alternatives in order to show a definite "That's it" or "That's not it" of things. But the same thing is both "That's it" and "That's not it." To adhere obstinately to "That's it" of an entity is to discriminate against alternatives. In doing so, one is obstructed from seeing the reality of the Tao.

What Zhuang Zi says here about the "Eight Powers" is reminiscent of Aristotle's doctrine of things in *Metaphysics* and *Categories*. Aristotle makes a distinction between substance and qualities, generation and alteration, doing and being-affected, and so forth. For instance, he claims that among many things that can be spoken of an entity's "what-it-is," there is only one way we speak of it as a substance, the rest being qualities. For Zhuang Zi, getting deeply involved in such disputes as whether an ox or a pack of flesh and bones is a substance is getting away from the Tao, because one fails to see another side of reality. For example, in distinguishing between an ox as substance and a pack of flesh and bones as a potentiality of the substance, one fails to see that what can be said of an ox as a substance can also be said of the pack of flesh and bones. The aggregate of parts, like the ox, can be treated as a "substance" that has certain properties. To know the Tao is not to discriminate against alternatives, but to be open to them. Therefore, obstinately holding that the entity is only an ox or a pack of flesh and bones is grossly one-sided. Zhuang Zi remarks:

To weary the intelligence by trying to unify things without knowing that they are the same I call "three every morning."

What do I mean by "three every morning?" A monkey keeper handing out nuts said, "Three every morning and four every evening." The monkeys were all in a rage. "All right then," said he, "Four every morning and three every evening." The monkeys were delighted. Without anything being missed out either in name or in substance, their pleasure and anger were put to use; his too was the "That's it" that depends on circumstance. This is why the sage smooths things out with his "That's it, that's not it," and stays at the point of rest on the potter's wheel of Heaven. It is this that is called "letting both alternatives proceed".[32]

Here Zhuang Zi advocates the view that everything belongs to the Tao. He criticizes those who fail to realize this as "[obsessed with] three every morning 朝三." Zhuang Zi's criticism also applies to Aristotelians who hold that an individual entity has only one primary being. The Aristotelians are trapped in a hierarchical way of thinking. For them, one has to give a definitive "either/or" type of answer between things like "three every morning and four every evening" and "four every morning and three every evening," and only one answer can be right.

Zhuang Zi does not deny that there is some difference between "three every morning and four every evening" on the one hand, and "four every morning and three every evening" on the other. But he believes that the difference is not significant enough for one to hold an obstinate adherence to one against the other. From the viewpoint of the Tao, the two are rooted in the same one. The monkeys fail to see that "three every morning and four every evening" and "four every morning and three every evening" amount to the same. Aristotelians are also obsessed with "three every morning" because they hold that only one answer is ultimately right and they fail to see that, from the point of view of the Tao, "being an ox with the property of having the pack of flesh and bones" and "being an aggregate of parts and having the property of being an ox" amount to the same thing. These are two different ways of being the same thing. Disputing which has the absolute primacy is like the monkeys fighting over whether they have three nuts every morning and four every evening or four every morning and three every evening. The sage, understanding the pivot of the Tao, would see the oneness of the two sides and remain flexible.

Recognizing that an entity can be both a "this" and a "that," Zhuang Zi is willing to judge as better or worse views of what an entity is on the basis of practice. This is what he means by saying that the "that's it" of things "depends on circumstance."

In the second chapter of *Zhuang Zi* 庄子, we find a conversation between Nie Que 齧缺 and his master Wang Ni 王倪:

> "Would you know something upon which all things agreed 'That's it?'"
> "How would I know that?"
> "..."
> "... When a human sleeps in the damp his back hurts and he gets stiff in the joints; is that so of the loach? When a human sits in a tree he shivers and shakes; is that so of the monkey? Which of these three knows the right place to live? Humans eat the flesh of hay-fed and grain-fed beasts, deer eat the grass, centipedes relish snakes, owls and crows crave mice; which of the four has a proper sense of taste? Gibbons go for gibbons, buck mates with doe, loaches play with fish. Mao Qiang 毛嬙 and Xi Shi 西施 were beautiful in the eyes of men; but when the fish saw them they plunged deep, when the birds saw them they flew high, when the deer saw them they broke into a run. Which of these four knows what is truly beautiful in the world? In my judgment the principles of good will and duty, the paths of "That's it" and "that's not it," are formless; how could I know how to discriminate between them?"[33]

Here through Wang Ni's mouth Zhuang Zi expresses his own view. He is targeting the issue of a universal "That's it" in a broader sense, extending to the ethical as well as to the aesthetic. It certainly includes the metaphysical. For him, the fact that there is no consensus on a universal "That's it" shows not only that we cannot reach such a state because each of us is always situated in circumstances, but also because there is no such reality. An entity has its being and functions. How we approach and value it really depends on the practice in which we are involved. Saying that the entity is an ox and saying that it is a pack of flesh and bones are two ways of approaching the same entity. As to which way is right, it really depends on the context in which the entity is recognized. The appropriate way to recognize an entity depends on the purpose we have for it, and the purpose varies from time to time and from place to place. For example, if we use the entity as farm animal, it is better to recognize it as an ox; for Cook Ding, seeing no whole ox shows that he has found his way in the world. It is very important for Cook Ding that an ox is not only a whole animal, but also an aggregate of parts. For only as a non-whole, as a pack of flesh and bones, is it possible for Cook Ding to find "plenty of room" in between to ply his blade. For him, the entity as a pack of flesh and bones is by no means merely a potentiality as Aristotle holds. It is a real being to deal with. In this way, Zhuang Zi's relativistic metaphysics and his emphasis on practice are linked.

An Aristotelian perhaps would not straightforwardly deny that sometimes it makes more sense to treat the entity as a pack of flesh and bones instead of as a whole ox. She may try in two ways to avoid an obvious contradiction with her metaphysical view that the entity is primarily an ox. First, she may maintain that, there are two entities, one ox and one aggregate of parts; while the ox is primarily an ox, the pack of flesh and bones is primarily an aggregate of parts. As I have pointed out earlier, in this way the Aristotelian not only goes against Aristotle himself but also inflates the number of entities in the world by duplicating entities. Second, she may choose to say that there is only one primary substance; while the primary substance is the ox, sometimes it is useful to focus on its potentialities rather than on primary substance; the case of Cook Ding is such an example.

This latter view, however, has two disadvantages in comparison with Zhuang Zi's view. First, for Aristotle, matter cannot exist without form and potentiality cannot exist without actuality. If the pack of flesh and bones is merely a potentiality, it cannot exist actually. This is obviously untrue. It is not the case that the pack of flesh and bones is actualized as flesh and bones only after the ox is killed. It is a pack of flesh and bones even while the ox is still alive. For we would say that after the ox is killed, it is the *same* pack of flesh and bones that remains. For Cook Ding, the aggregate of parts is a real being that does not depend on anything else. Zhuang Zi's account, therefore, works better here. Second and more important, treating the pack of flesh and bones merely as potentiality by the Aristotelian account, we can only approach the aggregate of parts through the ox. It is an indirect approach. In contrast, Zhuang Zi's account enables us to directly approach the entity as the aggregate of parts. Because the entity is really a pack of flesh and bones, instead of taking the entity *as* a pack of flesh and bones for convenience, we take the entity as the entity in its real being. In other words, we treat it as a pack of flesh and bones because it itself is an aggregate of parts. Thus, Zhuang Zi's metaphysics provides a suitable foundation for his practical philosophy, and the latter reinforces the plausibility of his metaphysics.

Transformation of the Butterfly

The third contrast between Aristotle and Zhuang Zi on the matter of "being" is found in their views as to whether the same entity can survive a substance sortal concept change. Substance sortal concepts are such concepts as "ox" and "horse." Such concepts designate Aristotelian substances. Going through a substance sortal concept change would mean becoming a different kind of substance. The question here is whether an entity can retain its identity through such a change.

Aristotle links an entity's essence to its species: "Essence, then, will belong to nothing which is not a species of a genus, but only to a species of a genus."[34] For an entity, to maintain what it is, to possess its essence, is to belong to the species to which it actually belongs. Therefore, ceasing to belong to its species amounts to ceasing to possess its essence, which amounts to the destruction of the entity. This means that no entity can survive a substance sortal concept change.

This Aristotelian view is very influential in contemporary debates over the issue of identity. For instance, David Wiggins, a contemporary Aristotelian, holds that the substance sortal or kind concept into which an entity falls is essential for the entity's identity. Namely, for an x and any kind f, if f is a substance kind, then if x belongs to f, x always belongs to f, in other words, "to *be*, for such a thing just is to comply with this ultimate or near ultimate concept f."[35] For example, the entity is an ox. It is the same entity as long as it is an ox and thereby falls under that same substance sortal concept of "ox." Accordingly, when an entity no longer falls under the same substance sortal concept, the entity is no longer the same entity. In this way, the concepts of primary substance, essence, and necessity are linked. The entity is primarily an ox, it is essentially an ox, and it is necessarily an ox. As a primary substance, the entity cannot be the same entity without being an ox.

Zhuang Zi again disagrees. In *Zhuang Zi* we have a story of his butterfly dream:

> Last night Zhuang Zhou 庄周 dreamt he was a butterfly. Spirits soaring, he was a butterfly, and did not know about Zhou. When all of a sudden he awoke, he was Zhou with all his wits about him. He does not know whether he is Zhou who dreams he is a butterfly or a butterfly who dreams he is Zhou. Between Zhou and the butterfly there must be some difference; this is what is meant by the transformations of things 物化.[36]

Here Zhuang Zi suggests that it could be that he is Zhuang Zi (Zhou) who dreams he is a butterfly or that he is a butterfly that dreams he is Zhuang Zi. He might never know which but, in either case, he would be the same individual. Losing his species status as a human does not mean destruction, but a different way of the being of the same individual. That is, it is not necessary that he is a man but not a butterfly. He might be a butterfly and still maintain his identity as the same individual.

If an entity can survive a substance category change and remain the same individual as Zhuang Zi believes, one might want to press further by asking "the same what?" To this question neither "the same man" nor "the same butterfly" can be the right answer. Even "the same animal" would not do it, because we normally do not consider a man and a butterfly the same animal. Zhuang Zi, however, does not follow this way of thinking. He does not deny that there is some difference between being a human and being a butterfly. But he believes that, from the viewpoint of the Tao, the difference only shows "the transformation of things." In Zhuang Zi, the transformation of things takes place when the boundary between "this" and "that" is dissolved and the oneness of the world is revealed.[37] In such a state, whether he is a human or a butterfly does not matter much not only because from the viewpoint of the Tao, everything in the world belongs to the oneness of the Tao, but also because this could be two ways of being the same self. The notion of the transformation of things becomes more plausible in the light of Zhuang Zi's view on the unity of the "that" and the "this" of the same entity. He would reject that there is essence and that the identity of an entity is determined by anything like essence. Accordingly, to say an entity is essentially or primarily a man or a butterfly is already to be misled. For him an entity can be both a "this" and a "that"; it may remain the same entity while transforming from one category into another.

This view is probably the most difficult to accept for those who are accustomed to the Aristotelian way of thinking. It is, however, an extension to the temporal or chronological dimension of what Zhuang Zi has said about the simultaneous coincidence of different ways of an entity's being. The view that a thing may survive a substance category change is grounded in traditions of Chinese thought. In Chinese classic mythology, we are told again and again that an individual maintains its identity after going through substance category changes. For example, the Monkey Sun 孙悟空 in *The Journey to the West* 西游记 is said to come from agate and to be able to change itself into seventy-two varieties. It can be a fish or a temple, an old man or a young girl. Yet it is the same Monkey Sun. Its identity as that individual entity transcends any particular category with which the entity is associated. The hero in *The Dream of the Red Chamber* 红楼梦, Jia Baoyu 贾宝玉, is said to have been transformed from a piece of jade. The heroin of *The Romance of the White Snake* 白蛇传 is said to be in the process of transforming from a white snake into a beautiful woman. This is hardly a real argument for Zhuang Zi and against Aristotle. It suggests, however, that in this culture it is not inconceivable for an entity to maintain its identity through category changes. On the contrary, such kind of transformabiltiy is deeply seated in people's thinking.

Suppose at time t_1 an entity is a member of a species S, and at time t_2 it ceases to be an s and becomes an a. After t_2 we can point to the entity and say "it used to be (or was) an s at t_1 but now it is no longer an s but an a." This sentence makes perfect sense. In order for the sentence to make sense the two "it's" must refer to the same thing. What is "it"? Zhuang Zi would say it cannot be an either/or and it has to be both. For example, in the case of the ox, it is that which is both an ox and a pack of flesh and bones. This intuition would support Zhuang Zi when he told his story of the dream, although he did not go further to give an argument for it.

In Zhuang Zi, the question how "this" (substance) and "that" (substance) are identical does not arise. If it is asked how "this" way of being and "that" way of being are identical, the answer is simply that they are not identical. But the entity that has both ways of being is self-identical. It is the same entity. This view of being fits well into the picture depicted by contemporary physics. At the micro-level of the world, there is no ultimate substance-brick of the world. What are particles are also energy. To ask for the substance or primary being of the world is futile. It is no more particles than energy-packets; nor more energy-packets than particles. It is both. The fact that we are more comfortable with the idea that it is particles is not a legitimate reason for us to take particles as primary substances and energy-packets as secondary.

From the above discussion, we can see that, although Zhuang Zi did not provide a systematic metaphysical theory as Aristotle did, he nevertheless indicated an alternative metaphysics. Perhaps the biggest difference between Zhuang Zi and Aristotle on being is that, while Aristotle sees things as primary being or substances, Zhuang Zi does not accept this notion. For Zhuang Zi, things have their ways of being. A thing can be a "this" and a "that." While being a "this" is a way for it to be, being a "that" is another way of its being. Both "this" and "that" are different ways for the same entity to be. Thus, from his point of view, not only is the world a world of diversity, but also the being of an entity is a diversity. One thing we can learn from Zhuang Zi is to open our mind to the diversity of the being of entities, and allow an entity to have both "this" and "that," and possibly any number of ways, as its real being.

One-Only versus One-Many Identity

Zhuang Zi's ontology of midsized objects thus may be called an aspect/perspective ontology.[38] It is the view that the identity of an entity consists in its aspects, namely, in its ways of being in the world, and each of these ways of being is contextually situated and can only be presented in perspective when we approach it. Therefore the identity of any entity always consists in a synthesis of its various ways of being. This ontology is shared by Chinese philosophers of various schools.

Even though the Confucians, largely preoccupied with ethico-political philosophy, have expressed little interest in discussing metaphysics of midsized entities, they do accord with Zhuang Zi in this regard. Confucius was quoted in *The Book of Change* 易经 (*Yi*

Jing) as saying that "different paths lead to the same destination."[39]
Wing-tsit Chan comments:

The idea of a hundred roads to the same destination is a direct
expression of the spirit of synthesis which is extremely strong
in Chinese philosophy. It is the Confucian version of Chuang
Tzu's [Zhuang Zi] doctrine of following two courses at the same
time.[40]

"Two courses" here of course does not literally mean just "two." It
can be more than two. Although Confucius did not elaborate on his
ontology, from this statement we can say that, in spirit, he is in
accord with Zhuang Zi's ontology. For example, for the Confucian, a
person is a son, a father, a husband, a teacher, and so on. Being a
son or a father is not merely a property in addition to his being; they
are (part of) his identities; they are his ways of being. Without this
ontology, the Confucian socio-ethical theory would be without base.
This ontology lays a metaphysical foundation for the worldviews of
Confucians as well as Taoists and directly affects their ways of life.[41]
    Zhuang Zi's notion of identity may be characterized as one-many
identity, in contrast to Aristotle's notion of one-one identity. It is
notable that Zhuang Zi's notion of one-many identity is shared by
other Eastern philosophies. It also appears in Hindu deities. For
example, Krishna, who appears in the guise of Arjuna's charioteer
in the *Bhagavad Gita*, is Vishnu, the god nourishing and sustaining
life; who is also Matsya, a huge fish that saves the ancestor of all
human beings during the great flood. Theologians usually rational-
ize this by saying that Vishnu is the god who has many forms of
incarnation such as Krishna and Matsya. Hence, the real identity of
the god is Vishnu. However, even the identity of Vishnu is not all
that clear-cut. Sometimes Vishnu appears to have been fused with
Shiva, another supreme god, into a single figure *Hari-hara*. In an
effort to reconcile this apparent discrepancy, later theologians
created an artificial notion of "One God in three forms"—Brahma-
Vishnu-Shiva. Despite this effort, in popular Hindu religion Vishnu
and Shiva are still worshiped as two different supreme gods.[42] For
the Hindus, all these forms of deity, Vishnu or Krishna alike, are
manifestations of Brahman, the ultimate reality.
    Another manifestation of this notion of one-many identity in
Hinduism is the identification of Brahman (the Absolute) and *ātman*

(the individual self). In a way, one can say that, since the individual self is a particular and the Brahman is the universal, they are different. Yet to say Brahman and *ātman* are identical is to say that they are one, not two. How is this possible? One may want to say that, instead of the individual self, "*ātman*" here refers to "the self of all." But the self of all cannot be separated from the totality of individual selves. In the *Upanishads* it is evident that the search is twofold, both for the eternal "self" (*ātman*) within a person and for the eternal ground of the universe outside him (Brahman). The *Aitareya Upanishad* states, for instance,

> Oneself (*ātman*) is to be made happy here on earth. Oneself is to be waited upon. He who makes his own self (*ātman*) happy here on earth, who waits upon himself—he obtains both worlds, both this world and the yonder;

and

> "He who moves about happy in a dream—he is the Self," said he. "That is the immortal, the fearless. That is Brahman."[43]

In the *Bṛhadāraṇyaka Upanishad* Uṣasta Cākrāyaṇa questions Yājñavalkya, the sage. "Yājñavalkya," said he, "explain to me him who is the Brahman present and not beyond our ken, him who is the Self in all things." Yājñavalkya responds, "He is your self (*ātman*), which is in all things."[44] Brahman is *ātman*. This cannot be the case unless Brahman is manifold. And indeed the *Upanishads* repeatedly make this claim. For example:

> There are, assuredly, two forms of Brahman: the formed and the formless, the mortal and the immortal, the stationary and the moving, the actual and the yon. This is the formed—whatever is different from the wind and the atmosphere. This is mortal; this is stationary; this is actual. . . . Now the formless is the wind and the atmosphere. This is immortal, this is moving, this is the yon.[45]

These forms of Brahman are better described as ways of the being of Brahman rather than its properties or attributes. We may simply say that they are Brahman. In other words, Brahman does not exist beyond all these forms; it is all these forms because Brahman is one and many. Even though the Chinese have a different worldview from the Indians, they do share a similar concept of one-many identity.

While this notion of identity appears incomprehensible to many in the West, G. W. F. Hegel, a Western philosopher, has made it one of his central claims. Hegel criticizes the Aristotelian concept of identity as "abstract identity" (in the form of "$a = a$"). It is the notion of identity entirely excluding difference. Hegel regards this notion of identity as the "key" to distinguishing good philosophy from the bad.[46] For Hegel, the real identity, the one that is philosophically interesting, is identity with difference. This notion can be put into a paradoxical yet very insightful form: instead an abstract "$a = a$", a is both a and non-a. To apply this formula to the above case of Hindu philosophy, we may say that *ātman* is both Brahman (i.e., in that they are fundamentally the same) and non-Brahman (i.e., in that there is some difference between them).

A recent Western philosopher whose ontology appears similar to Zhuang Zi's is Martin Heidegger. Heidegger believes that Aristotle was mistaken when he reduced the question of being into that of substance. Against Aristotle's view that a man is a substance with various properties, Heidegger uses the term "Dasein" for human being ("the kind of entity we are"). Dasein is not a substance. For Heidegger, "the 'essence' of Dasein lies in its existence."[47] As an entity, Dasein exists through ways of being. For instance, Heidegger writes: "Being-true as Being-uncovering, is a way of Being for Dasein"[48]; "the knowing which asserts and which gets confirmed is, in its ontological meaning, itself a *Being towards* Real entities, and a Being that *uncovers*"[49]; and "[Dasein's] asserting is a way of Being towards the Thing itself that is."[50] As understanding, asserting, knowing, and uncovering are all *ways* or modes that constitute Dasein.[51] For Heidegger, it is not the case that there is Dasein ontologically prior to its understanding, asserting, knowing, and uncovering, nor is it the case that Dasein has these actions as its attributes or properties in addition to its real being. Rather Dasein, or the Being of the "there (*Da*)," consists in these *ways* of Being. In the following chapter I will look into Heidegger's philosophy in some detail.

Truth

Confucius and Heidegger

I t would seem that from their earliest beginnings, truth and philosophy have been associated together. In Plato, for instance, philosophy is the pursuit of truth. Chad Hansen sounded shocking when he asserted that "Chinese philosophy has no concept of truth."[1] Huston Smith, however, sees the matter differently. Smith observes that "truth" has different references in India, East Asia, and the West: "India tied truth to things, East Asia to persons, and the West to statements."[2] Before we can ask the question "Who is right?" on this issue, we need to ask another question: "Are they talking about the same thing?"

Smith appears to be using the word "truth" in a broader sense. For Indians, the question of truth is primarily the truth of ultimate reality, namely the Dharma. For Westerners, the question of truth is usually seen as a matter of verifiability of propositions or statements, a matter of correspondence between words and facts. For East Asians, the Chinese specifically, truth is neither a person-transcendent reality nor a correspondence between words and facts. Smith writes:

> Truth for China is personal in a dual or twofold sense. Outwardly it takes into consideration the feelings of the persons an act or utterance will affect (one thinks of the normality of white

lies and keeping one's mouth shut when appropriate). Meanwhile, inwardly it aligns the speaker to the self he ought to be; invoking a word dear to the correspondence theorists we can say that truth "adequates" its possessor to his normative self. The external and internal referents of the notion are tightly fused, of course, for it is primarily by identifying with the feelings of others (developing *jen*) that one becomes a *chün tzu* [*jun zi*] (the self one should be).[3]

In other words, "truth" in China has (primarily) to do with a person's character and ethical behavior.

Does the Chinese "truth" have anything to do with the notion of "truth" in the West? Is the word here merely a homonym? Is Chad Hansen right after all that Chinese philosophy has no concept of truth? In this chapter I will explore these questions. To avoid confusion, I will call the notion of truth as Smith uses it in the Chinese case "pragmatic truth." I will call the notion of truth as a value applied to statements or beliefs which correctly or adequately reflect facts "semantic truth" (more by its content) or "propositional truth" (more by its form). I will show that "truth" here is by no means a mere homonym and that the link between the two notions of truth is substantial and should not be neglected.

This can be demonstrated, I believe, by a historical perspective upon Confucianism and by a reading of Martin Heidegger. Specifically, I will first examine truth as an ontological concept in both Heidegger and Confucianism, then turn to the ethical implications of this concept in each case and the connection between truth and freedom. A comparative study of these two philosophies will show how semantic truth was marginalized in Confucianism as a result of its preoccupation with the ontological-ethical dimension of truth, not as a consequence of the peculiar structure of Chinese language as Chad Hansen has claimed.

Truth as an Ontological Concept

Heidegger was one of few Western philosophers who had some philosophical affinity with Eastern philosophy. As a Western philosopher, Heidegger was deeply rooted in the Western philosophical tradition even though he rebelled against its metaphysics. He also developed insights that are close to Eastern thought.[4] A reading of

Heidegger may prove instrumental in making connections between the Chinese and Western notion of truth.

Let us first look at how Heidegger developed his concept of truth through an ontological twist by reworking the Western traditional concept of truth.

In Heidegger, truth is understood as "true-being" or "being-true (*Wahrsein*)." He defined "being true" as "unveiling (*aletheia*)."[5] In both *Being and Time* (1926) and *On the Essence of Truth* (1930) Heidegger explicitly criticized the Western traditional concept of truth that reduces truth to a matter of "correctness," the correctness of the relation of the intellect to the known object.

In the correspondence theory of truth, the essence of truth lies in the agreement of the assertion with what is being asserted. But an assertion does not literally "agree with" an object or reality, which is a nonassertion. "With regard to what do *intellectus* and *res* agree?" Heidegger questions. "In their kind of Being and their essential content do they give us anything at all with regard to which they can agree?"[6] The answer is of course "no." After all, it is impossible for *intellectus* and *res* to be equal because they are not of the same kind or same nature. Therefore, truth cannot possibly have the structure of an agreement between knowing and the object in the sense of a likening of one entity (the subject) to another (the object).[7] Correspondence between the statement and the thing cannot signify a thing-like approximation between dissimilar kinds of things.[8]

Then, what can truth be? Heidegger proposes:

> To say that an assertion "*is true*" signifies that it uncovers the entity as it is in itself. Such an assertion asserts, points out, "lets" the entity "be seen" in its uncoveredness. The *Being-true* (truth) of the assertion must be understood as *Being-uncovering*.[9]

For him, that an assertion is "in agreement with" or "corresponds with" an object is possible only in the sense that an assertion points out or reveals what has been hidden or covered. Therefore, the truth of an assertion, or more appropriately, an assertion's being true, lies in its "being-uncovering."

In this way, the truth of an assertion lies in its function of uncovering what is being asserted as it is. If this is the essence or underlying meaning of truth, then nonlinguistic behavior can also be true: speaking pragmatically, a hammer is being true when it reveals the being of the hammer—when it is presented in a contexture in which hammers exist; for example, when a hammer functions in a typical hammering way, not as a paperweight. Understood this way, the "locus" of truth is not in assertion or language per se but in the entire realm of being. The ontological status of being true is no longer merely one of knowing but also one of being. Thus, the semantic concept of truth now has turned into an ontological one with a shift in emphasis from "being *true*" to "*being* true." Consequently, propositional truth, the truth of a statement of a fact, is derivative from and based upon the truth of being. We can know something to be true only if it is true in the first place.

Heidegger did not finish here. In truth, entities are uncovered as they are. Heidegger maintains that they are true only "in a second sense": "What is primarily 'true'—that is, uncovering—is Dasein."[10] For him, entities cannot be uncovered unless there is "uncovering." Uncovering is a way of Being of Dasein.

Then, in what way does Dasein uncover? Dasein is that which understands. In understanding, Dasein intends itself and finds itself in its Being-in-the-world. In Dasein's world "there is" a functional referential contexture in which entities are. Only within this holistic contexture are things what they are in the way they are, and thus have meanings. In other words, the uncoveredness of entities within-the-world is *grounded* in the world's disclosedness, and disclosedness is the basic character of Dasein "according to which it *is* its 'there (Da).'"[11] Heidegger concludes,

only as Dasein *is* (that is, only as long as an understanding of Being is ontically possible), "is there" Being. When Dasein does not exist, "independence" "is" not either, nor "is" the "in-itself." In such a case this sort of thing can be neither understood nor not understood. In such a case even entities within-the-world can neither be discovered nor lie hidden.[12]

Without Dasein there is no uncoveredness, no disclosedness, and therefore no truth.

In truth, whereas entities are being uncovered, Dasein is being disclosed and is doing the uncovering. The "roots" of entities' being what they are can only be found in Dasein, and the foundation of their being true is in Dasein. Truth is a way of being of Dasein itself, of Dasein's existence. To put it another way, Heidegger states that

> In so far as Dasein *is* its disclosedness essentially, and discloses and uncovers as something disclosed to this extent it is essentially "true." *Dasein is "in the truth."*[13]

Heidegger maintains that this assertion has ontological meaning. Instead of an "agreement" between two things, truth is that in which Dasein uncovers entities in the world. It is a way of Dasein's Being— "a Being-towards uncovered entities."[14]

Furthermore, Dasein cannot uncover entities unless it is itself disclosed to the world. Heidegger uses "disclose" (*Erschliessen*) and "disclosedness" to mean "to lay open" and "the character of having been laid open."[15] To say that Dasein is laid open is to say that Dasein is Being-in-the-world in which Dasein unveils itself in a referential whole; it is within this referential totality that Dasein understands its being. In this disclosedness Dasein obtains familiarity with its world and upon this familiarity lies the very possibility of Dasein's explicit ontologico-existential interpretation of relations and entities in the world.[16] The disclosedness in the form of familiarity is, in turn, constitutive of Dasein. That is, in this disclosedness lies the very Being of Dasein. In such a way, truth is a fundamental character or state (*existentiale*) of Dasein; or in Heidegger's own words, disclosedness is the primordial truth and the truth of existence.[17]

The common Chinese rendering of the English word "truth" is *"zhen li* 真理." *"Zhen"* means true, real, genuine, and authentic; *"li"* means pattern (like in marble or wood), reason, and (natural) law. In Chinese, this concept as it is presently used has an ambiguous status of both the ontological and the epistemic. For example, during the late 1970s nationwide campaign on the "criterion of truth" it was said that "the criterion of truth is practice."[18] If it is about theories and ideas, as some articles then published suggested,[19] what makes theories and ideas true should be reality or facts, not practice; practice can only be the process that shows whether theories or ideas are consistent with the facts or reality. Then, how can it make sense to say that "practice is the only criterion of truth" as the then dominant view claimed? It does not unless it is presupposed that practice and reality are somehow the same thing. The campaign itself was politically oriented and did not really touch this metaphysical issue. The issue, however, was later picked up in another great discussion in the early 1980s, which was centered on Marx's early concept of "humanized nature," the idea that the reality for humans is one that is mixed with human labor, therefore a humanized reality. The notion of a humanized reality dissolved the apparently presupposed dichotomy in the earlier debate: theories and ideas on the subjective side and reality and facts on the objective side.

The usage of *"zhen li"* is fairly recent in China and is probably a hybrid of the Chinese traditional notion and a Western import. In order to understand the notion in its own tradition, we need to look into its history in the Chinese tradition.

One of the earliest uses of the word *"zhen"* can be found in *Tao Te Ching* 道德经.[20] Chapter 21 of the Taoist canon states, "In it [Tao/ Way] is the quintessence which is very *zhen"*; and chapter 54 says, "Cultivate the Way yourself, and your virtue will be *zhen."*[21] However, *Tao Te Ching* offers no exposition as to what the word means. In *Zhuang Zi*, *"zhen"* was used in contrast to *"wei"* (伪, human-made, artificial, false) for the first time. *Zhuang Zi* states: "How can Tao be so obscured that there are truth [*zhen*] and falsity? How can speech be so obscured that there are right and wrong?"[22] It should be noted that here associated with Tao is the matter of truth and nontruth, whereas associated with speech is the matter of (moral) right and wrong, not the other way around. In other words, truth is a matter of being; speech a matter of moral conduct. It is also in *Zhuang Zi* the term *"zhen zhi"* (真知, *chen chih*—true knowledge, real knowledge) first appeared: "There must be the true person (真人, *zhen ren/chen jen*) before there can be true knowledge (*zhen zhi*)." The true person (*"ren"* 人 in Chinese is gender-neutral) is one who does not see Heaven (天, nature) and human beings as in opposition against each other.[23] Only such a person can know the Tao. Hence, there must be the true person (*zhen ren)* before there can be true knowledge (*zhen zhi*). Evidently *"zhen zhi"* (true knowledge) is derivative of *"zhen ren,"* meaning the kind of knowledge that the true person possesses. Therefore the primary meaning of *"zhen,"* upon which *"zhen li"* (truth) is built, has to be found in the use in *"zhen ren."* "True" in "the true person" is used in an ontological sense; it can only mean "true to the Tao" or "[someone] lives truly."[24] It is a way of being.

In *Zhuang Zi* "*zhen*" was defined in terms of "*cheng*" (诚 *ch'eng*): "*zhen* is *cheng* in its ultimacy."[25] According to Chang Tainien 张岱年, in *Zhuang Zi*, "*zhen*" and "*cheng*" are synonymous, and in Confucianism, *zhen* is *cheng*.[26]

"*Cheng*," as it is used in contemporary Chinese, literally means "sincere" or "sincerity." As a Confucian philosophical concept it also means "real," "true," and "genuine."[27] Etymological evidence as seen in *Zhuang Zi*, however, at best gives us some clue as to how words transformed over time. In order to see what *cheng* has to do with truth in Confucianism, we need to look into how *cheng* is understood in the Confucian classics.

In *Analects* 论语, the central concept was "*jen* 仁," not "*cheng*." In *Mencius* 孟子, "*cheng*" was used numerous times, but Mencius's focus appears to be on "*xing*" (性 human nature, or characteristics), not "*cheng*." It is in *The Doctrine of the Mean* 中庸 that the concept of *cheng* emerges as one of cardinal importance.[28] This work is attributed to Zi Si 子思, Confucius's grandson and Mencius's teacher. Some scholars, however, have dated the work after Mencius.[29] If the latter account is true, there might be a thread of conceptual development from *jen* to *xing* and then to *cheng*.[30] What is clear, as I will show here, is that there is a close connection between *jen* and *cheng*.

Chapter XXV of *The Doctrine of the Mean* explicates "*cheng*" in terms of its root component which is also pronounced "cheng" but means "completion": "*Cheng* is self-completion (*Cheng zhe, zi cheng ye* 诚者, 自成也). . . . [It is] the beginning through the end of things." In this way, *cheng* is a process of completing things. The text also states: "*Cheng* is the Way of Heaven" (chapter XX);[31] and

> The ultimate *cheng* is ceaseless. Being ceaseless, it is lasting. Being lasting, it is manifesting. Being manifesting, it is infinite. Being infinite, it is extensive and deep. . . . It is because it is infinite and lasting that it can complete all things. (XXVI)[32]

Here *cheng* is presented as the creative power in the cosmos, or simply the dynamic reality or "the Real." This dynamic reality creates itself and creates through human beings. Through *cheng*, human beings participate in the creation of the Way.

Hence, "To think how to be *cheng* is the Way of humanity. He [who is *cheng*] . . . is naturally and easily in harmony with the Way. Such a person is a sage. He who tries to be *cheng* is one who chooses the good and holds fast to it." (XX) For the Confucians, *cheng* is not merely a transcendent heavenly power but also a human power. The Way of Heaven is also the human way. In *cheng* the two are one.

Cheng is the way of the unity of Heaven and human. We may designate as "the truth" the ultimate yet ever changing reality, of which humans are a part. Then the active human participation in the Heavenly way may be rendered as "(humans') being true." For the Mencian branch of Confucianism, to which *The Doctrine of the Mean* is attributed, human nature is Heaven-endowed and hence is in accord with the Way (e.g., *Mencius*, 7A:1). To be *cheng* is to be true to one's Heaven-endowed nature, and to be true to one's Heaven-endowed nature is to follow the Way.

It is probably in this sense that D. C. Lau translated "*Cheng* is the Way of Heaven" in *Mencius* as "being true is the Way of Heaven."[33] Tu Wei-ming maintained that "*cheng*" in this context "definitely points to a human reality which is not only the basis of self-knowledge but also the ground of man's identification with Heaven"; in other words, "*Cheng*, so conceived, is a human reality, . . . by which a person becomes 'true' and 'sincere' to himself, in so doing, he can also form a unity with Heaven."[34] Forming this unity means participating in, and becoming one with, the Way.

To form this unity, however, is by no means an easy task. It first of all requires devotion and persistency. *The Doctrine of the Mean* states:

Study it [the way to be *cheng*] extensively, inquire into it accurately, think it over carefully, sift it clearly, and practice it earnestly. . . . If another person succeeds by one effort, you will use a hundred efforts. If another person succeeds by ten efforts, you will use a thousand efforts. If one really follows this course, though stupid, one will surely become intelligent, and though weak, will surely become strong. (XX)

In order to be a unity with Heaven, one must strive earnestly. One must really want it from the bottom of one's heart; one must be sincere in this long journey of pursuit after the Way. *The*

Great Learning 大学, another Confucian canon, explicitly makes the *cheng* of one's will a precondition for rectifying one's mind and cultivating one's life. In this sense, *cheng* is the psychological state of sincerity. The will that consistently pursues what it wants is a sincere will.

Therefore, in Confucianism, *cheng* can be analyzed on two levels. On the first level, it is the true human way of being; it is humans' way of participating in the process of Heaven's creation of reality. We must remember that the Way of Heaven is not only an ontological determination, but also an ethical one for the Confucian. Because of this dual character of the Way of Heaven in Confucianism, *cheng* is an ontological-ethical concept.

On this level, it can be argued that *cheng* as the fundamental concept in Confucian metaphysics is more primordial than any other Confucian virtue concept and accounts for all other concepts. For example, why should one be *jen*? The Confucian answer is that because to be *jen* is to follow one's Heaven-endowed nature, and is to be true to one's ownmost nature. Therefore *The Doctrine of the Mean* states that "Without *cheng* there is nothing." (XXV)

On the second level, *cheng* has psychological implications. To be true means to be true to oneself and to be sincere with oneself, allowing no self-deception. At this level, *cheng* also has prescriptive ethical implications. *The Great Learning* explains "sincerity of the will (诚其意 *cheng qi yi*)" by using the analogy of one's disliking a bad smell and liking a beautiful color (chap. 6). The disliking of a bad smell and the liking of a beautiful color are real; they allow no deception. Pretending to like a smell that one dislikes does not make one like it; pretending to dislike a color that one likes does not make one dislike it. In following the Way, one must get real as one dislikes a bad smell and likes a beautiful color. That is, to know one's way and sincerely abide by it.

Following this way of thinking, *cheng* also has epistemic implications. For one thing, being-true cannot be separated from knowing-(what-is)-the-true, and vice versa. Therefore Mencius said "one who knows one's own nature will know Heaven."[35] According to Fung Yu-lan 冯友兰, to know Heaven (知天 *zhi tian*) is a (necessary) step toward serving Heaven (事天 *shi tian*) and being one with Heaven (同天 *tong tian*).[36] The person who is one with Heaven is a person of *cheng*. Of course, all these implications are derivative of the onto-logical notion of truth (being true). For in Confucianism as well as in

Heidegger, feeling-true (sincere) and knowing-the-true are ways of being-true.

Now we can see some resemblance between Dasein's being true in Heidegger and the Confucian person's being true. First of all, truth is primarily a matter of being instead of a matter of knowing. Second, it is Dasein or human beings, not mere propositions or beliefs, that are being-true. The locus of truth is human *being*. Third, being-true, in Confucianism as well as in Heidegger, is not a given state; it is rather a ceaseless process in which we find our own unique way of being in the world. In this process we define and make who we are and what we are. The Confucians thus would see the concept of *cheng* at work in Heidegger. Had Heidegger seen that in Confucianism *cheng* belongs to the Tao he would have been equally encouraged, just as he understood in the ancient Greeks truth (unhiddenness) belonged to the *logos*.[37]

Neither Heidegger nor Confucians accept the Cartesian dichotomy between ideas and reality, mind and body, the signifier and the signified, thought and action. Therefore truth for them cannot be a matter of correspondence between *intellectus* and *res*. A common conviction shared by Heidegger and the Confucians is this: Understood ontologically, truth is essentially involved in our being, or truth is (and ought to be) our way of Being. Our being true is more primordial than our knowing that something else is true; yet our knowing that we are being true is an inseparable part of our being true. Therefore, whereas for the Confucian *cheng* is the way of Heaven and striving to be *cheng* is the human way, for Heidegger being-true is the fundamental condition for our being able to be in the way in which we exist as Dasein.[38] What makes Heidegger closer to the Chinese is, for one thing, his making truth an ontological notion. Truth, for Heidegger as well as for the Chinese, Confucians in particular, is primarily an ontological concept. Truth, or being-true, is understood as a way of being, instead of a property or value of statements or beliefs.

This affinity between Heidegger and Confucians may help us answer a question raised earlier in this chapter: is the word "truth" used in Western traditional theories of truth and in Chinese philosophy a mere homonym? I have shown that Heidegger's notion of truth is an ontologized notion of the Western traditional epistemic notion of truth. Because "truth" in Heidegger and in Western traditional theories is not a mere homonym, "truth" in Western traditional theories and in Chinese (mainly Confucian) philosophy is not a mere homonym either. All three share the same root metaphor of disclosedness.

Ethical Implications

Because both Heideggerian and Confucian truth are a matter of our being in the world, it is appropriate to examine the ethical implications of their notions of truth. Confucian humanistic ontology affirms and emphasizes humans' potentiality for self-realization into being fully human or sagehood. For the Confucians, because truth or being-true pertains to being a good person, it is a profoundly ethical matter. In the view of many Confucians, Heidegger was not an ethicist for he did not extend his ontology of truth to moral considerations, at least not to the degree the Confucians would like to see. For example, Shu-hsien Liu writes, "Heidegger only gives a phenomenological description but refuses to make value judgments."[39] This observation echoes the view of many Western Heidegger scholars.[40]

Even though Heidegger claims that his ontology of being is an "original ethic," Heidegger scholars are divided on whether Heidegger's existential ontology of being has ethical implications. John Caputo denies any ethical implications in Heidegger's ontology. In fact, Caputo sees it as a fundamental defect in Heidegger and condemns it.[41] In *Against Ethics*, Caputo even goes as far as to attribute to Heidegger the idea that "we do not need ethics."[42] Lawrence J. Hatab, on the other hand, does not agree with Caputo's interpretation of Heidegger and tries to "explore the ways in which his thinking can make an important contribution to ethics."[43] Frederick A. Elliston takes "leaping-ahead (*vorausspringt*)" as a "positive form of solicitude" in Heidegger but maintains that "leaping-ahead" is primarily a *descriptive* category: it delineates one possible way to care for others. Elliston holds that, because of its connection to truth as disclosure, the category of leaping-ahead has "an amoral *evaluative* component [italics in original]."[44] That is, it can be used to evaluate the degree to which the Being of others is revealed to themselves, but this kind of evaluation is not a moral evaluation.

Lawrence Vogel presents three ways to interpret Heidegger's standing on ethics, namely the existential, the historicist, and the

cosmopolitan interpretation.[45] The best-known existentialist inter-
preter of Heidegger is Jean-Paul Sartre. Sartre's reading of
Heidegger laid the cornerstone for the existentialist interpretation:

> When we speak of "abandonment"—a favorite word of
> Heidegger—we only mean to say that God does not exist, and
> it is necessary to draw the consequences of his absence right
> to the end. . . . The existentialist . . . finds it extremely embar-
> rassing that God does not exist, for there disappears with Him
> all possibility of finding values in an intelligible heaven. There
> can no longer be any good *a priori*, since there is no infinite and
> perfect consciousness to think it. . . . Everything is indeed per-
> mitted if God does not exist, and man is in consequence forlorn,
> for he cannot find anything to depend upon either within or
> outside himself.[46]

According to this interpretation, authenticity in Heidegger does not
have any positive consequence in being ethical, for there are no rules
or principles in the world that one can authentically rely upon for
one's actions. One has to live "beyond good and evil." This interpretation, though popular, is not without difficulty. As Vogel points out,
the existentialist interpretation implies an individualistic idea that
the subject makes himself because he is absolutely free to create his
own values, and this idea "presupposes the very metaphysics of
subjectivity from which Heidegger distances himself when, in his
'Letter on Humanism,' he calls fundamental ontology a 'fundamental ethics' and denies that he is an existentialist."[47]

The historicist interpretation sees in Heidegger not only transcendence but also facticity and regards the two equally primordial
in Dasein's being in the world.

Heidegger defines Dasein as "Being-in-the-world" and maintains
that, after being thrown into its "there," every Dasein has been
factically submitted to a definite "world"—its "world";[48] and

> World is that which is already previously unveiled and from
> which we return to the beings with which we have to do and
> among which we dwell. We are able to come up against
> intraworldly beings solely because, as existing beings, we are
> always already in a world. *We always already understand*
> *world in holding ourselves in a contexture of functionality*
> [italics added].[49]

Dasein always understands itself in its being; its understanding is always interpreting; in its interpretation Dasein at the same time projects its possibilities for its own being. Dasein's interpretation and hence projection are not arbitrary or groundless; they are conditioned by the "fore-" structure, namely, fore-having, fore-sight, and fore-conception. Therefore, Dasein is not "a free-floating 'I'."[50]

Obviously the historicist interpretation of Heidegger is a strong antidote to the existentialist interpretation. But it inevitably carries with it a relativistic and provincialistic tendency.

Upon examining the inadequacies of these two interpretations, Vogel offers a third, namely the cosmopolitan interpretation. According to this interpretation, Dasein is being-with, and can develop liberating solicitude for others. Vogel writes:

When one includes this third aspect in the picture, the possibility opens up that moral authority in *Being and Time* lies not only in the choosing individual and the inherited past but also in the freedom of others in the face of whom I own up to my own possibilities and whose existence is honored not when I subordinate them to my own needs but when I let them be free for their own possibilities.[51]

That means, for Vogel, the authentic individual is subject to the imperative not to treat others merely as a means. From here a Kantian Heidegger is born.

Of course, it remains debatable which of the three interpretations is the authentic Heidegger. To the Confucian ear, the historicist and the cosmopolitan interpretations are more attuned than the existentialist interpretation. The Confucian self is not a free-floating "I" either. It is situated contextually in the family, the community, and the society. All these are historically structured. They are all outcomes of what they have been. Because of this contextuality of the self, the question of "who am I?" cannot be addressed without taking into consideration who I have been.

On the other hand, following the Confucian notion of "*shu*" (恕 reciprocity, extending one's mind to others) and Confucius's golden rule, one may come close to the cosmopolitan Heidegger. Confucius said:

Never do unto others what you do not want others to do to you;[52]

and

Wishing to establish his own character, also establishes the character of others, and wishing to be prominent himself, also helps others to be prominent.[53]

Perhaps Confucius's teachings for being moral cannot be reduced to the golden rule. It is, however, at least one thread that goes through his way of thinking about morality. It is safe to say that in this regard Confucius and the cosmopolitan Heidegger have something important in common.

If my interpretation above is correct that, in Confucianism "*cheng*" is more primordial than all other concepts including "*jen*," and *jen* has to be justified in terms of *cheng*, then the Confucians will see a lot to their liking in Heidegger's "original ethic."

In Heidegger, authentic existence cannot be justified in terms of the moral good. If one is to show why and how authenticity is preferable to inauthenticity, it has to be based on truth, not goodness.[54] Understood this way, the difference between Heidegger and the Confucian is not whether the fundamental question for being is, so to speak, "to be true or not to be true"; in that regard they concur. To be *cheng* and to be authentic are to be true. Rather, the difference between Heidegger and the Confucian is whether from "being true" we can derive "being ethical." Whereas the Confucian sees a direct and necessary link, Heidegger, at least in the existentialist interpretation, sees none.

For the Confucian, from *cheng* follows the moral. If one follows the Heaven-endowed nature in being *cheng,* one will develop the moral potential endowed by Heaven. Perhaps in Heidegger's eyes, this entails a Confucian leap of faith in the goodness of Heaven-endowed human nature and it is not well founded. The Confucians perhaps would say that, by refusing to make the move into the ethical, Heidegger has severely undercut his own philosophy, and despite Heidegger's deviation from the modern Western tradition, he is still deeply rooted in it as he presupposes a fundamental gap between truth and good.

Whereas Heidegger sees that Dasein's being-true or being-disclosed leads to its authentic existence, the Confucian sees that *cheng* leads to enlightenment. Enlightenment as a state of one's accomplished self-realization presupposes *cheng*, and *cheng* as one's self-realization of the Tao entails enlightenment.[55] As has been mentioned previously, for the Confucian, there is a direct connection between *cheng* and the moral good: one cannot be *cheng* without knowing the good.[56] The enlightened person knows the moral good and therefore can be *cheng*. Thus, *cheng* is at the core of Confucian morality.

Compared with Heidegger, who sees social norms mostly as presentations of the "they (*das Man*)," the Confucians are more acceptive of social norms. However, social norms, or for that matter any norms, are not all there is to Confucian ethics. For the Confucians, to live an ethical life is to live toward self-realization. According to *The Doctrine of the Mean*, *cheng* is also the completion of the self (XXV). Confucian ethics can be called a "person-making ethics" in the sense that it focuses on and emphasizes the self-realization of the person. *Cheng* is the process of self-realization. As made clear by Confucius himself, to live an ethical life is by no means merely to follow social norms.[57] The ethical life is a life of *cheng*. Although following social norms is important, one cannot become *cheng* by merely following a set of social norms.[58] On the contrary, only a person of *cheng* sees the need for and is capable of establishing the social norms. *The Doctrine of the Mean* states:

> Only those who are absolutely *cheng* can order and adjust the great relations of humankind, establish the great foundations of humanity, and know the transformation and nourishing operations of heaven and earth. (XXXII)

The difference between a moral life and an immoral life is one between *cheng* and un-*cheng*. Without *cheng*, morality is groundless. The Neo-Confucian Zhou Dunyi (周敦颐 Chou Tun-Yi, 1017–73) said: "*Cheng* is the foundation of the Five Constant Virtues and the fountainhead of all moral conducts. . . . Without *cheng*, the Five Constant Virtues and all conducts will be wrong."[59] The five Constant Virtues are: *jen* (仁 humanity, human-heartedness), *yi* (义 righteousness), *li* (礼 propriety, rituals, rules of proper conduct), *zhi* (智 *chi*, wisdom), and *xin* (信 *hsin*, good faith). The Confucians are not against conduct following social norms as long as it is rooted in one's true heart. However, for them, without *cheng* no real moral life is possible. Mencius said that: "There is no greater joy for me than to find, on self-examination, that I am *cheng*."[60]

Even with the "faith" in the goodness of human nature, the Confucian would nevertheless share with Heidegger the vision that the "burden" of finding our own way in the world is on ourselves, not on a god or something else. The person of *cheng* must find his way to a meaningful moral life within his own heart. In this regard, Heidegger has much to say.

Heidegger's existential-ontological interpretation of truth has led him to two related conclusions: First, truth is Dasein's disclosedness, and second, Dasein is equiprimordially both in the truth and in untruth.[61] Here, the second is perhaps as important as the first. Precisely because Dasein is the only being that can disclose beings in the world, it finds itself in an inescapable struggle for truth: it exists between truth and untruth. In other words, the very process of disclosing presupposes the "background" of the undisclosed; the very process of uncovering presupposes the "background" of the covered. Dasein can only uncover from the yet-to-be-uncovered and disclose from the yet-to-be-disclosed.

It is certainly not without reason that, in *Being and Time*, Heidegger includes a discussion of truth in the chapter titled "Care as the Being of Dasein." He maintains that the question of Being, to which "care" is a key concept, can be answered only if the phenomenon of truth is ontologically clarified.[62] This concept of truth directly leads to the being of Dasein as care.

For Heidegger, in disclosedness Dasein is care (*Sorge*). In care, Dasein makes itself an issue; that is, having been thrown into the world, Dasein is concerned with its own being and projects its own being ahead of itself. In such a way, Dasein finds in itself its own ability-for-being-one's-self. In care, Dasein carries a commitment and involvement with what it discloses. It is by no means indifferent.

The German word "*Sorge*" is not an exact equivalent of the English word "care." But Heidegger regards it as "fortunate" that the English word has connotations of love and caring.[63] These connotations have a resemblance to *jen*, the core idea of Confucian ethics.[64]

The call of care, Heidegger maintains, is conscience.[65] As Dasein in its everydayness tends to lose itself, to cover itself up, conscience calls. The call of conscience, however, may come in different voices. The everyday conscience calls Dasein to live up to existing social norms that claim to be "universally binding."[66] It makes Dasein feel "guilty" when failing to do so. However, instead of making Dasein disclosed, authentic, and true to itself, the everyday call actually covers it up; in everyday conscience "truth" is external, imposed from outside, therefore in it Dasein loses its authenticity. In such a state, Dasein falls into untruth.[67] It becomes one of the "they (*das Man*)." In order to be true to itself, to move toward its ownmost ability-for-being, conscience must reach further into Dasein's inner depth and summon it to its ownmost ability-for-being. With such an *existential* conscience Dasein is able to be resolute, that is, to "choose to choose."[68] In its resoluteness, Dasein is rejoined into its disclosedness, into truth. Therefore the "truth of existence" lies in Dasein's authentic self-disclosure or self-projection into one's own innermost possibilities.[69]

Authenticity, however, does not mean that Dasein simply chooses a way of being. Many people do more or less choose their ways of life, yet they may not all be said to be authentic. To be authentic means to choose Dasein's own way of life. In order to do this, Dasein has to choose the way that it has to choose. In this sense there is a paradox: on the one hand, Dasein is free and makes its own choice; on the other, its choice ought not to be just any choice. In an interview in his later years Heidegger said that "man is only man when he stands within the disclosing of being."[70] That is, a human is human in the proper sense only when one stands in truth.

In *Heidegger, Being, and Truth*, Laszlo Versenyi explicates this point as follows:

> Heidegger's "authenticity" of existence is, after all, but a new name for the age-old concept of *aretē*: the excellence in being what one is, the fulfillment of one's own particular functions; true self-realization in the sense of self-disclosure and self-fulfillment. Authenticity is a demand for man because human Dasein is characterized by both facticity and existentiality: it has necessary possibilities (functions to fulfill), but these possibilities that it is "thrown into" are not already realized (by nature) but have to be realized—disclosed and fulfilled—by Dasein itself, and Dasein is aware of this fact.[71]

To what extent Heidegger's notion of authenticity resembles *aretē* may be open to debate. Versenyi, however, does put the point in perspective. Understood the way Versenyi understands it,

Heidegger's authentic existence is similar to the Confucians' in "form" if not in content.

The Confucians believe that, as born and uncultivated, humans are characterized by "facticity," to borrow Heidegger's terminology; but we, as this facticity, are also that through which the Tao is manifested in our being *cheng* (or "existentiality" in Heidegger). On the one hand, *cheng* is a moral necessity; on the other, we need to choose the path of *cheng*. In other words, humans as humans have the Tao imparted to our nature by Heaven, and therefore have the ability or potential (or "potentiality-for-Being") to manifest the Tao through self-realization; every person has the potential to become a sage.

Tu Wei-ming writes:

> The person who embodies *cheng* to the utmost is also a most **genuine** human being. It is in this sense that he completely realizes his own nature. The person who realizes his own nature to the full becomes a paradigm of **authentic** humanity [boldface added].[72]

In *cheng* lies the most authentic human existence. Heidegger would most likely agree with this as he writes:

> Dasein discloses itself to itself in and as its ownmost potentiality-for-Being. This *authentic* disclosedness shows the phenomenon of the most primordial truth in the mode of authenticity. The most primordial, and indeed the most authentic, disclosedness in which Dasein, as a potentiality-for-Being, can be, is the *truth of existence*.[73]

Being-true is the authentic way of Dasein's being. It is the ultimate realization of Dasein's innermost potentiality-for-Being.

The difference between the Confucians and Heidegger is that the former have specifically identified their innermost potentiality as *jen*, a moral character, whereas the latter does not make this kind of move.

I have indicated that in Heidegger there is an essential tension between truth and untruth. He writes, "In its full existential-ontological meaning, the proposition that 'Dasein is in the truth' states equiprimordially that 'Dasein is in untruth.'"[74] For example, in communicating with others, Dasein tends to stabilize truth in the form of assertion. However, truth as disclosedness cannot be stabilized as a given. In such attempts Dasein inevitably covers and closes up, and, therefore, falls into untruth. Dasein's falling into untruth is by no means accidental. Heidegger writes: "The world is always the one I share with others. The world of Dasein is a with-world";[75] and "Dasein is for the sake of the 'they' in an everyday manner, and the 'they' itself articulates the referential context of significance."[76] Because Dasein is essentially "Being-with," the "they" is essentially part of Dasein's positive constitution.[77]

Strictly speaking, Dasein's two types of existence, authentic and inauthentic, cannot exclude one another; they both constitute Dasein. Nevertheless, because of this coexistence the very being of Dasein is in the tension, hence a struggle, between truth and untruth. Just as there are various degrees of inauthenticity, there can be various degrees of authenticity in Dasein. To live an authentic life is thus to be constantly on guard against falling into untruth. Thus in Heidegger, living an authentic life is like Sisyphus rolling the stone uphill: one may never overcome the struggle between truth and untruth, yet it is in struggling that truth takes place.

Similarly, the Confucians see self-realization as a constant lifelong struggle. The very notions of self-realization and self-cultivation imply that one is not yet fully *cheng* and that there are both truth and untruth. A person of full truth is one who is completely one with Heaven. Confucius is said to have achieved this stage when he was seventy years old. Presumably this rarely happens among ordinary people. Confucius was supposedly a "sage" and in his time few people lived so long. In effect the Confucian belief is that one's struggling between truth and untruth never ends.

The Confucians also see "others" as an indispensable part of one's constitution, that is, one's identity. Unlike Heidegger, they emphasize the positive effect of the presence of the public to one's approaching truth; the most difficult part of self-cultivation occurs "when one is alone." When one is alone, away from the public eyes, one tends to be off guard and uninhibited, and may go astray from the Tao; that is, one becomes un-*cheng* and untrue to the self. Therefore, one who is a person of *cheng* must be very "watchful over oneself when one is alone."[78] If one keeps cultivating oneself, eventually one will succeed and become a person of *cheng*, a person of freedom.

Truth and Freedom

In Heidegger, when Dasein is in the truth, when it chooses to choose for its ownmost potentiality-for-being, Dasein is free. When Dasein makes one choice out of its projected possibilities, it nullifies all other possibilities. "The nullity we have in mind belongs to Dasein's Being-free for its existentiell possibilities. Freedom, however, *is* only in the choice of one possibility."[79] Dasein is free only when it is in the resoluteness, that is, when Dasein is true to itself.

I have mentioned that Dasein is disclosed and uncovers within the referential totality of Dasein's world. However, it would be wrong to think this referential structure of contexture of Dasein's world as a fixed given. The relation between Dasein and the referential structure is twofold and bidirectional: on the one hand, in this contexture Dasein finds its world, and Dasein's understanding is based on this structure; on the other, through its activity or being, Dasein also participates in the constant formation and reformation of the referential totality. It is within this twofold characteristic of being that Dasein finds itself in the truth and is free.

In *On the Essence of Truth* Heidegger claims that "the essence of truth is freedom."[80] By "essence" Heidegger means "the ground of the inner possibility of what is initially and generally admitted as known."[81] This ground for truth, Heidegger suggests, is Dasein's freedom. Dasein in its freedom, or simply Dasein as freedom, lets beings be the beings that they are, and reveals itself as letting beings be.[82] Here "letting" means "making" in the active sense instead of the usual connotation as "leaving something alone." In this sense "letting-be" is exercising freedom. In "letting-be" Dasein discloses and uncovers.

This freedom is, however, not caprice. Heidegger writes that in letting beings be, Dasein

> sets man free for his "freedom" by first offering to his choice something possible (a being) and by imposing on him something necessary (a being), human caprice does not then have freedom at its disposal. Man does not "possess" freedom as a

property. At best, the converse holds: freedom, ek-sistent, disclosive Da-sein, possesses man.[83]

In freedom the authentic Dasein makes choices. Given the fore-structure of Dasein, its choices are by no means arbitrary. It is only through its freely choosing its possibilities that Dasein moves forward in its being-in-the-world.

Thus, in Heidegger, the question of the essence of truth finds its answer in the proposition "the essence of truth is the truth of essence."[84] The truth of essence is Dasein's authentic being in which Dasein remains free by choosing its own possibilities for being. Without this kind of authentic being, there is no freedom.

Interestingly, in Confucianism freedom is also grounded in truth, that is, *cheng*. *The Doctrine of the Mean* states that

> *cheng* is the way of Heaven. To think how to be *cheng* is the Way of humanity. The *cheng* person hits upon what is right without effort and apprehends without deliberating. He is naturally and easily in harmony with the Way/Tao. Such a person is a sage. (XX)

Sagehood is the state of ultimate freedom. When a person is so persistently true to himself, he is perfectly in alignment with the Tao and his way is the Way of Heaven, and vice versa. Following Heidegger, we may say that such a person does not possess *cheng* as a property; the converse is true: *cheng* appropriates the person. The person's being appropriated by *cheng* should not be viewed as passive. It is the ultimate harmony with the Way.

The Book of Change also states that the gentleman (君子 *jun zi*) acts toward the completion of virtue, and such a great person forms the same virtue with Heaven and Earth, produces the same illumination with Sun and Moon, generates the same order with the Four Seasons, and shares the same fortune with the spirits; "when [he] acts before Heaven acts, Heaven does not go against him, when [he] acts after Heaven, he enhances Heaven's course."[85] A person of completed virtue is a person of the Way. His course of action is one with the course of Heaven. Therefore, such a person is free. When, at seventy years, Confucius could do whatever he willed and still remain in the Way, he was in this state of freedom.[86]

It should be noted that the Confucian freedom is not an absolute freedom without external constraints. The Tao has its way; whether we like it or not. In this regard, the Confucians find Heidegger again on their side in opposition to Sartre's absolutism of freedom. Heidegger maintains:

> Care does not characterize just existentiality, let us say, as detached from facticity and falling; on the contrary, it embraces the unity of these ways in which Being may be characterized. So, neither does "care" stand primarily and exclusively for an isolated attitude of the "I" towards itself. . . . In Being-ahead-of-oneself as Being towards one's ownmost potentiality-for-Being, lies the existential-ontological condition for the possibility of *Being-free* for authentic existentiell possibilities. For the sake of its potentiality-for-Being, any Dasein is as it factually is.[87]

As a basic component of Dasein's being-in-the-world, care is not detached from the external conditions of its existence. As essentially being-in-the-world, Dasein is only "free-in-the-world," namely, free for its authentic possibilities.

Here emerges the Confucians' own problem of the inevitable tension between the "is" and the "ought" of human existence. *The Doctrine of the Mean* states that "The Tao cannot be separated from us for a moment. What can be separated from us is not the Tao" (I). The words for "cannot" are *"bu ke* 不可*."* Like its English counterpart, *"bu ke"* carries with it an ambiguity between impermissibility ("ought not to") and impossibility ("being incapable of"). The text does not specify whether "cannot" is a metaphysical description or an ethical prescription. Here a question arises. If the Tao necessitates that we "follow our nature," then how is freedom possible? If the Tao cannot be separated from us in a metaphysical sense, we certainly have no freedom. On the other hand, if it is only in the moral sense that we ought to participate in the Tao, where is the basis for (moral) necessity?

Perhaps Heidegger's twofold characteristic of Dasein's being-in-the-world, which we discussed earlier in this section, can shed some light on this issue. Similar to the way in which, in Heidegger, Dasein is thrown into a world that is already organized in a factual contexture, the Confucians also find themselves living in a human world in which the Tao is already under way. The Tao is already so deeply rooted in the world that it cannot be reversed. The Confucians have a choice to make: they either choose to be carried away passively by the Tao or choose to actively participate in the ceaseless unfolding of the Tao, the ceaseless formation and reformation of the world. Only in resolutely choosing the latter can the Confucians find freedom. Thus, paradoxically, freedom is manifested when we actively engage in our Heaven-imposed activity of self-realization. That is to say, only by being *cheng*, can we be free. In this sense, for the Confucian the essence of *cheng* is freedom.

Why Semantic Truth Has Been Marginalized

So far I have examined the concept of truth and its implications for ethics and human freedom in both Heidegger and the Confucians, and thereby have given a qualified "yes" to the question of whether Chinese philosophy has a concept of truth. I say "qualified" because the Confucian truth is not semantic truth. When Chad Hansen asserted that "Chinese philosophy has no concept of truth," he apparently meant semantic truth or propositional truth. The notion of semantic truth in the Confucian has been largely marginalized, if not entirely ignored. But why so? Is it because of the Chinese language structure as Hansen claimed? I do not think so.

Adopting a linguistic approach, Chad Hansen argues that "a pragmatic interpretation of classical Chinese is a more explanatorily coherent theory than a semantic (truth-based) alternative."[88] Pragmatics, as defined by Charles Peirce, is the study of the relation of language and its users, whereas semantics deals with the relation of language and states of affairs. Of course, if one adopts also a realist assumption about the text as Hansen does, one has to say that a pragmatic interpretation of classical Chinese is more explanatorily coherent *because* classical Chinese philosophers had primarily pragmatic instead of semantic concerns for truth.

Then the question becomes, why didn't Chinese philosophers develop semantic concerns of language that would have enabled them to deal with propositional truth? Hansen's answer focuses on language itself. He argues that most Chinese verbs are "two-place action" verbs and they take direct objects instead of propositional clauses; therefore Chinese sentences are not propositions, which are required for expressing semantic or propositional truth.[89] This line of argument suggests that the Chinese did not develop a concept of semantic or propositional truth because they lacked the linguistic tool to do so. Here Hansen appears to have put the cart before the horse. Language is a tool for our use. When there is a need, people will develop or invent new tools. If other languages and modern Chinese can express semantic truth, it seems only reasonable to think that the ancient Chinese would have developed their language to do the same if there had been such a need. Moreover, Heidegger certainly did not lack the language to develop his concept of propositional truth. Why did he not develop such a concept? Perhaps the real answer lies not in the language. Perhaps a study of Heidegger will help contemporary Confucian scholars solve the puzzle.

It is certainly not the case that Heidegger was unaware of issues of semantic truth. In fact, as shown earlier in the chapter, semantic truth is where Heidegger started his investigation of truth. I claim that it is Heidegger's preoccupation with Dasein's being and truth as being-true that precludes him from devoting more attention to semantic truth. Analogously, we may propose as a hypothesis that Confucian philosophers did not fully develop the concept of semantic truth because their preoccupation with the ontological-ethical conception of truth precluded them from getting deeper into the concept of semantic truth.

Let us look at the case in Heidegger. First, Heidegger was overwhelmingly preoccupied with his effort to safeguard Being. Everything else must serve this goal. His attitude toward other kinds of learning and knowledge is clearly shown in his discussion of modern science:

> Every sort of thought, however, is always only the execution and consequence of a mode of historical Dasein, of the fundamental position taken toward Being and toward the way in which beings are manifest as such, i.e., toward truth.[90]

For Heidegger, Dasein cannot seek semantic truth for its own sake. Semantic truth, as commonly understood to be used typically in modern science, does not have value of its own. It is subordinated to ontological truth.

Second, the concept of semantic truth generally presupposes the existence of the object to be known. The object usually has to be taken as a "given" before one can pursue further how true knowledge is possible. In Heidegger, however, this object is never a "given." It is its very being that is at issue. That is, we must inquire into the context of Being that provides the support for the relational totality of the *intellectus-res* structure of truth.[91] The question is primarily ontological and truth has to be investigated as an ontological issue. Heidegger holds that entities have meaning only within a referential contexture that cannot be separated from Dasein. Therefore, semantic truth can only be treated as an extension of ontological truth. The question of semantic truth cannot be answered unless ontological truth is clarified and the question of being is answered; after the ontological concept of truth is worked out, there is little left for additional exploration of semantic truth since semantic truth is entirely dependent on ontological truth.

Third, in Heidegger, "to know" is primarily and essentially "to know how," and "knowing how" only takes place in the existence of Dasein. Interpretation as theoretical knowing or "knowing-that" cannot be separated from, and is predicated on, understanding, or "knowing-how." Therefore, "knowing the truth" is a matter of "being in the truth" or simply "being true." What is traditionally the semantic has become the ontological in Heidegger.

Finally, Heidegger also extends his notion of the truth of assertions, in which the locus of the traditional studies of truth lies, as "uncovering" things as they are, to the notion that nonlinguistic actions can also uncover things as they are. This move puts linguistic acts into a much larger category of actions and thereby makes linguistic acts merely a subcategory within this much larger primary category, the investigation of which received priority or primacy. In this way, the study of the concept of semantic truth per se has to be de-prioritized and consequently marginalized.

Similar reasons may explain why semantic truth has been marginalized in the Confucian tradition. First, the Confucian starts from the premise that the Way of Heaven and the human Way are one and the same. The human Way is not something that is given in a ready form in advance. And human knowledge cannot be obtained without the knowledge of Heaven. Tu Wei-ming interprets the Confucian doctrine that the Way cannot be separated from humanity as meaning that "transcendental truth, devoid of any human content, is certainly not the Way (of *The Doctrine of the Mean*)."[92] "To know Heaven" is to become aware of our own being in this profound cosmological system. The only Way for human beings to know, and hence to join the Way of Heaven, is to participate in the process of the self-creation of the Way. So the primary question is how one participates in the Way of Heaven.

Hall and Ames interpret the Confucian "know" (知 *zhi, chih*) as follows:

> *chih* [zhi] is a process of articulating and determining the world rather than a passive cognizance of a predetermined reality. To *chih* [zhi] is to influence the process of existence within the range of one's viable possibilities.[93]

In this regard the Confucians would agree with Zhuang Zi that "There must be the true [*zhen*] person before there can be true [*zhen*] knowledge."[94] It follows that the Way to find true knowledge is to find the true person, and the Way to be knowledgeable is to become a true person, namely a person of *cheng*. For the Confucians, the knowledge of the Way cannot be separated from participation in the Way.

This is why Wang Yang-ming (王阳明, 1472–1529) is able to maintain that knowing and practicing (i.e., knowledge and action) are one. In Wang Yang-ming "*zhi*" (知 "know") is understood almost entirely as practical knowledge, or precisely, moral knowledge. For Wang Yang-ming, to know is to attain the knowledge of the good (良知 *liang zhi*); the knowledge of the good is grounded in the Way; one cannot know the good unless it shows in the self and it shows only when it is practiced—only when one is *cheng*, that is, true to oneself. In this way, what knowledge of the good can be known depends on how true one is to oneself—depends on *cheng*.

Wang Yang-ming says: "Suppose we say that someone knows filiality and someone knows brotherly respect. Before he can be said to know filiality and brotherly respect, he must have actually practiced them. We cannot say that he knows filiality and brotherly respect if he merely shows them in words."[95] To know filiality is to know how to practice it. Therefore, what is to be known is never a "given" object merely for reflection. While the study of semantic truth does not necessarily presuppose a "given" object, as long as the being of the "object" is yet to be investigated, the ontological question of being naturally preoccupies the Confucian philosophers. If knowledge is seen as knowing some objective facts as a given, such as "water is H_2O," it hardly makes sense to say as Wang Yang-ming does that knowing and practicing are one.

Second, the Confucians agree with Socrates that knowledge is good for its consequences, but probably would not agree with him that it is good for its own sake. For the Confucians, to know is always to know for the purpose of fulfilling one's nature.[96] With such a goal, the Confucian understanding of knowledge is saturated with practical and axiological significance. The real thing to know is not the myriad things themselves, but the "*li*" or "*tian li*" (天理 *t'ien li*, the principle of Heaven), which is present in myriad things. *The Great Learning* makes it very clear that "investigation of things," as the first in the eight-step practice, has the ultimate goal of manifesting one's illuminating character to the world. It begins with "investigating things," then progresses through the intermediate links of "extending knowledge," "making one's will sincere," "rectifying one's mind," "cultivating one's life," "regulating one's family," "ordering the state," and finally ends with "manifesting one's illuminating character to the world." With such a goal in mind, the Confucians naturally would give priority to and put paramount weight on knowledge that shows a direct relevance to this goal. Wang Yang-ming simply rules out "investigation of things" as a necessary step toward the goal. Pure semantic knowledge, knowledge that does not show such a direct relevance, is consequently undervalued or devalued, if not entirely ignored.

Thus, the Confucians inevitably discriminate between two kinds of knowledge: that which would directly serve this goal and that which would not; and hence creates a tension between the two. Confucius said that "the gentleman cannot undertake trivial knowing but can be relied upon for important undertakings; the small people cannot be relied upon for important undertakings but can undertake trivial knowing."[97] "Trivial knowing" is "*xiao zhi*" (小知 *hsiao chih*), literally "petty knowledge." It is not entirely clear here as to what exactly "petty knowledge" denotes. We can be sure, however, that since it came from Confucius it must mean something other than moral knowledge. Later, in a sharp contrast between two kinds of knowledge the Neo-Confucian Zhang Zai (张载 Chang Tsai, 1020–77) makes the point clear: "Knowledge gained through *cheng* and enlightenment is the innate knowledge of one's Heaven-endowed character. It is not the trivial knowledge of senses."[98] For

Zhang, knowledge obtained from seeing and hearing is knowledge obtained through contact with things. It is not knowledge obtained through one's moral nature. Knowledge obtained through one's moral nature does not originate from seeing or hearing. Understood this way, even if there are things in the world that are objects of semantic truth, they possess only marginal significance. A person merely rich in factual knowledge and semantic truth is nevertheless ignorant.

In sum, between moral knowledge on the one hand and knowledge of facts or semantic truth on the other, the Confucians make a judgment on the values of these two in great favor of the former. This value judgment may have enhanced moral education in society, but it inevitably has had a negative impact on the advancement of physical science. Given the deep Confucian conviction in the priority of moral knowledge over knowledge of material things, the matter of knowing these things and the issue of their semantic truth can only be marginalized. This partly explains why it makes sense in following Huston Smith's line of thinking to say, even at great risk of exaggeration, that Chinese philosophers are ethicists, while Indian philosophers are metaphysicians, and Western philosophers are epistemologists.

Language

Pragmatic versus Semantic

As I indicated in chapter 2, Chinese philosophers have been primarily concerned with the pragmatic dimension of truth and language, and consequently have not paid much attention to semantic theories of language. In sharp contrast to this, the primary concern with language in the West appears to be with the semantic dimension. Whereas the Chinese are interested in the appropriate use of language and its social functions, the Westerners are usually interested in whether what is being said is true. In this chapter, I will explore this difference by examining some Confucian thoughts on language, specifically on names, with an emphasis on the pragmatic dimension, and then examine a contemporary Western semantic theory of language, namely Saul Kripke's direct reference account of names. His account, if right, would undermine the foundation of the Confucian understanding of language. I shall show that, while Kripke's account is supported by a strong intuition about names, it has a serious flaw, and therefore fails to undermine the foundation of the Confucian conception of language.

Rectification of Names

One of Confucius's most important political-ethical doctrines is the rectification of names (正名 *zheng ming/cheng ming*). In the *Analects* there is a dialogue between Confucius and his disciple Zi Lu 子路, who asked what Confucius would do first in government. Confucius replied:

> It must be the rectification of names.... If names are not rectified, then [our] language will not concord with what it means. If language does not concord with what it means, then things cannot be accomplished. If things cannot be accomplished, then rites and music will not flourish. If rites and music do not flourish, then punishments will go astray. If punishments go astray, then people will not know how to move hand or foot. Therefore, the gentleman will give only names that can be described in speech and say only what can be carried out in practice.[1]

Here Confucius gave paramount importance to language and the use of names for administering government. Confucius lived in a time when "social rules were broken and music deteriorated (礼崩乐坏 *li beng yue huai*)." He took as his mission the restoration of the social order of the Zhou (周 Chou) dynasty. For him, the starting point was the rectification of names.

The Chinese word for name is "*ming* 名," which means "that by which something/someone is called," or "that for which something/someone is known." The character consists of two components, one for the waning moon symbolizing night, the other for the mouth. The ancient Chinese lexicon *Shuo Wen Jie Zi* 说文解字 explicates that "in the dark things cannot be seen, therefore use mouth (sound) to call them." This apparently includes all designating functions of language. "*Ming*" therefore not only includes proper names but also kind names; not only natural kind names but also non-natural kind names; and not only names in the sense the English word usually means but also descriptions. However, Confucius's concern is not so much with proper names as with names as general terms, that is, kind names and descriptions.

Fung Yu-lan explains the above passage of Confucius as follows:

> Every name possesses its own definition, which designates that which makes the thing to which the name is applied be

that thing and no other. In other words, the name is that thing's essence or concept. What is pointed out by the definition of the name "ruler," for example, is that essence which makes a ruler a ruler. . . . For if it is brought about that ruler, minister, father and son all act in real life in accordance with the definitions or concepts of these words, so that all carry out to the full their allotted duties, there will be no more disorder in the world.[2]

The definition of the name is its connotations, namely, the set of attributes constituting the meaning of the name. It should be pointed out that the first occurrence of "essence" in this passage is the rendering by the translator of *"yao su* 要素*,"* which in Chinese means "key element(s)." The clause "that essence which makes a ruler a ruler" is a liberal rendering of *"jun zhi suoyi wei jun zhe* 君之所以为君者*,"* which means "that which makes the king the king" or "that by which the king is the king"; the word "essence" here is an insertion by the translator. The use of the word "essence" presents an essentialistic overtone that may not exist in Fung Yu-lan. The whole passage nevertheless represents a classical interpretation of Confucius's words on the rectification of names.[3]

This interpretation is supported by a statement in the *Analects* where Confucius said that good government consists in *"Jun jun, chen chen, fu fu,* and *zi zi* 君君, 臣臣, 父父, 子子*."*[4] Here *"jun"* is the word for "king," *"chen"* for "minister," *"fu"* for "father," and *"zi"* for "son." Given the flexibility of ancient Chinese grammar, the sentence itself may be interpreted in two ways. If we read the first word as a verb and second as a noun, then it can mean "treat [only] the king as king, treat the minister as minister, treat the father as father, and treat the son as son." A similar grammatical structure can be found in Mencius's statement of *"qin qin* (亲亲 *ch'in ch'in)."*[5] It means "treating the parents as parents," with the first *"qin"* as a verb and the second a noun. The other way is to read the first word as a noun and the second as a verb. Then it means "the king ought to behave like a king, the minister like a minister, the father like a father, and the son like a son." The first interpretation would provide a guideline for a person's behavior in relation to people of different roles in society; the second provides guidelines for different people with respect to their own social roles. While the sentence itself does not indicate what Confucius meant, the context of the statement makes the second interpretation more plausible.

Confucius was conversing with Duke Jing of Qi 齐景公 on good government. In response to Confucius, the duke said "Indeed if *jun bu jun, chen bu chen, fu bu fu, and zi bu zi,* although I may have all the grain, shall I ever get to eat it?"[6] The Chinese negation word *"bu* 不" is usually followed not by a noun but by a verb or adjective.[7] If the second word is not a noun but a verb, it has to mean "not be" or "not behave like (a king or a minister)." Then the duke's sentence must be "the king is not (behaves not like) a king, the minister is not a minister, the father is not a father, and the son is not a son." Assuming that the duke understood Confucius correctly, we can say that the second interpretation is more appropriate. That is, by *"Jun jun, chen chen, fu fu, and zi zi"* Confucius meant that "the king ought to behave like a king, the minister like a minister, the father like a father, and the son like a son."

For Confucius, names like "king," "minister," "father," and "son" imply a person's proper role in a nexus of social relationships and also imply social responsibilities. For him, "being the king" implies "being kingly," and "being the father" implies "being fatherly." Evidently being something such as a king, a minister, a father, or a son is understood and defined functionally; namely, defined by what one in the role does. And it is not just whatever one in the role does; it is only those functions that one in the role ought to perform.

Then what are these functions that a person in the role ought to perform? The Confucian understanding of the proper role of a person is deeply embedded in Confucian ethics. For example, the king is supposed to be wise, capable of exercising authority properly, and most of all, benevolent. When the person in the role of the king is not performing this way, then he is not fit for the name of the king; for instance, if instead of being benevolent, he is being cruel. The person in the role of the king must therefore constantly remind himself what it means to be the king. On the other hand, if one is not in the role, one should not overstep one's own role limits. Confucius said that "when not in the post, one must not meddle with its affairs."[8] If everyone does what one's role prescribes, the Confucians believe, the world will be in good order.

Therefore, saying "the king [ought to be] king, the minister minister, . . ." is not a simple tautology. For example, when the minister seizes too much power and consequently the king is no longer really in charge, the king is no longer the king nor the minister the minister; when the father is no longer kind and taking father's responsibilities, the father is no longer the father; and when the son no longer honors and respects his parents, the son is no longer the son. Cheng Chung-ying puts it in a nutshell:

> This doctrine does not just require definitional consistency, but implies a recognition of principles: that is, recognition of standards of action that can be used to judge what is true, good, and right, on the one hand, and what is false, bad, and wrong, on the other. To rectify names therefore is to establish standards of the true, the good, and the right.[9]

To indicate and reinforce the true, the good, and the right, and therefore the oughtness, is the primary purpose of names for the Confucians. And to make sure that names perform this function is the Confucian project of rectifying names.

Confucius believed that names have connotations and their connotations determine the way the named "ought to" be, or the features the named "ought to" possess. That is, names are both descriptive and prescriptive. They are descriptive of the ideal states that the names designate, as in the case of the sage Shun 舜 as the son and later the king; they are prescriptive for ordinary people. For an ordinary king, minister, father, and son, these names prescribe the duties that each has to fulfill.

It should be noted that the prescriptive function of names does not only apply to people but also to things in general. For example, Confucius said: "(When) a *gu* is no longer a *gu*, how can you call it a *gu*?"[10] "*Gu* (觚 *ku*)" refers to an ancient eight-cornered bell-shaped wine vessel with the large opening on the top. It symbolizes harmony among people of all directions: east, west, south, north, southeast, northeast, southwest, and northwest. The first part of the sentence here in Chinese is "*gu bu gu* 觚不觚." "*Bu*" means "not" or "no longer." As the grammar requires, the first "*gu*" is a noun, the second a verb. Apparently Confucius was unhappy when he saw that the wine vessel no longer had the shape it was supposed to have. For him, a *gu* must fit its name, which implies certain features. When something does not possess the features of *gu*, it is not a *gu* and should not be called by that name. Therefore the utterance may be rendered as:

When the (so-called) *gu* (the object) is no longer a *gu* (the eight-cornered bell-shaped wine vessel with the large opening on the top), is it (really) a *gu* (the eight-cornered bell-shaped wine vessel with the large opening on the top)?

For Confucius, *"gu"* by definition is an eight-cornered and bell-shaped wine vessel. For anything to be a *gu*, it must be eight-corned and bell-shaped, or it is not a *gu*. On the one hand, a name contains descriptions that the named must fit. On the other, nothing that does not fit the descriptions of the name should bear the name.

Following Confucius, Mencius also believed that the actuality must fit the name or it is no longer the same thing. In *Mencius* we find the following conversation:

King Xuan of Qi 齐宣王 asked, "Was it a fact that Tang 汤 banished King Jie 桀 and that King Wu 武王 marched against King Zhou 纣?" Mencius replied, "According to the records, yes." The king said, "Is it permissible for a minister to murder his king?" Mencius said, "He who injured humanity is a bandit. He who injured righteousness is a savage. Such a person is a despot. I have heard of killing a despot Zhou, but I have not heard of murdering him as the king."[11]

Mencius was evidently concerned with the propriety of using names. For him, the king is one who fits the definition and image of the (Confucian) king. When Zhou no longer fitted that notion, he was no longer the king and should not be called "the king." The people should not rebel against the legitimate king; but when the king loses the qualities that make a king, a revolution is justified under the name of fighting the despot, as opposed to fighting the king, who, by definition, must be just, based on the word's prescriptive function.

Neither Confucius nor Mencius, however, elaborated further on names. It is Xun Zi (荀子 Hsün Tzu, fl. 298–238 B.C.E.), the naturalist Confucian, who explored in some details what kind names are and how names supposedly work. Being "the most logical of all ancient Confucianists,"[12] Xun Zi developed a realist theory of names. He believed that there are different things in the world and therefore was a need for different names in order to denote these actualities. In "actuality" Xun Zi included objects, natural events, and human affairs.

First, how do things in the world fall into different categories (under different names)? Xun Zi believed that we humans classify things into categories according to the way we perceive things in the world:

Why are there similarities and differences in names? It is because of the natural senses. The senses of the same species with the same feelings perceive things in the same way. Therefore, when things are compared, similar things are sorted together. In this way conventional names are given and their meanings are known.[13]

Our five senses register different qualities. Our eyes perceive different colors and shapes; our ears hear different sounds; our noses smell different scents; our tongues taste different flavors; and our bodies feel different touches and temperatures. Based on these different perceptions, we classify things into different categories.

Here Xun Zi did not speculate about what kinds of things there are in themselves apart from human awareness. It is clear that, for him, naming and classification are the same process; it is we who do the classification on the basis of our experience of things.

But sometimes our senses may give us different perceptions of the same thing, and sometimes the same perception of different things. How can we keep track of them? Xun Zi said:

There are similar things but in different places, and there are things that are not similar but in the same place. They can be distinguished. When two things of the same appearance are in different places, although they are same, they are called two actualities. When the appearance changes but the actuality remains the same, it is called transformation. When a thing endures transformation but remains no different in actuality, it is called one actuality. This is how actualities are examined and their number is determined. This is the fundamental principle for instituting names.[14]

As our senses are in contact with outside things and the two work together we acquire knowledge. Xun Zi also called this kind of knowing "*neng* 能," which in Chinese literally means "capability" or "dynamic capacity." It indicates the active role of the knower in the process of knowing. Xun Zi also used the expression "*xin zheng zhi*"

(心征之 the mind/heart collects it [the sensed]). *"Zheng"* can mean both "to verify" and "to summon." Wing-tsit Chan noted that this expression implies that the mind/heart is active, not just receiving knowledge passively.[15] In knowing, the mind/heart is not passively dependent on what the senses register. It processes what the senses register and produces judgment on what things are and how to name them.

Second, Xun Zi believed that the need for names is for human knowledge and for human activities. We respond differently to different qualities and we need to know different things. For that purpose, we need not only to classify things into different categories but also to use different names for them. Xun Zi expressed this view in a passage, which Wing-tsit Chan translated as:

If the five organs register it without knowing what it is, and the mind collects it without understanding it, then everyone says there is no knowledge. These are the causes for the similarities and differences in names.[16]

"Without knowing" in Chinese is *"bu zhi* 不知*."* It does not have an object following the verb *"zhi"* in the original sentence, which needs to be made complete in English rendering by adding "what it is."

Xun Zi differentiated the function of the senses and the function of the mind/heart. It is the mind/heart that processes sense data to identify the whole object being sensed; the objects of the senses are qualities such as colors and sounds. Our senses have direct acquaintance with what is perceived. For example, it is impossible to feel pain yet not recognize it as pain, even though it is possible to fail to identify it under the name "pain" if such a name is lacking. Therefore, here "what it is" cannot mean what is being felt; it can only mean "the name of it (what is being felt)." If so, it is better to make it explicit in the English rendering.

"Without understanding" is *"wu shuo* 无说*."* It does not have an object either. *"Shuo"* in Chinese means "to speak" or "to tell." *Shuo Wen Jie Zi* explicates this word in terms of *"shi* 释*,"* which means "explaining" and "releasing." Rendering *"shuo"* as "understanding" is too much of a stretch. If we reconstruct the missing object following *"wu shuo"* to be "the name(s)," it seems to me that "without telling" is a better way of rendering this sentence than "without understanding." Also, as usual in Chinese, the original sentence does not specify whether what the five senses register here is a singular or a plural. In Xun Zi names are not only for objects (e.g., "bird," "animal") but also for qualities (e.g., "black," "white"). The five senses register various objects and qualities. Therefore, the plural may be appropriate here. This passage may be more appropriately rendered as follows:

If the five senses register different things without knowing [their names], and the mind collects them without telling [their names], everyone would say we do not know these things. This is why there are various names.

In other words, we need different names for different things in the world because we need to know these things, and we need to know them for human benefit. Even though individual sensations are particulars, we need to group them together under different names as different kinds of things. Without names, our senses would not be able to register that they are perceiving the same thing, and our mind/heart would not be able to collect knowledge about things in the world.

Third, Xun Zi saw a hierarchical structure in names based on different degrees of generality and specificity in things. According to him, at the highest level there is the "great general name (大共名 *da gong ming*)," called "*wu*" (物 thing). Under it are lesser common names such as "animal" and "bird." Xun Zi said:

There are myriad things. But sometimes we want to speak of them altogether and call them "things." "Thing" is a great common name. We go from specific to general, and to even more general, until there is nothing more general. Sometimes we want to speak of one type of things and so we call them (for instance) "animals." "Animals" is a lesser common name. We go from general to specific, and to even more specific, until there is nothing more specific.[17]

This is Xun Xi's idea of taxonomy. For Xun Zi, we name things at different levels because we have a need for them. Sometimes we need to speak of things at a more general level and sometimes at a more specific level. So we break things down into sections accordingly.

Fourth, Xun Zi believed that names are governed by convention. He believed that the wise ancients named different things with different names. Initially names were arbitrary. They were fixed by convention. Xun Zi said:

Names have no appropriateness of their own. They are given by convention. It is by convention and custom that names are called appropriate names. If they do not comply with convention, they are inappropriate names. Names do not refer to actualities by themselves. Convention makes them to refer to actualities. It is by convention and custom that they become names of actualities.[18]

In other words, names have no essence. They are given by social convention. Nevertheless, Xun Zi does not believe all names are equally well given. He maintains that while some names are felicitous in themselves, some are not. When a name is direct, easy to understand, and self-consistent, Xun Zi calls it "felicitous (善 *shan*)." Accordingly, people who give felicitous names must be wise persons. At Xun Zi's time, the only persons who were regarded wise enough to do this were the sage-kings. He believed that after the wise sage-kings named various things and people accepted them, names became appropriate names. Here Xun Zi's view of naming is similar to the view in the Confucian classic *The Book of Rites* (礼记 *Li Ji*), which says in chapter 23 that "the Yellow Emperor rectified the names of myriad things to clarify the people's minds (黄帝正名百物 以明民 *Huang Di zheng ming baiwu yi ming min*)."

Fifth, following Confucius, Xun Zi did not fail to note the importance of rectification of names. He said:

Knowing that things with different actualities should have different names, we should let all things with different actualities have different names. They should not be confused.[19]

Because there are different actualities that need to be differentiated, there must be different names for doing so. Confusing different names will cause confusion of actualities, which will have grave consequences.

Xun Zi believed that in society there were the noble and the base. When they were called by false names, the noble and the base were not properly distinguished. Confucians emphasize the distinctions within the social hierarchy. This is not only reflected in the belief that people of different social positions must have different "names," that is, titles, but is also reflected in the fact that the same person had different names for different functions.

Traditionally, a Chinese may have two different names, *ming* 名 and *zi* 字, for distinct functions. The *ming* is the name by which one refers to oneself humbly or by which the superior person calls the inferior. The *zi* is the name by which the inferior person addresses the superior or by which peers address one another. For example, Confucius's *ming* is "Qiu 丘," and his *zi* is "Zhong Ni 仲尼." Within the social hierarchy the same person stands in different relations to people of different social positions. Different uses of names have the function of indicating the social relations that different people are in. It has been considered very important to follow propriety in using the names of the person. Confucius referred to himself as "Qiu" while his disciples referred to him by "Zhong Ni." It would be considered highly inappropriate if it were the other way around. In this way of understanding, names are by no means merely labels. For the Confucians, who think highly of the importance of social propriety, naming is part of social institutions, names carry social relationships, and a person's names indicate that the person's identity is socially constituted.[20]

Xun Zi believed that many social problems were caused by the confusion of names. Statements like "to kill a robber is not to kill a person" and "a white horse is not a horse" had made people confused. This kind of confusion will cause problems in society. He said:

When sage-kings instituted names, they fixed names and distinguished actualities. The Tao prevailed and the sage-kings's wills were understood. Then people were carefully led on the same path. Therefore, quibbling with terms and arbitrarily making up names to confuse appropriate names, thus confusing people's minds and bringing about much litigation, are called great wickedness. It is a crime similar to manufacturing illegal credentials and measurements.[21]

When people rely on correct names and avoid incorrect names, they are honest, like using only valid credentials and accurate measurements. When people are honest, they will be easily employed and will single-mindedly follow the law and carefully obey orders. This way will result in the highest point of good government.

In brief, Xun Zi's theory of naming includes the following points. Names are fixed by social convention and they have connotations. The connotations of a name have prescriptive force on the being of the named. Therefore there is an oughtness for the being of the named; a bird ought to have wings just as a son ought to honor and respect his parents. Confusion and misuse of names have bad social consequences; they may confuse people's minds and be causes of social disorder. Therefore, it is important to include the rectification of names as a necessary step to restore and maintain social order.

In the terminology of contemporary philosophy of language, the Confucian "theory" of name is a description theory. It may be subject to criticism in many ways. For one thing, many names that the Confucians discussed were actually used to denote the name-bearers regardless of their being good or bad. For instance, "*jun* 君" was not only used to denote these who were good kings, but also those who were bad kings. This is why there is the difference between a good wise king ("明君 *ming jun*") and a bad stupid king ("昏君 *hun jun*"). In this context, the word "*jun*" simply denotes the person who occupies the kingship. "*Gu*" obviously had been used to denote the object that Confucius thought was no longer a *gu*; otherwise Confucius would not have complained. The Confucians may argue, of course, that when words like "*jun*" were used both ways they were not used in the way they were supposed to be, and it showed the need for rectification of names.

There appears to be a built-in paradox in this Confucian position. For in order for the statement "*jun jun*" ("the king should behave like a king") to make sense, it must make logical sense to state its negation, that is, "*jun bu jun*" ("the king is not behaving like a king"); in order for "*jun bu jun*" to make sense, the first "*jun*" has to mean "the person who occupies the kingship," not "the king as he is supposed to be," or the sentence of "*jun bu jun*" would be an utter contradiction. Since from our reading above we know that it is not a contradiction, the word "*jun*" has to be used in two senses, both as "the person who occupies the kingship" and "the king as he is supposed to be."

However, any criticism or comparison between the Confucian account of name and other accounts must not forget that they deal with very different issues. For one thing, the Confucians' primary concern is social and ethical, not purely linguistic. Instead of providing a semantic theory here, the Confucians are trying to show how the use of language may contribute to the ethical dimension of society. We should realize that in an important way the Confucians are right about using certain kinds of names. When someone says something like "I cannot do that in front of my children; I am the *father*," he suggests that being a father implies he should or should not do certain things. The Confucians are more concerned with making sure that the person as king or father is aware that one must do the right things in order to deserve the name of a king or father. Moreover, today when we say that a cruel criminal is not a human being but a brute, we suggest that common names like "human being" imply what kind of thing the named are supposed to be. Hence when we say to the criminal "you must not forget that you are a human being, not a beast," we are in line with the Confucian doctrine of rectification of names.

Another aspect of the Confucian account of language that appears most irrelevant today is its reliance on the myth of the sage-kings. It should be noted, however, sage-kings in Chinese legends were also "scientists," just as the ancient Greek philosophers were also early scientists. For example, the Great Yu 大禹 was a flood specialist, Shen Nong Shi 神农氏 was an agriculturalist and a botanist, and Sui Ren Shi 燧人氏 introduced the use of fire. It is likely that early scientists contributed a great deal to the naming of things. Of course, whether these legends are historically accurate may be another matter. I would suggest, however, what makes this Confucian view of names still relevant today is that it stands for an intuitive insight that cannot be easily dismissed, namely, the use of names has social and ethical implications.

Another weakness in Xun Zi's account of names lies in his assumption that naming and classification of things are the same process. This assumption is also debatable. We can know types of things without knowing their names. If so, then classification and naming are not necessarily the same process, even though they may be done at the same time. Xun Zi's argument would work better if it were based on the need for communication rather than the need for knowledge.

In contrast to the Confucian account of names, what lies at the other end of the spectrum is another intuition that feels that names are mere labels without connotational meanings. This intuition also has its accounts and justifications. One notable example is Saul Kripke's "direct reference" account. By examining some serious problems of the theory, I will show that Kripke's account, even though it makes good sense in some ways, is problematic and hence fails to undermine the Confucian account.

Rigid Designation

Semantically, the Confucian account of naming implies that names cannot be separated from their connotations. Without connotations, a name is no longer a name; without connotations of names the project of the rectification of names would be groundless. The Confucian insistence on the connection between names and their connotations is not without allies in the West.

As far as language is concerned, the Western tradition is much concerned with its semantic aspect. This is particularly evident in the recent linguistic turn in contemporary analytic philosophy. In this tradition, the critical questions have been "Do names have meanings?" "How does a name refer to its object?" and so on. The standard Western traditional view, since John Locke at least, is that names, including general terms, have intensions and their intensions determine their extensions.

John Locke maintains that names are words that stand for our ideas of things in the world. He calls these ideas the "nominal essences" of objects.[22] The nominal essence of gold for which the name "gold" stands is, Locke writes, the complex idea of "a body yellow, of a certain weight, malleable, fusible, and fixed."[23] Gottlob Frege in his now classic article argues that a name has both sense and reference and it is connected to its reference through its sense.[24] The sense is attached to the name through descriptions. Bertrand Russell holds that names are abbreviated descriptions.[25] Despite their differences, these writers all believe that names refer through their intensions or connotations. This view has an orientation different from the Confucian view on names, but it is in general not in conflict with the Confucian view.

This description theory of names has been vigorously challenged in the last two decades. One outstanding challenger is Saul Kripke. In *Naming and Necessity*, Kripke developed an account of naming and reference that "stood analytic philosophy on its ear."[26] Kripke calls names and descriptions "designators." He maintains that names are generally rigid designators and descriptions are mostly nonrigid designators,[27] and that there is a fundamental difference between the two. Contrary to the Confucian view, Kripke holds that names, "natural kind" names as well as proper names, do not pick out their reference through connotations; they make their reference directly.

Kripke argues that the descriptions that are associated with the name cannot be its meanings. For if "Aristotle," the name, meant "the man who taught Alexander the Great," a description associated with the name, then saying "Aristotle was the man who taught Alexander the Great" would be a tautology. It is not a tautology: a tautology is necessarily true; the statement "Aristotle was the man who taught Alexander the Great" is not necessarily true. It is certainly possible, even if unlikely, that one day we will discover the statement to be false that Aristotle actually did not teach Alexander the Great. Should that happen, "Aristotle" and "the teacher of Alexander the Great" would not designate the same individual; Aristotle nevertheless would remain Aristotle. Therefore, Kripke concludes, *"being the teacher of Alexander the Great* cannot be part of [the sense of] the name."[28]

We must admit that this is an extremely powerful argument. This argument makes Kripke's own account of naming an obvious alternative to the traditional one. If Kripke's account is correct, it will undermine the foundation of the Confucian project of rectification of names. From the point of view that names do not have connotations, even if the Confucians might have been right about some description terms, they would be definitely wrong about names (in the usual sense of the English word as other than descriptions).

Kripke confines his account of naming to natural kinds. The question with his account is whether the kind of direct designation of natural kind terms without connotations is possible at all. He believes that when a natural kind is named, the name is directly linked to the kind in the world, just as we fix a label to an object when we put a tag on it. I claim that Kripke failed to see the indeterminacy of kind terms and that, without connotational meanings, the reference of a name cannot be fixed.

In naming a natural kind, we cannot have the *kind* right in front of us. Kinds are not classes. Even if we could collect all instances of a kind that currently exist, we nevertheless do not have the kind at hand, because a kind is supposed to include instances that have existed in the past and instances that will come to be in the future.

That is to say, in naming we do not have direct access to a kind as we (at least seemingly) have access to an individual. This characteristic of naming natural kinds, as I shall show, has direct consequences in determining what is being named.

According to Kripke, a natural kind can be named by ostension through paradigmatic instances of a kind.[29] For example, we point to a glass of water and say "let's call this (liquid) 'water.'" In doing so, we have directly named a kind of thing, namely water. We might be wrong about the properties of the kind being named; water might turn out not to be colorless and tasteless even though we think it is. Should that happen, we would not think that we have named something that does not exist, but rather that we have been wrong about the kind of thing we have named. This is so because, according to Kripke, in naming we fix the reference directly to what is named, and what we have named is not dependent on the properties we have thought it to possess. In other words, in naming a kind, we directly name *"that kind of thing."*[30]

But what *kind* of thing? A natural response to this question would be *the* kind of which the instances that have been used in naming are paradigmatic. By answering this way one has assumed that a group of instances can be paradigmatic of only one definite kind. This is by no means a simple matter.

On the issue of the relation between an object and its kind(s), there are at least three views. First, one may think that an object can be in or of only one kind. For example, one may think that since an object has only one essence, it has to belong to only one species, which is determined by its essence, and only biological species terms are natural kind terms. Holding this view, however, will drastically reduce the scope of the direct reference theory and leave out most natural kind terms (e.g., genus terms and subspecies terms) unaccounted for. The theory of direct reference has been proposed as a theory for naming in general. It should have explanatory power for all "direct reference" terms. If a genus term is introduced into the language through the same mechanism as a species term, it should have the same direct reference character as a species term does. Thus this path would lead to very odd consequences for the direct reference account. As a matter of fact, Kripke does not seem to have taken this path. He thinks "common names" is an expression "quite appropriate" for natural kind terms and uses "cow" as an example, which stands for the mature female of the genus *Bos*.[31] Unless he changes his view in a drastic way and greatly reduces the scope and power of the theory, I assume Kripke would not desire this option. He would like his account to apply to all natural kind terms, including species and genus terms.

The second view is represented by writers such as Bruce Goldberg, W. V. Quine, John Dupré, and Philip Kitcher.[32] They have argued that one item may have membership in overlapping natural kinds or classes at the same taxonomic level. For instance, Quine writes, "Kinds can, however, overlap; the red things can comprise one kind, the round another."[33] Whether this is true of natural kinds has been a matter of dispute. In biology, for example, Willi Hennig in his celebrated book *Phylogenetic Systematics* maintains that only one taxonomic system can be regarded as privileged, and accordingly one organism cannot properly belong equally well to two overlapping kinds (at the same taxonomic level).[34] Kripke would agree with Hennig and reject the second view.

There is a third option. It is the view that there is one correct taxonomic theory and one object or instance belongs to only one species and one genus, but not to two or more overlapping kinds at the same taxonomic level. Holders of this view usually rely on the idea of scientific taxonomy, the idea that it is up to the scientists to find out the taxonomic structure of natural kinds. This view is favorable to Kripke's account of direct reference. On the one hand, it would allow a broad application of his direct reference theory to both genus and species terms as he intended, and on the other hand, it would avoid some difficulties that have been raised by those following the Quinean view. For the sake of argument, I will assume the third view is the only correct one.

Following this line of reasoning will distinguish my argument from many anti-Kripkean philosophers. Mark Wilson's argument, for example, relies heavily on examples of artificial kinds and contends that the thesis, which seeks to sharply distinguish between natural kinds and artificial kinds and to limit the Kripkean account to natural kinds, is "incoherent." Since many people believe that there is or at least should be a distinction between natural kinds and artificial kinds, an argument that does not rely on the rejection of this distinction is needed. My argument is also different from the one presented by Hartry Field, who is primarily concerned with scientific terms such as "mass" and draws his motivating examples entirely from Kuhnian "scientific revolutions."[35]

For the sake of simplicity, I use "taxonomy" in a very broad sense and use "species" to include element and chemical compound kinds. What I say about species and genus applies to biological species and genus as well as element and chemical compound kinds. Also "species" and "genus" are used in the way they are used in logic, namely, "genus" means a relatively larger kind and "species" means a relatively smaller kind or subkind of the genus. Thus, when "species" is used along with "genus," they are intended to mean, in addition to biological concepts, concepts of two adjacent levels within the taxonomical hierarchy in general.

Holding the third view, however, does not imply that an object can be in only one natural kind, because both species and genus are natural kinds. Cow (the mature female of the genus *Bos*) is a natural kind *per* Kripke; one has every reason to say that a species of the genus *Bos* is also a natural kind. Similarly, we can say that apple is a natural kind as well as that Red Delicious apple is a natural kind. This view poses a difficulty for Kripke. A Red Delicious apple can be an instance of the kind *Red Delicious* and it can also be an instance of the kind *apple*. In other words, natural kinds are nested in a taxonomic framework. Within this framework, instead of a one-one relation there is a one-many relation between an individual and its kinds. Now, when we point to some Red Delicious apples and name "that kind of thing," the question is, what kind of thing has been named?

To illustrate this, let us imagine a possible world *W* (or, for those who do not like the possible world language, an isolated island people with their own language) in which there are no fruits and consequently there are no such natural kind terms as "apple" in the *W* people's language. Now let us throw a number of Red Delicious apples into that world. Suppose the *W* people point to the Red Delicious apples and name that kind of thing "ABC." Let us further suppose the *W* people endorse Kripke's account of direct reference and believe that ABCs do exist even though they might have been mistaken about the properties of these objects, such as roundness, sweetness, and the like. The problem is that there is a taxonomic hierarchy (e.g., Red Delicious/Delicious/Apple/ . . .) in which kind terms such as "ABC" have to be nested. What "ABC" means depends on the level of the taxonomic hierarchy at which the term is posited, and its level cannot be clearly determined through paradigmatic instances alone.

In the case of ABC, what kind of thing has been named? Red Delicious? Delicious? Apple? Or something even broader in the taxonomic system? At this stage there would be no way to tell. If we ask the *W* people what "ABC" means, they would probably say a natural kind represented by those Red Delicious apples. If we press further and ask whether by "ABC" they mean Red Delicious, Delicious, apple, or something broader than apple in the taxonomic system, they would look at us, puzzled, and probably ask us, what is the difference? Of course there is a difference. *We* know there is a big difference. If ABC is Red Delicious, a Macintosh apple would not be an ABC. If ABC is something broader than apple, not only a Macintosh apple, but also a pear would probably be an ABC. The point is that the *W* people have no clue as to that difference.

One may contend that whether the *W* people realize any of these differences or not is irrelevant, and what ABCs are is something they need to discover in the world, not something to be decided by them. In other words, the issue is ontological, not epistemological. This objection confuses the issue. Here I do not suggest that the way we name objects can change objects in the world. Assuming the realist claim about the independent existence of natural kinds in the world is correct, the above problem for the account of direct reference remains. For if the existence of species is objectively independent of our mind, the existence of genus and subspecies is also objectively independent of our mind. An object is an instance of both a species and a genus, which are both natural kinds. The issue here is how names are connected to natural kinds in the world, and in particular, how a name is connected to a species instead of a genus or vice versa. It is a matter of naming. We cannot expect a natural kind term to have reference even before the term has been adopted into language. Nor can we discover what ABCs are before we understand what it takes for there to be ABCs. Assuming the Kripke's realist view of natural kinds is correct, ostension through paradigmatic instances alone does not determine what natural kind has been named.

To be sure, taking place in a certain context, an ostensive definition does exclude objects from the kind. For example, perhaps no one in *W*, unless extremely mistaken, would wonder whether a table is an ABC. However, in our case, nothing in the *W* people's mind could definitively determine whether Macintoshes are also ABCs. When naming a kind, the namers usually do not specify characteristics of the kind in great detail as the criteria of the kind that is being named. Also, as Kripke himself points out, they may be wrong about these features. Because the contrast between Red Delicious apples and Macintosh apples does not occur in the W people's mind at the time of naming, the issue whether ABC includes Macintoshes simply does not arise until after the name has been put in use. And after the name has been put in use, it does not bear enough import to determine whether a Macintosh is also an ABC. The problem with the W people is this: on the one hand, Macintosh apples share sufficient similarities with Red Delicious apples to be one kind (i.e., apple); on the other hand, they also bear sufficient dissimilarities with Red Delicious apples to be a different kind (of apple). Therefore, the W people have to make a decision as to whether a Macintosh apple is an ABC, and this decision cannot be dictated by what they had in their minds at the time of naming ABCs.

Kripke would like to say that it is up to the scientists to find it out. Scientists in W, however, can do no better than *decide* whether a Macintosh apple is also an ABC. Shifting the burden to scientists does not change the nature of the issue. The naming of a natural kind cannot be accomplished once and for all by using paradigmatic instances. The only way to find out more about what kind of thing has been named "ABC" is to show the W people some fruits other than Red Delicious apples and ask them whether these fruits are also ABCs. If we show them some Macintosh apples and they call them "ABCs," then probably "ABC" does not mean "Red Delicious." If, in addition to Red Delicious apples, the W people call pears "ABCs," then "ABC" cannot merely mean "apple." However, it is not the case that the W people make a judgment according to a fixed criterion, because there is no such established criterion. In further focusing on what is named, they need to *decide* whether a Macintosh apple is also an ABC.

This sort of decision is also a decision about what nature or sameness relation is involved in the kind and what kind of thing ABCs are. Hilary Putnam, who basically shared Kripke's view, maintained that the kind is determined by a certain sameness relation among its instances.[36] What sameness relation? A Red Delicious apple bears a certain sameness relation to other Red Delicious apples insofar as they are Red Delicious apples. It also bears a certain sameness relation to Macintosh apples insofar as both Red Delicious apples and Macintosh apples are apples. The W people need to make the decision because the initial ostensive definition does not bear enough import regarding whether, for instance, a Macintosh apple, which bears a sameness relation with Red Delicious apples at the taxonomic level of apple, is an ABC.

We should note also that the decision is not merely a matter of whether we *call* some objects "ABCs." It has been decided to call both a financial bank and a river bank "bank," yet it does not make them the same kind. To decide to call both Red Delicious apples and Macintosh apples "apples" is to recognize a certain sameness relation between Red Delicious apples and Macintosh apples, and it does indicate that they are in a sense the same kind of fruit: apple. That is, to decide whether Macintosh apples and Red Delicious apples are both ABCs is to decide what kind of sameness relation is required for an instance to be that of ABC. It has to do with what ABC is or what nature ABC has.

One may think that since the W people use Red Delicious apples as paradigmatic instances, ABC must be Red Delicious apple. In making this assumption one has hastily ruled out the possibility that, if we later show the W people a Golden Delicious apple or a Macintosh apple, they might accept it as an instance of ABC, which I do not think entirely unlikely. The history of biology shows a history of discovering new species and subspecies that belong to some kinds that have been named. To see why it is not entirely unlikely for the W people to accept Macintosh apples as ABCs, let us look at another natural kind term, "elephant." The term "elephant" applies to animals of two different species, the Asian elephant and the African elephant. The Chinese counterpart of "elephant" is *"xiang* 象*."* The term must have been first used to designate the Asian elephant, because that was all the Chinese could know when they started using the term. Today *"xiang"* designates both the Asian elephant and the African elephant. It is reasonable to think the Chinese first used the Asian elephant in fixing the reference and later included the African elephant under the kind name *"xiang."* In the same way, it is possible that the W people also take Macintosh apples as ABCs.

In deciding what to call an "ABC" the W people are not compelled by necessity to call or not to call a Macintosh apple an "ABC." If there were such a necessity, there would be an exact cross-cultural correspondence between natural kind terms in two cultures that have the same natural kinds. Obviously we do not have such a uniformity. For example, in Chinese, *"lao-shu* 老鼠*"* stands for both mice and rats, while *"yan* 雁*"* and *"e* 鵝*"* stand for wild geese (which fly) and domestic geese (which do not fly) respectively. It is possible that, with the same paradigmatic instances, the Chinese have made decisions differently from the English in introducing these natural kind terms. The Chinese think mice and rats bear a certain sameness relation in terms of both being *"lao-shu,"* while the English think *"yan"* and *"e"* bear a certain sameness relation in terms of both being geese. Scientists may agree that they are both right: while one way focuses on the species, the other focuses on the genus. This difference indicates the possibility of going either to species or to genus from the same paradigmatic instances.

One should not confuse our case with that of reference changes of natural kind terms. Sometimes terms do change their references. Our case, however, is different. When the Chinese decided that *"xiang"* also refers to the African elephant, it is not the case that the reference of the kind term has been *changed* from a narrower taxonomic kind to a broader one. It would be the case only if the status of the kind term had been determined. Before the decision was made, the taxonomic status of the term was far from being determined. An ostensive definition alone does not complete the process of naming a natural kind, if by naming we mean fixing the reference rigidly to a specified scope that draws a clear line between what is and what is not of the kind. Decisions following an ostensive definition to further specify the kind are also part of the process of naming. The *W* people would not need to make a decision until they encounter something different from, and yet similar enough to, Red Delicious apples (e.g., Macintosh apples) for them to seriously wonder whether it is also an ABC, and they might not encounter such objects in a million years or at all. Even after they encounter some objects of this sort, further decisions will still be needed. Generally speaking, when we come across a new object *O*, which makes us seriously wonder whether it belongs to a kind that we have already named without further focusing to determine whether objects like *O* are or are not instances of the kind, we need to *decide* whether it is of the same kind.

Therefore, the ultimate reference (or the scope) of a natural kind term is pending and hence indeterminate as long as the entire process of naming is not finalized. The process can never be finalized. Of 500 million species of animal and plant life estimated to have existed on Earth, 99.75 percent are extinct. There are at least 500 species of fleas and 100 species of mosquitoes.[37] There are always new species emerging. Besides, we can always imagine an instance that makes us seriously wonder whether it belongs to a kind that has been named but not further focalized to determine whether that instance is one of the kind. The dispute over the identity of water itself shows that the taxonomic status of the natural kind term "water" needs further focusing.[38] The very fact that we are debating over the issue whether something that resembles H_2O in every aspect but has the chemical formula XYZ is water indicates that the taxonomic status of the term "water" has not been finally determined.

Names as Prescriptions

If my argument is correct, naming as Kripke has it would never be able to reach its reference, and any direct link between names and the named would be impossible. It has appeared that the only way for the namer to fix the reference of a name is to fix it by descriptions or, which is the same, by connotations of the name. If so, Kripke's whole theory of direct reference collapses.

If a name is linked to its reference by connotations, then the reference of the name is determined by the use of the name in the language, because the use of a name reveals its connotations. Saying "a bird has two wings" reveals that "having two wings" is a connotation of the word "bird." Saying "someone has a bird" reveals that "capable of being possessed" is also a connotation of "bird" as opposed to "rainbow." What a name is a name of and how a name is used are inseparable.

This way of thinking has at least two consequences in the Confucians' favor. First, it supports Xun Zi's "taxonomy," which does not distinguish natural kinds and artificial kinds, both being "things." We divided "things" further and further into lesser general categories depending on our needs. Therefore we may say that both "bird" and "*gu*" (the wine vessel that Confucius complained about) are names, the references of which are fixed in the same way.

Second, it also diminishes, if it does not entirely eliminate, the Kripkean distinction between names on the one hand and descriptions on the other. For example, the reference of "father" can be fixed by the connotation of "male parent." "Father" can also be used as a description in such statements as "X is the father of Y." "Father" can thus be both a name and a description.

If names are necessarily embodied with connotations, the very use of a name gives us a certain expectation about the named when we know what a name means. For example, if someone tells me that John is the father of Johnny, I would expect that John parents Johnny. If John fails to do so, I would say that either there is something wrong with John or the name "father" has been misused on John, that is, he really does not deserve the name "father." In the same way, if I am told that there is a bird, then I would expect to see the thing with two wings. If it turns out that the thing does not have two wings, then either the name "bird" has been misused or there is something wrong with that thing.

This expectation in the named generates in us a sense of "oughtness." It means that names not only have a descriptive function, but also a prescriptive power. This sense of "oughtness," this prescriptive power, is the basis of the Confucian doctrine of rectification of names.

Chi-yun Chen recently argued that, in his doctrine of rectification of names, Confucius's focus is on language or how to use language (言 *yan/yen*), not names. According to Chen, when we use names properly, we create "propositions with truth contents," and these truth contents can be analyzed, confirmed, rectified, or falsified.[39] Chen's interpretation may carry too much of an overtone of semantic truth, which was not Confucius's primary concern, but Chen is right in pointing out that, in Confucius's doctrine of rectification of names, the matter is more of the use of language than merely a relation between names and the named.

I have shown that names have to refer through connotations, and the relation between names and the named can only be determined through connotations. If my analysis is right, then the only way to determine the relation between names and the named is through the use of language. Thus, the matter of the relation between names and the named on the one hand and the use of language on the other are not opposed in Confucius. As a matter of fact, for Confucius, the only way to set right the relation between names and the named is through appropriate use of language. If we assume that the matter of the relation between names and the named is more a matter of semantics, and the matter of appropriate use of language is more a matter of pragmatics, Confucians are clearly more concerned with pragmatics than semantics.

This analysis reconfirms what has been indicated in chapter 2. Whereas in the West people's concern with language is primarily on semantic truth, in China it is mainly a matter of appropriate use. It is an ethicopolitical issue, on which I will focus in the next chapter.

Ethics

Confucian *Jen* and Feminist Care

As a philosophy, Confucianism is ethicopolitical in character. Some of its values are different from those in Western mainstream philosophies. Differences in value assumptions often make another philosophical system appear less accessible than it is. I believe that the most important aspect of understanding another philosophy such as Confucianism is to understand its way of thinking. In this chapter I shall examine Confucian ethical thinking from a comparative perspective by comparing two views that have seldom been brought together: Confucianism and feminism. Specifically, I will compare the idea of *jen* 仁, the central concept of Confucian ethics, and the idea of care, the central concept of feminist care ethics.

By "care ethics" I mean the feminist ethics with care as its foundation, instead of rights or justice. This ethics is represented by feminist philosophers such as Carol Gilligan and Nel Noddings. I do not regard care ethics as the only feminist ethics. Just like feminism itself, feminist care ethics is not a uniform theory. The views of feminist care ethics discussed in this chapter are held by some influential feminist philosophers, although other feminist philosophers may not consider them to be authoritative.

With origins in a feudal society, Confucianism has been typically patriarchal. Like most ethicoreligious traditions in the world, Confucianism historically has given little recognition to women. Feminist care ethics, however, is relatively new. One striking feature of this ethics is that it is antipatriarchal. This means that it is opposed not only to male dominance in society but also to what has been characterized as the "male/masculine" (i.e., rights-based, principle-oriented) way of thinking in general. One might suppose that Confucian ethics and feminist ethics are diametrically opposed to each other. And many philosophers have noted their differences and even used feminism as a weapon against Confucianism.[1] In doing so, however, they often neglect important similarities between these philosophies. In fact, Confucianism and feminism share important common ground, and this common ground may make it possible for them to learn from and support each other.

Self and Society: The Foundation of *Jen* and Care

Morality concerns the code of acceptable human behavior in society and our understanding of the nature of morality has much to do with our understanding of the nature of the self and its relation to society. In investigating Confucian *jen* ethics and feminist care ethics, we should first note some important similarities between the Confucian notion of the self and society on the one hand and the notion of the self and society advocated by care-perspective philosophers on the other.

Feminist researchers have noted that women see themselves in a way different from the way men traditionally view themselves in the West. Men see "the primacy of the self" over all other things in the world. Roderick M. Chisholm, for example, examines three possibilities of how one individuates one's self:

1. The only thing one (directly) individuates is one's self; one individuates other things only by relating them to this self;

2. One individuates one's self as well as other things;

3. One only individuates certain other things and individuates one's self only by relating one uniquely to some of these other things.[2]

Chisholm believes that only the first is true:

Whenever I do identify *per se* some individual other than myself, then I am in a position also to identify that individual by
reference to some unique relation that individual bears to me.
If I can now pick you out as being *that man*, then there is some
way of perceiving which is such that I can now pick you out as
being the thing I am now perceiving in that particular way.
If I were *not* in a position to identify you by thus relating you
uniquely to me, then I wouldn't be able to identify you *per se*.[3]

The way of thinking represented here by Chisholm presumes the
logical and ontological primacy of one's individuality. According to
this view, the self per se can be determined prior to considerations
of other beings in the world; moreover, a direct understanding of the
self per se is the precondition for any considerations that one could
give to others. Thus, the individuality of the self ontologically pre-
cedes the relations in which the self exists.

Some woman philosophers, however, see the self differently and
speak of it in a different voice. For example, in exploring feminist
epistemology, Lynn Hankinson Nelson writes:

The question, again, is whether when we say "we know," the
"we" in question is a collective entity or merely a collection of
individuals, me and you and you . . . , each of whom, individu-
ally knows. Alternatively put, the question is whether we know
because each of us knows, or each of us knows derivatively
because *we* know. I am advocating the latter; when we say "we
know," "we" is, in fact, a primitive term.[4]

As indicated in chapter 2, "knowing" is a way of being; what we
know cannot be separated from what we are. To take "we" as a
primitive term, a term more primitive than "me and you and you,"
means to take the self as essentially connected to others. This view
is in diametrical opposition to the view that "human individuals are
ontologically prior to society," the view that "human individuals are
the basic constituents out of which social groups are composed."[5]

In her book *In a Different Voice*, Carol Gilligan divides women's
moral development into three levels or perspectives. On the first
level, women focus on their own individual survival. This emphasis

on individual survival is often viewed as being selfish. On the second level, women turn away from self-centeredness and turn to care for other people. At this level they view the good as self-sacrifice and seek others' approval by caring for others in conformity to conventional social norms. Finally at the third level, women focus on the dynamic relationships between their own selves and other people, and thereby dissipate the tension between selfishness and responsibility through a new understanding of the interconnection between other and self.[6] At each level, there is an implicit understanding of who they are, namely, what kind of self they have. And at each level this understanding is different.

Nel Noddings views this transition from the first level to the third as a transition from the "actual self" to the "ideal self." The ideal self is the self that the morally mature person strives to become. In the process of striving for the ideal self, there is the "ethical self." Noddings writes:

> The ethical self is an active relation between my actual self and a vision of my ideal self as one-caring and cared-for. It is born of the fundamental recognition of relatedness; that which connects me naturally to the other, reconnects me through the other to myself.[7]

The ideal self is one of fundamental relatedness. To recognize this ideal self, the self one ought to be, is to recognize that the real self is not isolated or disconnected from the rest of the world. In this concept of self, to be is to be related. The ethical self as an active relation is an active force to drive one toward the ideal self. One feels separated from others and feels a sense of the lonely self only when one fails in following the ethical self moving toward the ideal self.

In the Confucian context the self is the person. The question "what is the self?" is the question "what is the person?" The issue of "what self one has" is the issue of "what kind of person one is." We can examine this Confucian notion of self in two ways. First, diachronically, the self is a dynamic "making process." The self is not a "given." One is not born with a definitive self or a ready-made soul. One has to make one's self. This is the Confucian belief of "person-making" and "self-cultivation." Consequently what kind of person one ends up to be depends on how well one is cultivated. In this sense one cannot take one's personhood for granted. As Tu Wei-ming points out, "Personality, in the Confucian perception, is an achieved state of moral excellence rather than a given condition."[8] It takes effort to attain it and takes effort to make a good person. Furthermore, this effort is a lifetime process. Confucius, the sage and role model for Confucians, sets an example:

> At fifteen my heart was set on learning. At thirty I had stood my feet firm upon the ground. At forty I no longer suffered from perplexities. At fifty I knew the Mandate of Heaven. At sixty I was at ease with whatever I heard. At seventy I could follow my heart's desire without transgressing moral principles.[9]

Learning is most important in one's becoming human. To learn is to develop and cultivate oneself. If one keeps cultivating oneself, the older one gets the more mature and the more respectful one becomes. The Confucian value of respecting the old is a reflection of this ideal: with the Confucian ideal of life, the more time one has lived, the more likely one is to be better cultivated. In the Confucian culture, reminding a person of his or her age is often a way of reminding a person of his or her moral responsibilities. In a strong sense, we are not born with a personhood, we earn it. We are not born with dignity, we earn it. We are not born (fully) human, we earn it.[10] We progress from "human being" as potential to "being human" as actualization.

Second, synchronically, one's self is not an atomic entity. It is the focus of a network at most. Using Roger Ames's metaphor, the Confucian self is a "focus-field." In Ames's model, the self is a center or focus that fades off into a ritually ordered society.[11] The focus, of course, exists only in the field and exists only as long as the field exists. The existence and identity of the focus depend on the field. It is from this focus, this center, that one gradually reaches out to form one's identity. Accordingly, person-making does not take place in a vacuum. It always takes place in a social context. The social context is first of all one's family and community. It is through interactions with other people and through establishing social ties with these people that one gradually earns one's membership in the human community.

Tu Wei-ming describes the Confucian self as an open system that

> in the genuine sense of the word is expansive and always receptive to the world at large. Self-cultivation can very well be

understood as the broadening of the self to embody an ever-expanding circle of human relatedness.[12]

Similar to the woman's self depicted by Noddings, the Confucian self is also a process for relatedness.

Such a self is never an abstract. It always exists through specific relationships. Who and what one is depends on who and what one is in this human community, and depends on what one is to other people in this human community. In this way, the self is defined in these social relations. Cut off from them, there is no longer a real self. One gets into a social relation by fulfilling a particular social role, as a son or daughter or a father or mother within the child-parent relationship, or as a student or teacher within a student-teacher relationship, and so on. To make oneself a good person means to do well as one's roles require. One does not have a self apart from one's roles. On the contrary, these roles are constitutive of one's identity. There is no question that one can develop one's roles. However, the development of new roles has to be based on one's existing roles.

It is interesting to note the difference between introducing someone in China and in the United States. In China, when people introduce a visiting relative to someone, they may say "this is my nephew" or "this is my cousin," often without mentioning the person's name. It is considered an adequate introduction to situate a new person in relation to someone whom people already know. One knows someone if one knows that person is the neighbor's nephew or cousin. In the United States, people do not feel they know someone unless they know the person's name, as if the name, not the relations of the person, bears more of the person's identity. Even though they may not have in mind Kripke's account of names, they surely share his direct reference intuition about names. The Confucians would say that a person's name becomes meaningful when it bears some description of the person.

In the Confucian view, this self is not an independent agent who happens to be in certain social relationships. The self is constituted of, and situated in social relationships. An evaluation of how good oneself is, will be an evaluation of how well one has been in these social roles and how well one has nurtured and maintained these social relations. Therefore, our self-knowledge can only be reflective; it can only be gained through knowing people with whom we are in relationships. This is very different from the traditional Western view, which, according to Chisholm, is that an individual has "direct knowledge of himself," or in Russell's term, the man may be said to be "directly acquainted with himself."[13]

In accord with the individualistic view of the self, an influential Western social theory sees the society as based on a contract between rational beings with self-interests and certain rights. Individuals enter the society as if they had signed a social contract with one another for the purpose of mutual gains, and by this contract their individual rights are guaranteed. Thus the relation between members of a society is like a contractual relation. In contrast, the Confucian views the society as a large family in which the ruler's relation to the subjects is like that of a father to his children.[14] For Confucius, just as there is no contract within the family, there is no contract in the society either. The philosophy of managing a good family and that of managing a good society are essentially the same. The Western division of "public sphere" and "private sphere" simply does not exist in Confucianism.

Some feminists see a similar analogy between a family and a society. Virginia Held, for instance, criticizes the assumption that human beings are independent, self-interested, or mutually disinterested individuals. She believes that "relations between mothers and children should be thought of as primary, and the sort of human relation all other human relations should resemble or reflect."[15] The relation between mothers and children is to a large extent nonvoluntary and hence noncontractual.[16]

This way of understanding the nature of human societies is crucial for the unfolding of Confucian ethics as well as feminist care ethics. If the society is a contractual society, justice is served only if each participant's rights are guaranteed; and as long as these rights are not violated, morality is satisfied. Neither Confucian nor feminist care ethics bases its morality on individual rights. As Gilligan observes, women's moral understanding is based on a "very strong sense of being responsible to the world," not on the primacy and universality of individual rights.[17] On this understanding, the moral dilemma is not "how to exercise one's rights without interfering with the rights of others," but how "to lead a moral life which includes obligations to myself and my family and people in general."[18] For Confucius, the concept of individual rights has no place in morality.[19] Morality is a matter of fulfilling one's proper role in the society, as a son, a brother, a father, and, further, as a ruler or a subject under the ruler. In this noncontractual society, for the Confucian, the key concept to guide human relations is *jen*, and for the feminist of this perspective, care.

Jen and Care as the Central Moral Ideals

The concept of *jen* occupies a central place in Confucian philosophy. In the *Analects* Confucius mentioned *"jen"* more than one hundred times, but he never formally defined it. In a study of the semasiology of Confucian concepts, Peter Boodberg observed that *"jen"* belongs to a group of words with the starting initials *"j"* or *"n,"* including the word later used specifically for "Confucian" *"ju"* (儒 *ru*), that

> appear to be derived from the same etymonic nucleus and to be conveying as words such notions as can be expressed in English by the following terms: softness, weakness, mildness, pliancy, lenity, comity, temerity, mansuetude, forbearance, the quality of being soft but tough, slender, graceful, complaisant, patient and tender, tolerant, yielding, and coddling (in both senses of the English "coddling": to treat tenderly and to "tenderize" by cooking).[20]

It is not without justification that, in the English world, scholars have translated *"jen"* by many terms, some of which share with the above in connotation, namely benevolence, love, altruism, kindness, charity, compassion, magnanimity, human-heartedness, humaneness, humanity, perfect virtue, goodness, true manhood, manhood at its best, and so forth.

These translations reflect the two senses in which Confucius used the word *"jen," "jen* of affection," and *"jen* of virtue".[21] In the sense of *"jen* of affection," *jen* stands for the tender aspect of human feelings and an altruistic concern for others.[22] Confucius said, *"Jen* is to love others."[23] One can readily experience the sense of *jen* if willing to do so. Confucius said, "Is *jen* so far away? If we really want *jen*, we should find that it is at our very side."[24] In Mencius, *jen* is treated almost exclusively in the sense of affection. Mencius made *jen* as affection the foundation of his ethics. He said, "No man is devoid of a heart sensitive to the suffering of others. . . . The heart of compassion is the seed of *jen*,"[25] and "for every man there are things he cannot bear. To extend this to what he can bear is *jen.*"[26] Sympathy naturally arises in one's heart when one sees other people suffer. One cannot bear to see sufferings. To extend this feeling to other things in the world and thus make it a general disposition is characteristic of *jen*. In this sense, *jen* is benevolence, love, altruism, tenderness, charity, compassion, human-heartedness, humaneness, and so on.

In the other sense, the sense of *"jen* of virtue," *jen* is a general virtue that has to be realized among other virtues. For example, Confucius said, "one is *jen* if everywhere under Heaven one can practice the five: courtesy, breadth, good faith, diligence and kindness."[27] In this sense, a person of perfect *jen* is a morally perfect person, and *jen* may be translated as "perfect virtue," "goodness," "true manhood," and "manhood at its best."

Although the relation between *"jen* of affection" and *"jen* of virtue" is open to interpretation, one thing is certain: a person cannot have the latter without the former. A person who has *jen* as a general virtue cannot lack *jen* as affection. In order to understand Confucian ethics we must first of all understand the concept of *jen* as affection.

The word *"jen* 仁" in Chinese consists of a simple ideogram of a human figure and two horizontal strokes suggesting human relations. What are these relations? If benevolence, love, altruism, kindness, charity, compassion, human-heartedness, and humaneness all translate the concept of *jen*, what do all these terms have in common? The answer, I think, is "caring-about." Taken as a virtue of human relations, "caring-about" is the essence of every one of these terms. If a person does not care about others, he or she cannot be described with any of these terms. For example, benevolence is the kindly disposition to do good and promote the welfare of others. If one does not care about others, he or she cannot be benevolent.

Confucius came closest to a definition of *jen* when he said *"Jen* is to *ai* others."[28] Although "love" is the common translation of *"ai* 爱," the English word expresses a sentiment stronger than *"ai." Shuo Wen Jie Zi* interprets *"ai"* as *"hui* 惠," that is, favorableness or kindness. In Chinese, *"ai"* is often used in phrases such as *"ai hu"* (爱护 "take good care of") or *"ai xi"* (爱惜 "cherish"). In the phrases *"ai mo neng zhu* 爱莫能助" and *"ai wu ji wu* 爱屋及乌," *"ai"* is best understood as "caring for tenderly." They respectively mean "I care about it but cannot help" and "caring about the house along with the bird on its roof." "Caring-about" is more appropriate in expressing this tender feeling one has toward people and things.

In Mencius, *jen* as "caring-about" is more evident. If a child were to fall into a well, why should one care? Mencius believed that a person cares because he or she has compassion. A person has a natural tendency or disposition to be *jen*, to care, and therefore to act to save the child. One does not have to love the child to save her. In situations like this, a person who holds a "who cares?" attitude is one without a human heart. Although the heart of *jen* is natural, Mencius also said that a moral person needs to develop the seed of *jen* in one's heart, along with the seeds of a sense of shame, of courtesy and modesty, and of right and wrong. "If a man is able to develop all these seeds that he possesses, it will be like a fire starting up or a spring coming through."[29] Moral cultivation and development will make the natural instinctual heart of *jen* a mature moral virtue.

Like Confucius, Mencius's ideal form of government is one of *jen*. He saw that princes of some states took the people away from their work during busy farming seasons, making it impossible for them to till the land and minister to the needs of their parents. Thus, parents suffered cold and hunger while brothers, wives, and children were separated and scattered. These princes did not care about their people. Mencius believed that in order to become a true king, one must care about his people and practice the governance of *jen* toward the people.[30] In other words, being caring, or *jen*, is the way to become a good ruler. Both Confucius and Mencius believed that if a government is one of *jen*, one that takes good care of its people, there would be no crime or poverty. If the ruler cares about his people, he will make sure that people do not miss their farming seasons, and thus they will have good harvests in good years and be prepared for bad years. When people have enough food, they behave themselves well and do not steal or rob. It is not that we do not have enough punishment; nor is it that we do not have enough taxation. It is that we do not have enough care, and this sometimes makes life unbearable. What we really need is care.

Whether Confucius and Mencius are right is open to discussion. They might have been idealistic about the consequence of good government. What we can conclude from their teachings is that, in Confucian philosophy, to be a person of *jen*, one must care about others. So, even if the entire concept of *jen* cannot be reduced to "caring-about," at least we can say that "caring-about" occupies a central place in this concept. As Lik Kuen Tong has properly concluded, Confucianism is a care-oriented humanism and the Confucian love (*"ai"*) is a caring, responsible love.[31] To understand the care orientation of Confucian ethics is the key to understanding the concept of *jen* as Confucius's central moral ideal.

At this point it may be useful to compare Confucius's conception of virtue with Plato's, which has been influential in the West. In Confucius, the three cardinal virtues are wisdom, courage, and *jen*.[32] Plato's four cardinal virtues are wisdom, courage, temperance, and justice. Confucius believed that in order to become a person of *jen*, one needs "to return to the observance of the rites through self-control."[33] That is, controlling one's desires in accordance with *"li* 礼," the Confucian proper social behavior. Hence it can be said that the concept of *jen* implies temperance. Now we can see that where Plato placed justice Confucius placed *jen*. For Plato, justice as the central moral ideal is achieved when reason prevails, and is achieved only when the other three virtues are duly practiced. But this ideal is missing in Confucius. Confucius, for whom *jen* is almost synonymous with the moral, would find it unintelligible for a morality not to include the element of care. This difference between the two major philosophers is not an accident. It reflects a major divergence between the two ethics. At this point Confucius would certainly find more common ground with feminist care ethics than with Plato's justice ethics.

On the feminist care perspective, the central ideal of morality is caring. In her study of women's ethics, Gilligan found that women's morality centers on care.[34] A moral person is one who cares for others, or as Noddings put it, "one-caring." Noddings writes, "It is this ethical ideal [caring], this realistic picture of ourselves as one-caring, that guides us as we strive to meet the other morally."[35] While Confucius believed that a person of *jen* is one who, "wishing to establish his own character, also establishes the character of others, and wishing to be prominent himself, also helps others to be prominent,"[36] a female interviewee in Gilligan's study equates morality with caring about others and considers responsibility to mean "that you care about that other person, that you are sensitive to that other person's needs and you consider them as a part of your needs."[37] Gilligan writes,

The ideal of care is . . . an activity of relationship, of seeing and responding to need, taking care of the world by sustaining the web of connection so that no one is left alone.[38]

She would agree with Confucius and Mencius that a good government as well as a good person is one that cares, and promotes care, for the people.

As the central moral ideal, care serves as the guide for one's moral behavior. In our world, things are often complicated. People may get into moral dilemmas that have no easy solutions. In such cases, all we can ask people to do is to care about those who will be affected by their decisions. An authentically caring person is not one who merely says to him or herself, "I care." We must make efforts to look into the situation and the effects of possible decisions. Afterwards, we may praise one for having been caring or blame another for not having been caring enough (therefore people may have been hurt). It is unreasonable to demand more than that. Circumstances are not perfect. We cannot require anyone to make them perfect. As long as one demonstrates reasonable care, morality is satisfied.

Only with care can one be a moral person. Only in the practice of caring, can one become a moral person. It is caring, not the consequences of it, that establishes moral values. At this point both Confucianism and the feminist care ethics differ widely from utilitarianism and consequentialism. *Jen* and care are not to be justified in terms of the consequences they bring about, though the consequences are generally desirable. As the central moral ideals, *jen* and care are inherently good.

Jen and Care: Ethics without General Rules

In the *Analects*, Confucius talked many times about how to become a person of *jen*. However, each time he came up with something different. He never gave a general guideline. This is by no means negligence. *Jen* cannot be achieved by following general rules.

In the broad sense of the word, of course, rules as moral principles can be found in all ethics. In the past two thousand years a vast number of rules have been developed in the Confucian tradition. For instance, there have been the rules that girls and boys older than seven should not sit at the same dining table, and a man would have to accept the bride picked by his parents, whether he liked her or not. However, we must note the differences between Confucian rules and rules in other ethics, for example, Kantian or utilitarian ethics. First, these rules are not an essential feature of Confucian morality. At the same time, different places often have different rules, even though they have all been called "Confucian." Over the years these rules have changed, many have even disappeared. Confucian ethics nevertheless remains. Second, these rules are specific rules, not general rules. They are not like the utilitarian rule that one should always maximize total net utility, or like the Kantian rule that one should always treat people as ends. In Confucianism, these specific rules are guidelines for young people to learn *li*, that is, proper social behavior. Rules of *li* are important, but learning to be *jen* is more important. Confucius indicated that, without *jen*, *li* is of no use.[39] For him, being ethical is being *jen*; it is not merely a matter of following rules.

Where Confucius talked about reciprocity, he talked about something akin to general rules. Confucius told his disciple Zeng Zi 曾子 that his philosophy had one thread running through it. When others asked Zeng Zi about it, Zeng Zi said "*zhong* and *shu*."[40] "*Zhong* 忠 " means conscientiousness or loyalty to one's cause. If one is loyal to one's cause, one should exert all one's strength to the cause. "*Shu* 恕 " means extending one's mind to others and being considerate of others. It is sometimes rendered in English as reciprocity. Confucius's notion of reciprocity goes beyond that of the rights and justice perspective. Proponents of the rights/justice perspective also believe in reciprocity. Their notion of reciprocity is the basis for the social contract: if you do not infringe upon my rights, I will not infringe upon yours. Confucius believed in his golden rule. He believed that a person of *jen* should help others develop their character if he wishes to develop his own, and help others to become successful if he himself wishes to succeed. That is, instead of leaving people alone, he should understand others" situations and care about them. Thus, Confucius extended the notion of reciprocity beyond the limit of the "rights perspective" to the "care perspective."

For Noddings, caring has the distinctive feature of motivational displacement. She maintains that, in caring, because one sees the other's reality as a possibility for oneself, one must act to eliminate the intolerable, to reduce the pain, and to fill the need to actualize the dream; caring implies "a total conveyance of the self to the other."[41] When one wants to do something, one should ask, "How would my action affect others?" "Would I want a person to do this if I were in his or her situation?" This way of thinking requires more than noninterference. This kind of reciprocity is different from rules in Kantian or utilitarian ethics. It demands that one should care about others.

To say "Always care about others" or "Be *jen*/caring!" is different from saying "always follow such-and-such a general rule." Traditional Western ethical theories have principles or general rules for people to follow. Utilitarianism, for example, follows the rule to maximize total net utility. In addition to general rules there is also the thesis of universalizability. This is the idea that if one person is obliged to do x under certain conditions, then everyone under sufficiently similar conditions is obliged to do x, with no exceptions. While the care perspective does not entirely deny that we can receive some guidance from principles, there seem to be no general rules to determine whether one situation is sufficiently similar to another. More often than not general principles do not solve problems for us. We need to inquire into individual cases. Noddings said that her feminist care ethics

> does not attempt to reduce the need for human judgment with a series of "Thou Shalts" and "Thou Shalt nots." Rather, it recognizes and calls forth human judgment across a wide range of fact and feeling, and it allows for situations and conditions in which judgment may properly be put aside in favor of faith and commitments.[42]

For example, there can be no general principles that will give a mother a definitive answer to whether she should send the money to charity or spend it on her child's favorite meal. It really depends on individual situations, and individual situations vary from time to time and from place to place.

What makes Confucian ethics more like feminist care ethics than justice ethics is not that they have or do not have rules, but that they both emphasize the importance of the intrinsic moral virtue of *jen* and care and remain flexible with rules. When a rule fails to work, instead of trying to make up another rule, as justice ethics would do, they will readily accept flexibility with rules. Noddings writes: "The one-caring is wary of rules and principles. She formulates and holds loosely, tentatively, as economies of a sort, but she insists upon holding closely to the concrete."[43]

In caring, a person may get into conflicts. Noddings gives us an example in which a professor receives a research proposal from graduate student *B*. *B* proposes to do research that requires deceiving the subjects involved in the research.[44] On the one hand, the professor does not want to hurt *B* by turning the proposal down. On the other hand, the professor is not sure whether the subjects would be hurt by the experiment. If they would not be hurt and *B* succeeds in the research, then everything would be fine. But what if they are hurt? In cases like this, there would be no general infallible rules or principles to follow. It is not to say there cannot be any rules. There are rules. However, rules cannot give us infallible solutions in conflicting situations of caring.

Moreover, even though we can follow rules, rules do not have the overriding power in deciding our actions. Noddings thinks that although general principles call for support to socially oppressed people, a caring person might fight along with her father and brother against the oppressed if they are on the opposite side of the oppressed.[45] While this may sound extreme, it does make the point clear: general rules are not absolute. This is so because, as Joan C. Tronto puts it:

The perspective of care requires that conflict be worked out without damage to the continuing relationships. Moral problems can be expressed in terms of accommodating the needs of the self and of others, of balancing competition and cooperation, and of maintaining the social web of relations in which one finds oneself.[46]

Under certain circumstances, a caring person needs to break the rules to preserve social relations.

Confucius, again, would share the view of these feminists. Unlike Plato's Euthyphro, who does not shy from charging his father of wrong-doing, Confucius believed that, even though we normally consider theft to be wrong, a son should not expose it if his own father stole a sheep from his neighbor.[47] He said, "In serving his father and mother a man may gently remonstrate with them. But if he sees that he has failed to change their opinion, he should resume an attitude of deference and not thwart them."[48] At first glance, this may sound immoral. However, if *jen* and care are the central moral ideals, it is only reasonable to follow Noddings's and Confucius's way, especially given the gradation of caring (which will be discussed later). Wm. Theodore de Bary remarked,

> Here the point lies not in any tangible quid pro quo but in the inviolability of family intimacy. If the most basic human relations cannot be respected and protected within the family where all virtue is nourished, if family members cannot trust one another, the whole fiduciary basis of society stands in jeopardy.[49]

It does not mean one must disregard right and wrong altogether in preserving social relations; that would be another rigid rule. Rather, one needs to work it out without ruining social relationships. In cases such as the father stealing a neighbor's sheep, one may find other ways to make up the damage and one always has opportunities to help one's parents to come to moral sense later if the relationship is preserved.

Often, Confucianism leaves the impression that one's filial duty to parents is absolute. This is not so. In Confucianism, a person has many duties. Besides filial duty to parents, one also has the duty of loyalty to the ruler (the country). The two duties may come into conflict. For instance, when the country is being invaded, a man has the duty to answer the ruler's call to fight at the front line. What if his aging parents also need his daily assistance? In situations like this one, Confucianism offers no general rules to solve the problem. It depends on individual circumstances, and, as long as one cares, he can be *jen* even though failing to perform some of his duties.

Focusing on *jen* of affection, Mencius seemed even more flexible on general principles. He said, "All that is to be expected of a gentleman is *jen*. Why must he act exactly the same as other gentlemen?"[50] For Mencius, "A gentleman need not keep his word nor does he necessarily see his action through to the end. He aims only at what is right (appropriate)."[51] This remark seems to suggest that a person of *jen* may not always live up to her words as long as what she does is right or proper. Here the doctrine of living up to one's words, which would appear as a general principle, does not always determine what is appropriate. Unlike Kant, who believed that a person should never tell a lie, Mencius suggested that sometimes telling a lie is acceptable. He told a story about the legendary filial son Zeng Zi 曾子 and his father Zeng Xi 曾皙. Living in poverty, after meals Zeng Xi would ask Zeng Zi whether there were wine and meat left for the family, and Zeng Zi always replied in the affirmative even when actually there was not any left. In this way, Zeng Zi was able to give his father more gratification.[52] Though being honest is a virtue, whether we should tell the truth or a lie depends on circumstances. There are no general principles to follow. A person of *jen* is one with practical wisdom who can make good judgment and knows what to do and when.

Noddings notes that even though not following general rules, a caring person is not capricious. Like Mencius, Noddings believes that moral life based on caring is coherent and one can be content if there has been no violation of caring.[53] No ethics can be entirely devoid of rules, general rules or rules of thumb. One difference between Confucian ethics and feminist care ethics on the one hand, and Kantian ethics and utilitarian ethics on the other, is that the former are not as rule/principle-oriented.[54] A person of *jen* or a caring person knows where and when not to depend on rules.

Jen and Caring with Gradations

As a person of *jen*, a person of care, ought one to care for everyone equally? On this issue feminist philosophers are divided. It is with some feminist care philosophers that the Confucian shares an important common ground.

Confucius distinguished between a person of *jen* and a sage. Once his disciple Zi Gong 子贡 asked him, "If a person confers benefits on the people universally and is able to assist all, what would you say of him? Would you call him a person of *jen*?" Confucius said, "Why only a person of *jen*? He is without doubt a sage. Even (sage-emperors) Yao 尧 and Shun 舜 fell short of it."[55] Only sages are able to practice universal love. It is noble and admirable but far beyond ordinary people's moral horizon. For ordinary people, the highest moral ideal is *jen*, not sagehood.[56]

Ought a person to care for everyone equally, or to care more for those close to him or her? Confucius and Mo Zi (墨子 Mo Tzu, 479–438 B.C.E.), the founder of Mohism, are opposed on this issue. Mo Zi, the major rival of Confucians of the time, also believed in *ai* or love. But he believed in universal love (兼爱 *jian-ai*) and urged everyone to "regard other people's countries as one's own country. Regard other people's families as one's own family. Regard other people's person as one's own person."[57] Mencius condemned Mo Zi's universalism as an ethic with "no father."[58] That is, by treating everyone equally, one fails to treat one's father as the father.

The difference here, however, is not whether one should love or care for other people universally. Mencius himself said, "A person of *jen* embraces all in his love."[59] Confucius also said that one should "love all people comprehensively."[60] However, Confucius and Mencius believed that a person practicing *jen* should start with one's parents and siblings and then extend to other people. This is called "*ai you cha deng* 爱有差等" or "love with gradations." In other words, although one should love both his father and a stranger, he should love his father first and more than he loves the stranger. Confucius believed that "the greatest application of *jen* is in being affectionate toward one's parents,"[61] and "filiality and brotherly respect are the root of *jen*."[62] A person of *jen* must love first his father and elder brothers and then, by extension, other people. Mencius said, "Treat with respect the elders in my family, and then by extension, also the elders in other families. Treat with tenderness the young in my own family, and then by extension, also the young of other families."[63] He believed that a person of *jen* should be *jen* to all people but attached affectionately only to one's parents.[64] This means that one's parents exert a greater pull on him or her. Thus, when both one's father and a stranger are in need, the doctrine of love with gradations justifies one's helping one's father before helping the stranger.

In this regard Confucius and Mo Zi had different perspectives. Mo Zi had a utilitarian approach. For him moral life is desirable because of the benefits it brings with it. He said, "What the person of *jen* devotes oneself to surely lies in the promotion of benefits for the world and the removal of harm from the world."[65] Mo Zi argued that only by universal love is it possible to generate the most desirable outcome of actions. For Confucius, moral life is desirable for its own sake. *Jen* demands that one love one's parents first and other people second. This is the ideal moral life to which one should devote oneself. If a man treats his father as he treats a stranger and vice versa, then he is neglecting the affectionate tie between himself and his father and hence fails to be *jen*.

In *Caring*, Noddings follows a similar line of thinking. She believes that morality requires two sentiments. The first sentiment is that of natural caring. Caring starts with a person's natural impulse to care. We naturally care for our own family and relatives and people close to us. The second sentiment "arises from our evaluation of the caring relation as good, as better than, superior to, other forms of relatedness."[66] This is the genuine moral sentiment. Because the most intimate situations of caring are natural, proximity is powerful in caring.[67] Noddings notes that

> my caring is always characterized by a move away from self, . . . I care deeply for those in my inner circles and more lightly for those farther removed from my personal life. . . . The acts performed out of caring vary with both situational conditions and type of relationship.[68]

In accord with the Confucian, Noddings rejects the notion of universal love, on the grounds that it is unattainable except in the most abstract sense, and hence it is only a source of distraction.[69] For Noddings, this gradation of caring is justified by the fact that a person's very individuality is defined in a set of relations.[70] This set of relations is one's basic reality. What is right for a person to do is defined in this reality. Thus, an ethics of caring implies a limit on our obligation.[71] For people too far away, even if we would like to care, we simply cannot. While neither Confucius nor Mencius put limits on the scope of one's practicing *jen*, given their emphasis on one's filial duty and its extension to other family members and relatives, one cannot possibly practice universal love directly toward all the people in the world. If care as a natural sentiment arises from our daily life, it is only natural for us to start caring for people around us and then by extension for other people away from us; and if this kind of caring is the base for the central moral ideal, then it is only reasonable to have gradations among those for whom we care.

In this regard, philosophers of the care perspective such as Noddings and the Confucian again jointly stand in opposition to Kantian and utilitarian ethics. Kantians and utilitarians subscribe to the concept of impartiality. For them all moral patients exert an equal pull on all moral agents. For the Confucian and the one-caring, parents and others who are closely related certainly have a stronger pull. Accordingly, although we should care for everyone in the world if possible, we do need to start with those closest to us. This is not to say that we should care only for people close to us. It means that starting with those close to us is the only reasonable way to practice *jen* and care. It would be perfect if a mother could care, in addition to her own baby and her neighbor's, for every little baby in the world who needs care. Unfortunately that is not possible. She should be content with giving her care to her own baby and, perhaps, her neighbor's. This is as far as she normally can go, and this is our way of life as people of *jen* and care. Giving priority to people near us is not merely justified by the fact that the closer the needy are to us geographically, the more efficient our aid is. Even if it were equally efficient, we would still feel more obliged to help the nearby. This feeling can be justified by the notion of care with gradations.[72]

How a Care Ethics Could Have Oppressed Women

For a long period of time Confucianism has been notorious for its history of oppression of women. Feminism is primarily a fighter for women's liberation. Is it possible for them to share philosophically significant common ground? My findings provide an affirmative answer. I have identified three major areas in which there are similarities between Confucianism and feminist care ethics. The similarities between the two are not in the ways they have treated women but in their philosophical thinking, in the way they view the nature and foundation of morality, and in the way they believe morality should be practiced. Based on these similarities, we can conclude that Confucian ethics is a care ethics.

If Confucian ethics is a care ethics, a question that naturally arises here is, how can it be possible for a care ethics to have been so uncaring toward women and to have oppressed women? Apparently there is a discrepancy. To shed some light on the problem and to dissolve the apparent discrepancy, in this section I will first show, through a historical examination of the development of Confucianism, that to a large extent Confucius and Mencius, the founders of Confucianism, are not responsible for its history of oppression of women. Then I will show why it is not impossible, and not contradictory, for a philosophy that is essentially caring in nature to have oppressed women. If either of the two accounts succeeds, the discrepancy is dissolved.

As we know, Confucianism was founded by Confucius. The major doctrines of this philosophy are in his *Analects*. Mencius contributed a great deal to Confucianism by providing substantial arguments for ideas propounded by Confucius. It is safe to say that by the time Mencius died, the basic doctrines of Confucianism were already well established. In China, Confucianism is called the "Philosophy of Confucius-Mencius" ("孔孟之道" *Kong-Meng zhi dao*). Confucian scholars of later ages modified and hence more or less altered the philosophy. These versions usually have a specific name attached to the generic term "Confucianism," for example, "the *Yin-yang* Confucianism 阴阳儒家" or "Neo-Confucianism." Because the basic doctrines of Confucianism were established by Confucius and Mencius, these doctrines without later modifications certainly well deserve the name of Confucianism.

It is a fact that under the name of Confucianism there has been oppression of women. But since when has it been so? If it can be shown that Confucianism became oppressive to women only at a later stage, since Confucianism had existed before it became so, one can say that oppressing women is not an essential characteristic of Confucianism, and hence Confucianism as propounded by Confucius and Mencius can be a care ethics.

The most notorious women-oppressive doctrine in the name of Confucianism is that the husband is the wife's bond. According to *Bai Hu Tong* 白虎通, the encyclopedia of *Yin-yang* Confucianism, a bond (纲 *gang*) gives orderliness.[73] It serves to order the relations between the superior and the inferior, and to arrange and adjust the way of humankind. Then why should the husband be the wife's bond? Why is it not the other way around? The principal justification of this is the *yin-yang* doctrine.

In Chinese philosophy, *yin* and *yang* are two mutually complementary principles or forces. The words originally referred to two natural physical phenomena, that is, clouds shading the sun and the sun shining, respectively. Later their meanings were expanded broadly to cover two general kinds of phenomena. *Yang* represents light, warmth, dryness, hardness, masculinity, activity, and so on, while *yin* represents darkness, cold, moisture, softness, passivity, and so on. In *Yin-yang* Confucianism *yang* has been considered as the superior and dominant principle, and *yin* the inferior and subservient or subordinate principle. Accordingly, all phenomena in the world are results of the interplay of these two principles. Between male and female, male is the *yang* and female the *yin*. From this it follows that, prior to marriage, a woman must listen and yield to her father, after marriage, to her husband, and after her husband dies, to her son. In reality, domination was translated into oppression. Under this philosophy, the wife is judged almost entirely on the basis of her relationship to her husband. She must remain obedient to her husband. For her, "to die of starvation is a small matter, but to lose integrity is a large matter."[74] To serve and please her husband is her destined duty. When there is absolute power/domination there is abuse of the power/domination. Women's fate was thus doomed.[75]

It should be noted that the *yin-yang* concept itself does not necessarily imply the inferiority of the female. A Taoist interpretation of *yin-yang* may make the female superior. The interpretation of this concept in *yin-yang* Confucianism, however, leads to the belief of men's superiority and women's inferiority. Then, when was this *yin-yang* doctrine incorporated into Confucianism? Confucius himself did not talk about *yin-yang*. Like most of his contemporaries, Confucius believed in the Mandate of Heaven, but he never went so far as to attempt to work out a cosmological system, let alone a systematic theoretical justification of the oppression of women. In the *Analects*, Confucius specifically mentioned women only a few times. He never suggested that men should dominate or oppress women. In one place it is recorded that Confucius went to visit Nan Zi 南子, the wife of the duke of Wei.[76] There Confucius did not make a statement in regard to relationships between men and women. In another place, Confucius did make a statement about women. He said,

Young women and small men are hard to rear. If you become familiar with them you lose respect, and if you keep aloof you provoke resentment.[77]

Here Confucius offered an observation of young women rather than a theory about women in general. It probably reflects a social prejudice that already existed in his time. Given Confucius's later illustrious status in China, this short comment on (young) women may have considerably influenced people's view on women in general in a negative way, and reinforced people's prejudice against women. However, there is no reason for one to think that this view is an inherent or essential part of Confucius's thought or an inevitable consequence of his general philosophy.

Like Confucius, Mencius did not talk about *yin-yang* either. He, however, mentioned women in his book. For example, Mencius believed that, although men and women outside of marital relationships should avoid physical contact with each other, a man definitely should pull his sister-in-law out of a pond, by whatever means possible, including bare hands, if she were drowning. Although Mencius suggested that obedience was a virtue for women,[78] his general attitude toward women was not negative. This is so perhaps partly due to his relation with his mother, who brought him up single-handedly after his father died young. One can hardly imagine that a person from such a family would advocate a philosophy of the husband's being the wife's bond.

According to Fung Yu-lan, the *yin-yang* school probably did not enter the Confucian school until after Mencius died, and it was during the Qin (Chi, 秦 255–209 B.C.E.) and Han (汉, 206 B.C.E.–23 C.E.) dynasties that the *yin-yang* doctrine came to be almost completely amalgamated with Confucianism.[79] Shu-hsien Liu also believes that Confucianism was transformed in the Han dynasty:

The Han Confucians liked to talk about the "interaction between Heaven and man" (天人感应 *tian ren ganyin*), combining Confucianism with *yin-yang* philosophy and eclecticism (杂家 *za jia*). [Hence] the Confucian transcendent Heaven fell and was mixed with the *yin-yang wu-xing* (五行 five agents) cosmology; in human affairs Confucianism became the *wu xing* . . . political philosophy.[80]

The philosopher most responsible for blending the *yin-yang* doctrine into Confucianism is Dong Zhongshu (Tung Chung-shu, 董仲舒 179–104 B.C.E.). As Liu points out, "Dong Zhongshu's mixing *yin-yang* [with Confucianism], absolutizing the *gang* and constants, were [already] a big tortuosity for the pre-Qin Confucianism."[81] Dong's high social position as the master of the state (博士 *bo shi*) and his great scholarship in Confucianism and the classics facilitated his effort in combining Confucianism with the *yin-yang* doctrine. A substantial portion of his major philosophical work,

Luxuriant Gems of the Spring and Autumn Annals (春秋繁露 *Chun Qiu Fan Lu*), deals with *yin-yang*.[82] Dong believed that *yin* and *yang* are two opposing forces that follow the constant course of Heaven. There is an intimate relationship between Heaven and humans. He said,

> The relationships between ruler and subject, father and son, husband and wife, are all derived from the principles of the *yin* and *yang*. The ruler is *yang*, the subject *yin*; the father is *yang*, the son *yin*; the husband is *yang*, the wife *yin*. . . . The *yang* acts as the husband, who procreates [the son]. The *yin* acts as the wife, who gives assistance [to the husband]. The "three bonds," comprising the Way of the King (王道 *wang tao*), may be sought for in Heaven.[83]

Thus, among the human relationships discussed by Confucius, Dong singled out three. He believed that in the human world, the relationships between the ruler and the subject, the father and the son, and the husband and the wife, are the same as that between Heaven and Earth. Corresponding to the *yang*, the ruler, the father, and the husband dominate over the subject, the son, and the wife respectively, who correspond to the *yin*, in the same way as Heaven dominates over Earth.

Now, we can suggest who is responsible for the elements oppressive to women in Confucianism. There is no evidence in works by Confucius or Mencius explicitly indicating that they had a view oppressive to women. If it is true that neither Confucius nor Mencius specifically spoke highly of women, it was so probably because women's social status was low during their times. Obviously, these philosophers were not liberators of women. Furthermore, there is no essential connection between their doctrine of *jen* on the one hand and their view on women on the other. It is Dong Zhongshu who was most responsible for incorporating the *yin-yang* doctrine into Confucianism, which resulted in a version of Confucianism oppressive to women.[84] The Song Neo-Confucians further developed this tendency.[85]

Now I will try to answer the question of how it is possible for a care ethics to have taken part in the oppression of women. The point I want to make is that people may hold the same principle while they disagree on the application of it. Later Confucians may have excluded women from the domain of the practice of *jen* because they did not believe that women are as fully persons as men are. The apparent discrepancy between the oppressive view toward women and the concept of *jen* may be explained away by the account that many Confucians had a limited application domain of the concept of *jen*.

In history, it is not rare for people to hold a certain principle while practicing something that would appear contrary to that very principle. Ancient Athenians believed in democracy. Yet their democracy was limited to "citizens." Slaves and women were excluded from participation in democracy because they were not citizens. Imagine that a political change took place in the city-state and consequently all slaves and women were allowed to participate in democracy along with the citizens. Now, should we say that the Athenians have changed their principle of democracy or that they continue to hold the same principle but expanded the domain of its participants? I think the latter is the appropriate answer.

A Christian may have held a strong belief in the brotherhood/sisterhood among her fellows, and yet at the same time may have taken a black slave. For her there was no contradiction simply because she sincerely believed that blacks were not among her fellow people to whom brotherhood/sisterhood would apply. Suppose later this person changed her view on blacks and realized that, after all, blacks were also her fellow people. Would one say that this person changed her principle of brotherhood/sisterhood or that she changed the application domain of the principle? I think the appropriate answer is the latter. Similarly, in America the change from believing that all *men* are born equal to believing that all men and women are born equal is a change of the application domain of equality, not the concept of equality itself.

The same logic holds true for our case on Confucianism. Assuming that Confucius and Mencius held restrictive views of women, it would not cause any conflict for them to maintain a care ethics. A care ethics may extend or reduce its application domain. For Confucius and Mencius, *jen* is a human relation. It does not apply to animals.[86] Today, a Confucian who is firmly convinced by Peter Singer's argument for animal equality may maintain that *jen* should be practiced on animals too. In the same way, if a Confucian was convinced that women were not fully persons, he might well have thought (wrongly, of course) that *jen* did not fully apply to women. If this is the case, changing the view to include women into the domain of the application of *jen* will only alter the application domain of the concept, not the concept itself.

So, is Confucianism a care ethics that has oppressed women? If by Confucianism is meant Confucianism after Dong Zhongshu's *yin-yang* philosophy, including Song Neo-Confucianism, the answer to this question is definitely affirmative. If one wants to say that the authentic philosophy of Confucius and Mencius is the one before Dong, then there is no evidence that the Confucianism of Confucius and Mencius was really oppressive to women.[87]

I have also shown that it is possible for a person to hold a philosophy that is caring in nature and at the same time excludes women from its application. If this possibility is real, then it is possible for Confucianism as a care ethics to have oppressed women. Furthermore, if this in turn is accurate, then it is possible for us to fully restore the concept of care to Confucianism by eliminating the women-oppressive doctrine from it.

Now we can see that care-orientation is not a characteristic peculiar to a particular social group or culture. Like feminist care ethics, Confucian ethics centers on human relatedness and responsibility instead of individual liberty and individual rights. This characteristic of Confucianism bears heavily on its relation to liberal democratic value as I will discuss in chapter 7. But before that I will examine one more area of Confucian emphasis on human relatedness and responsibility in the next chapter.

Family

Duty versus Rights

Based on her years of observation, Diane B. Obenchain writes on the importance of the family in the Chinese culture:

In China, family truly is the central symbol of more in human life than meets the eye. As a member of a family, stretching from the finite here and now into infinity backward and forward in time, a Chinese person is always aware that who he or she is, is family. Knowledge of self is knowledge of family. Cultivation of self is cultivation of family. Nurturing of family is nurturing of self. It is this nurturing of family that is at the core of Chinese cultural learning, past, and present.[1]

Obenchain is not exaggerating. The family is at the core of Chinese culture and Chinese philosophy. For the Chinese, the family is the center of and the most important aspect of a person's life. The family is the foundation of one's identity, one's morality, and the source of meaning of life.

Among many relationships within the family—between parents and children, husband and wife, between siblings—the Chinese philosophical discourse has focused most on the one between parents and children. The relation between parents and children is the most natural relation. By nature, parents generally care for their young when the young need care. Even animals have a natural inclination to care for their offspring. The inclination for adult children to care for their aged parents is usually much weaker. In animals this kind of care virtually does not exist. For humans, what is missing in nature may be found in morality. Confucianism is emphatic on the moral obligation of children toward parents, and particularly on grown children's obligation toward their aged parents.

People of different cultures hold different views on the issue of filial morality. This is one of the areas that deeply separate the Chinese tradition from the (contemporary) West. Many Westerners find this Confucian value hard to accept. For example, Bertrand Russell, who expressed much sympathy for Chinese culture after visiting China, commented:

> Filial piety, and the strength of the family generally, are perhaps the weakest point in Confucian ethics, the only point where the system departs seriously from common sense.[2]

Undoubtedly, in this regard many Westerners will find themselves in opposition to the Confucians.

Can filial morality be justified? If the answer is negative, as some people believe, then why is this so, and how can we account for the strong intuition in many cultures that such an obligation exists? If the answer is affirmative, then on what basis is this obligation founded? Perhaps the justification or non-justification of filial morality is deeply rooted in the culture. Perhaps something that is hard to justify in one culture may be justified in another. If this is true, the only way to look into this matter is to look into the culture itself. In this chapter I will first examine problems with some accounts of filial morality that have been put forth in recent years, and then turn to Confucianism and show how it provides a sensible alternative perspective.

Critiques of Some Recent Theories

It appears that today's American culture generally does not favor the notion of filial obligation, or at least not a strong notion of it. Arguments, however, have been put forth on both sides, pro and con. While Jane English has been a representative of the side against filial obligation,[3] there are writers who support it. However, as I will show, none of these writers seem to have been successful.

In her article "What Do Grown Children Owe Their Parents?" Jane English proposed a theory based on the concept of friendship.[4] She argued that grown children have no more filial obligation toward their parents than the kind of obligation toward friends or the people whom they love. According to her, if parents' earlier sacrifices for their children resulted in friendship and love in their children, parents may have the good fortune to be honored and served by their grown children. If parents' earlier sacrifices failed to produce friendship and love in their children, then the children have no filial obligation to serve and honor their parents. "After a friendship ends, the duties of friendship end," she asserted.[5]

English distinguished two kinds of relationships, indebtedness and friendship. Here "indebtedness" is not limited to literal debts, but understood broadly to include all situations where a favor has been done. "Favors create debts," English wrote.[6] If person *B* has done a favor for person *A*, then *A* is indebted to *B*. *A* ought to do something to reciprocate the favor. She maintained that, unlike indebtedness, friendship is characterized by mutuality rather than reciprocity; in friendship, a person can benefit from what her friend has done to or for her out of friendship, but she is not thereby indebted to him. She does not "owe" him anything.

Then why is the typical relationship between children and parents not characterized as "indebtedness"? Because, English argued, parents' earlier voluntary sacrifices for their children are not favors to their children, and therefore these sacrifices do not render their children "indebted" to their parents. When the children grow up and the parents need help, the children may lend a helping hand out of friendship and love—if parents' earlier sacrifices have resulted in friendship and love. No filial obligation exists beyond that.

Why are parents' earlier sacrifices for their children not favors, which should be reciprocated? English argued that parents' earlier sacrifices are not favors because their children did not request them. Obviously, the children were too young to request favors from anyone, including their parents. Therefore the children are not obliged to repay them when the parents are in need.

It may be debatable whether small children make requests. It is arguable that requests do not have to be verbal, which small children (infants) are certainly incapable of. Requests can be made through gestures, eye contacts, and so forth. Many pet owners think their pets do make requests in many ways. Therefore in a broad sense of the word, from the mother's point of view, a crying baby is making a request for help. For the sake of argument, however, let us grant English that small children cannot and do not make requests for their needs. Now, does it follow that parental care is not a favor to their children?

A favor results, according to English, when person *A*, at person *B*'s request, bears some burden for *B*, then *B* incurs an obligation to reciprocate.[7] English illustrated this as follows:

> New to the neighborhood, Max barely knows his neighbor, Nina, but asks her if she will take in his mail while he is gone for a month's vacation. She agrees. If, subsequently, Nina asks Max to do the same for her, it seems that Max has a moral obligation to agree (greater than the one he would have had if Nina had not done the same for him), unless for some reason it would be a burden far out of proportion to the one Nina bore for him.[8]

In this case, English maintained, Nina has done a favor for Max and, therefore, Max owes a favor to Nina. If "Max simply goes on vacation and, to his surprise, finds upon his return that his neighbor has mowed his grass twice weekly in his absence. [Then] this is a voluntary sacrifice rather than a favor, and Max has no duty to reciprocate."[9] In the latter case no favor has been done because, as English indicated, Max did not request the service from his neighbor.

Is a request necessary for a favor to take place? I do not think so. Whether a favor is done has more to do with whether a person being benefited would like the thing done to or for him or her. In English's case, imagine that, due to unusual weather Max's grass grew much faster than normal during his absence and without his neighbor's voluntary help Max would have received a substantial fine for breaking a city ordinance. Shouldn't Max consider his neighbor's voluntary help a favor?

Let us look at another case. Suppose on her way home to feed her one-year-old child, Nina's car broke down, and Max happened to drive by and offered her a lift home. Even if Nina did not request it,

Max has done a favor for Nina. Next time when Nina sees Max's car break down, she has a moral obligation to help, an obligation greater than the one she would have had if Max had not helped Nina when her car broke down, unless a burden much greater would result from helping Max. Perhaps Nina would feel a stronger obligation if she had requested a lift home from Max. In many cases favors are done without a request. Suppose that Nina's house is on fire, and Max happens to pass by and sees it. He manages to put out the fire and thereby suffers a financial loss due to missing a business appointment at the time of the fire. Even though she did not request it, it would be outrageous if Nina does not consider Max's sacrifice a great favor. It would be indecent if Nina does not think she has a moral obligation to lend a hand when Max later needs someone to take in his mail for a month. Under these circumstances, whether a request has been made is inconsequential to whether a favor has been done.

Since English did not deny that a person is morally obliged to return a favor, her entire friendship model depends on the argument that parents' earlier sacrifices are not favors to their children. Her argument in turn relies on the claim that a request is a necessary condition for a favor to occur. This claim, we have shown, is unwarranted, and, therefore, so is her conclusion that parents' earlier sacrifices are not favors to their children.[10]

Contrary to English, Raymond Belliotti argued for filial obligation. He proposed an argument from personal identity, which he characterized as the "Contribution to Self Principle." According to this view, "we have moral requirements of a special sort to those who contribute to and help nurture our identities, and those whose attachment is essential for our self-understanding."[11] Belliotti believed that, in addition to her failure to recognize unrequested favors, English assumed an atomistic notion of self. He wrote that English's position

> fails to capture the sense in which our families (partly) constitute our identities, not merely engage our volitional acts. It fails to understand and appreciate the role in the parent-child relationship of cognition and discovery (in contrast to volition and choice). In short, it ignores the way our parents affect directly our very identities, how we have moral requirements to them and in fulfilling these requirements we are, in a literal way, being true to our "selves."[12]

Accordingly, a person's filial obligation arises from one's identity, namely, who and what one is.

Belliotti's identity thesis bears some similarities with Confucianism, which I will discuss later in this chapter. It is also different from Confucianism in a substantial way. In brief, while Confucianism is both backward- and forward-looking, namely, looking both at what one has become and what one will/ought to become to determine one's moral duty, Belliotti's thesis appears solely backward-looking. His thesis relies solely on what parents have done to the person's identity. Therefore it is not unfair that Jan Narverson summarized Belliotti's principle as follows:

> Premise: Person A contributed factor X to the "identity" of another person, B.
> Conclusion: B morally *owes* something to A.[13]

One problem with this thesis is that of negative contribution. In a person's life there are countless factors that have contributed to her identity. Obviously we do not want to say that she owes everyone who has contributed to her identity. Narveson wrote, "Suppose you, my parent, endow me with a lifelong case of syphilis, or with mongolism. Presumably I'm not supposedly to be really grateful for *this* particular contribution to my identity."[14]

When Belliotti used the word "owe" he apparently meant "owing something good." For, in the normal sense of the word, we usually do not say things like "I owe you a good kick in the pants for a harm you have caused me." If Belliotti's thesis is to be taken as a general one as it appears to be, it would follow that a person has moral obligations to those who have made whatever contributions, both positive and negative, to his identity. One should love her father for having taught her to be a good barber and hate him for getting her into the profession that she dislikes. However, the notion of negative contribution to self and hence negative moral obligation seems inappropriate here because Belliotti was discussing what moral duties grown children have toward their parents, by which he evidently was discussing what good grown children ought to do for their parents. It is unclear what Belliotti would say on this problem.

Perhaps Belliotti can modify his thesis and say that we owe moral requirements only to those who have contributed something *positive* to our identities. Then there is the question of what counts as positive contributions. Suppose my father contributed a great deal to my being a fine barber and I hate my profession as a barber; should I be grateful for this contribution of his? Also positive contributions may come from different directions. We should not be grateful to all whose actions have resulted in positive contributions to us. Suppose I grew up in an orphanage, and a vicious man in the orphanage gave me all kinds of hardships, but as a result I have developed a strong character that enables me to endure future hardships on the way to a successful and splendid future. Should I be grateful for his *positive* contribution to my identity? Probably not. So, contributions to our identities, even limited to positive contributions, cannot serve as a solid foundation for filial morality.

In his article "On Honoring Our Parents," Jan Narveson favored filial obligations of grown children by arguing that

> parents do put themselves to much trouble to benefit their children, and if the children in question agree that the effects of those efforts really have been beneficial, then they should see to it that they are benefitted in turn to at least the degree that renders it non-irrational for the parents to have done this.[15]

Belliotti has called this the "prudent investor thesis."[16]

Narveson believed that one rational motive for people to do good to others is that of *investment*.[17] According to this conception, people tend to do good to one another "because they see the potential benefits of having everyone so disposed, and if we are to secure such a general disposition, we must instantiate it ourselves."[18] The rationale here appears to be a Kantian one: we are obliged to do what we need to do, in order for the kind of investment that we wish to be universally continued, to continue.

One difficulty with Narveson's thesis lies in the clause "if the children in question agree that the effects of those [parental] efforts really have been beneficial." As Belliotti pointed out, this clause "holds the existence of the moral requirements hostage to the child's judgment that she has been benefited by her parents' efforts."[19] Belliotti remarked that under this condition,

> a child can let herself off the ethical hook by simply denying that her parents' past efforts were benefits. Given human pro-

clivities for rationalization and good faith errors of judgment, this is dangerous.[20]

Belliotti is certainly right in this regard. A moral obligation, if it exists, is an obligation, regardless of whether a person likes it or not.

If, when Nina's life is in great danger, Max saves her without being requested to, Max does Nina a great favor. If Nina does not appreciate the favor and does not feel grateful, we say she has a very poor or bad sense of appreciation or she is ungrateful. Even if she does not feel she "owes" Max a great favor, it does not change the fact that she is under a moral obligation to reciprocate the favor in some appreciative way. Max, on the other hand, may graciously "waive" any moral obligation that Nina has to him and not expect anything in return. That is entirely Max's noble gesture. In the same way, if the parents have done a great favor to their children without being requested to, by giving them life and bringing them up, then grown children are under obligation to return the favor. Usually the best way to do so is to take care of their parents when they grow old and need care from their grown children.

A grown child normally should have love and friendship toward her parents and acknowledge that she has benefited from her parents' earlier sacrifices. Even if she does not, she is not thereby exempt from her filial obligation (if there is one). Similar to the case of Max's saving Nina's house from fire without being appreciated, a person may not feel grateful for her parents giving her a life and bringing her up. That only shows that she is ungrateful. The lack of love and friendship on her part does not exempt her from her filial obligation to serve her aged parents. Morality demands that one fulfill one's obligation regardless of whether one recognizes it or not.

However, the requirement that the child agrees that her parents' sacrifices have been beneficial to her does not seem indispensable to Narveson's thesis. For he could simply delete the phrase "the children in question agree that" and let the clause read "and if the effects of those efforts really have been beneficial, then...." By doing so Narveson could easily get himself off Belliotti's hook.

There is, however, another problem, which in my view is more serious than the first one. It is the question whether parents need a rational motivation for having children. Here I have no intention to attack the rationality talk (i.e., the demand for a rational justification for almost everything that we do) that has deeply saturated our philosophical discourse today. Perhaps we can give a rational justification for having children. However, it seems to me that parents do not have to have a rational justification for having children. The desire to have offspring, whether conscious or not, is rooted deeply in every species. Otherwise the species would no longer exist. In this regard, humans are not different from animals. A people that do not reproduce offspring simply cannot exist.[21] It means that regardless of whether we have rational justification for it, humans will continue having offspring. It is a law of nature, and a law of nature does not need a rational justification. Therefore, Narveson's notion that a child has filial obligation toward her parents because she should see that it is not irrational for parents to have children, is itself unjustified and perhaps unjustifiable.

In her article "Filial Morality," Christina Sommers proposed a theory of ethical duties that she called "the thesis of differential pull."[22] This thesis states that "the ethical pull of a moral patient will always partly depend on how the moral patient is related to the moral agent on whom the pull is exerted."[23] This thesis appears similar to the Confucian thesis of love with gradations.[24] Based on this thesis, Sommers argued that children have special moral obligations toward their parents because of their special relationship with their parents. She attempted to justify this special relationship as follows:

The presumption of a special positive obligation arises for a moral agent when two conditions obtain: (1) In a given social arrangement (or practice), there is a specific interaction or transaction between moral agent and patient such as promising and being promised, nurturing and being nurtured, befriending and being befriended. (2) The interaction in that context gives rise to certain conventional expectations (e.g., that a promise will be kept, that a marital partner will be faithful, that a child will respect the parent).[25]

Sommers argued that because of the existence of this parental "conventional" expectation of the children, children's failure to perform their expected behavior will cause unwarranted interference with the rights of the parents.

Although I agree with Sommers, as I do with the Confucian view, on the "thesis of differential pull," I do not think Sommers's argument is cogent.

By justifying moral obligations on the basis of conventional expectations, Sommers seems to have confused morality with mores. Simply put, the conventional is not tantamount to the moral. Good performance of conventionally expected behavior is not necessarily moral; failure to perform such behavior is not necessarily immoral. Much conventionally expected behavior is actually immoral and should be avoided. At a certain time in some part of the world it has been conventionally expected that if a man could not repay his debts, he should give away his wife or daughter to his creditor, or render himself a slave to the creditor. Yet this is not a moral practice. If I cannot repay my debts and refuse to render my wife or myself to my creditor, he may feel that his right has been violated. The fact of the matter may be that he has never had such a right, even though it is a conventionally expected practice. Under these circumstances, a breach of conventional expectations would be a morally justifiable behavior and should be encouraged and praised. Therefore, one cannot successfully argue for what ought to be the case merely from what is conventionally expected to be the case; one cannot argue for filial obligation by simply stating that it is conventionally expected.

Jeffrey Blustein has presented perhaps the most carefully argued and sophisticated work in recent years on the matter of filial morality.[26] His thesis is that grown children owe their parents many things and yet are not indebted to their parents.[27]

Blustein distinguished two kinds of duties, duties of gratitude and duties of indebtedness:

> Duties of gratitude are owed only to those who have helped or benefited us freely, without thought of personal gain, simply out of a desire to protect or promote our well-being. . . . Duties of indebtedness, in contrast, can be owed to those who were motivated primarily by self-interest or by the desire to help only insofar as this was believed to involve no risk or loss to themselves.[28]

A person with duties of indebtedness is subject to claims for repayment, while a person with duties of gratitude is not. Grown children's duties to their parents are typically duties of gratitude. With such duties, grown children ought "to express their gratitude in words or deeds or both,"[29] but the parents do not have claims for repayment from their children.

Blustein suggested that the occurrence of duties of indebtedness requires two conditions: (1) the giver does not have a duty to benefit the receiver; and (2) the receiver does not only receive, but also accepts, the benefit.[30] Blustein wrote,

> In order for claims to repayment to have any moral force, it must first be established that what parents claim repayment for is something that they were morally at liberty to give to or withhold from their children.[31]

A lot of things that parents do to or for their children are things required by their parental duty and demanded by the children's rights. "Children's claim rights," as Blustein insisted, "correlate with the obligations of their parents."[32] Mere fulfillment of duties does not create indebtedness. When person *A* owes person *B* $100, *B* has a claim right to get the money back. If *A* pays *B* the money, *A* only fulfills his obligation, and *B* is not thereby indebted to *A*.

Moreover, Blustein maintains that one cannot become indebted if one does not *accept* the benefit that one receives. If you, under no obligation, offer to maintain my lawn while I go on vacation and I accept your offer and benefit from the service, then I am indebted to you. If I refuse your offer, then you cannot make me indebted to you by maintaining my lawn. In the latter case I only receive, not accept, the benefit.

Blustein argues that, within the family, the parents do have a duty to provide care for their young children, and the children, while young, "cannot exercise genuine choice with respect to the benefits of early care."[33] Therefore, unless the parents have done something good for their children that is supererogatory to parental duty, and unless the children have accepted it or would have accepted if they could exercise genuine choice, the children do not incur duties of indebtedness to their parents.

One objection to Blustein might be that parental duty cannot be clearly defined. For example, is it a parental duty that the parents should get up in the middle of night to check and see if their child is sleeping well when they hear a little unidentifiable noise? Would it be supererogatory if the parents feed their children expensive fish instead of chicken on weekends? Would it be a supererogatory act if the parents spend two hours playing with their children instead of one hour? If a couple does more for their children than average parents and their children appreciate it, would that entitle the parents to some claims over the children for repayment? Social customs cannot help much in determining these issues. As soon as one starts drawing the line between what belongs and what does not belong to parental duty, one is treating the family as a group of self-interested strangers. Family members are not strangers.

However, this objection may be trivial. For Blustein can say that the main issue here concerns the large portion of parental sacrifices clearly required by parental duty; if parents cannot claim repayment for these services required by parental duty, then there is no basis for demanding that the children reciprocate these services. One cannot deny that parents do have a duty to care for their children. If fulfillment of duties does not create indebtedness, then it follows that children are not indebted by benefiting from their parents' service required by parental duty.[34] If this is the case, Blustein's goal is achieved.

I agree with Blustein that what parents do for their children should not be considered merely and literally as a loan to be repaid later. I also agree with him that children owe duties of gratitude to their parents for their earlier sacrifices. From a Confucian point of view, however, grown children "owe" their parents many things in a much stronger sense. The sense is so strong that grown children can be said to be "indebted" to their parents and that, from their grown children, parents are entitled to and can, with full moral force, *claim* "repayment," in terms of financial assistance, physical attendance, personal care, and the like.

I think Blustein, within his theoretical framework of rights, has presented a strong negative case that cannot be easily dismissed. His argument may be used against some of the above-mentioned authors who are in favor of a stronger notion of filial obligation. Perhaps Blustein is right that, from the rights perspective, filial morality cannot be justified. Perhaps this partly explains why so many people in this culture of individual rights do not accept filial morality. I will, instead of arguing against Blustein within his framework of rights, turn to an alternative framework, Confucianism, and see what light it can shed on this important issue.

The Confucian Perspective

Unlike in the West, where filial morality is rarely a philosophical topic, in China filial morality has long been at the center of philosophical discourse. Renowned Chinese scholars such as Chien Mu 钱穆 and Hsieh Yu-wei 谢幼伟 described Chinese culture as "the culture of filial morality (孝的文化 *xiao de wenhua*)."[35] One cannot understand traditional Chinese culture without understanding the role of filial morality in it.

The Chinese newspaper *People's Daily* 人民日报 (overseas edition) of August 25, 1993, reported that in Shandong Province of China a ninty-year-old woman took her two sons to court for failing in their filial duty. The woman's husband died young and left her with two sons, a one-year-old and a three-year-old. Through countless hardships she brought them both up. Now she was old and could no longer work. Neither of her two sons wanted to take care of her. The court's intervention resulted in her favor and the sons, who were relatively well-to-do, agreed to take full responsibility for her living and medical expenses.[36] In China the law requires that parents have legal duties to rear their young children and grown children have legal duties to support their aged parents.[37] It reflects a Chinese conviction that is deeply rooted in the social values of the culture, mainly Confucian culture.

Filial morality is one of the most important concepts of Confucian ethics and a cardinal virtue in the Confucian tradition. This may be seen through the fact that *The Classic of Filial Morality* (孝经 *Xiao Jing/Hsiao Ching*) and Confucius's *Analects* have been the two most widely read among Confucian classics.[38] *The Classic of Filial Morality* makes filial morality a cardinal virtue by stating that "filial morality is the unchanging truth of Heaven, the unfailing equity of Earth, the [universal] practice of the people" (VII).

What does filial morality mean in Confucianism? The Chinese word *"xiao* 孝*" (hsiao)* is usually rendered in English as "filial piety." It can also be rendered as "filial ethics" or "filial morality." The Chinese character consists of two components, one standing for the son or daughter (子 *zi*) and the other, the old. The word has the part symbolizing the old on top of the part symbolizing the son or daughter, meaning the son or daughter supporting or succeeding the parent. *Shuo Wen Jie Zi* defines *"xiao"* as "being good at serving one's parents" (善事父母者 *shan shi fu mu zhe*).

In ancient China filial morality included five types of behavior.[39] The first is supporting one's parents. *The Classic of Filial Morality* said "supporting one's parents is the filial morality (*xiao*) in common people" (VI). The second is honoring, revering, and obeying one's parents. Confucius said, "Filial morality nowadays means to be able to support one's parents. But we support even dogs and horses. If there is no feeling of reverence, wherein lies the difference?"[40] Mencius said "the greatest thing a filial son can do is to honor his parents."[41] On the relation between supporting one's parents and honoring them, *The Book of Rites* said "There are three levels of filiality: the highest is honoring one's parents, the secondary not disgracing them, and the lowest, [merely] supporting them" (chap. 24). The third type of filial behavior is producing heirs. Mencius said, "There are three ways of being unfilial. The most serious is to have no heir."[42] The fourth is to bring honor and glory to one's ancestors. *The Classic of Filial Morality* said "to establish oneself, to enhance the Way, and to leave a good fame behind, in order to make one's parents illustrious, are the ultimate goal of filiality" (I). Finally, after the parents's death, one should mourn and offer memorial service and sacrifice to them. *The Classic of Filial Morality* has ample discussions of this, particularly in chapters X and XVIII.

Among these five types of ancient filial behaviors, the one that appears most incomprehensible to many Westerners is the third. What does producing heirs have to do with filial morality? After all, filial morality has to do with treating one's parents well; one can certainly treat parents well even without producing heirs. People who think along these lines, however, have overlooked the religious dimension of Confucianism. It must be noted that there is no heaven, as in Christianity, to ensure an eternal life in Confucianism.[43] The Confucians have to look somewhere else for the meanings of life, and to satisfy the almost inescapable human desire for immortality. The place to find it, for the Confucians, is human-relatedness. Human-relatedness has multiple dimensions. One primary dimension is continuing the family line. Through reproduction, one can not only pass on one's family name, but also one's blood, and hence life, to later generations. Tang Chün-i 唐君毅, a renowned Chinese philosopher, said, "the lives of my offspring come from my life. Their existence is considered the direct evidence of the immortality of my life."[44] Also the meaning of life is realized when one is loved by the members of one's family, and after death remembered by the family members that follow. Therefore, one most important thing to avoid is to "discontinue the sacrificial burning of incense (断了香火 *duan le xiang huo*)" by not having later generations. The continuation of the family line is a necessary way for this purpose. Not having heirs means cutting off the family line that has been passed on by the earlier generations, and it therefore is unfilial. This doctrine may also have helped to sustain a stable population in the early times.

This line of thinking also explains the fourth and fifth types of filial behaviors. One would feel that life is (more) meaningful if one believes that one will be remembered and honored and even glorified by later generations.

Another often neglected implication is that, without raising children of our own, we cannot fully appreciate our parents' efforts in raising us. A Chinese saying is that "we do not really know our parents' kindness until we raise our own children (养儿方知父母恩 *yang er fang zhi fumu en*)." Having one's own children will give one the necessary experience to fully appreciate one's parents' love and care, and therefore is instrumental in helping to make a person filial toward the parents.[45]

The first filial requirement of supporting one's parents includes financial and moral support. In the old days, senile parents passed their entire assets to their grown children and hence put their livelihood in their children's hands. Financial support from their children was necessary for their survival. Today in China as in the West, many aged parents keep their own assets. What they need from their children is mostly moral support. The need for grown children's financial support exists only for those parents who do not have enough means on which to live.

The second filial behavior requires one to honor, revere, and obey one's parents. Most people in the West probably agree that children have a moral obligation to honor their parents,[46] even though such writers as Jane English may question such a moral obligation. It may be more controversial as to whether grown children have a moral obligation to revere and obey their parents. Some people are under the impression that Confucianism demands the son's absolute obedience to the parents. This notion of Confucian obedience may have been exaggerated.

Tu Wei-ming, for example, has argued that Confucianism does

not demand the son's absolute obedience.[47] There is the widespread proverb, attributed to Confucianism, "There are no erroneous parents under Heaven." Tu Wei-ming interprets "erroneous parents" as "wrong parents in the sense that they do not fit our ideals of parenthood"; it therefore does not mean that parents never make mistakes.[48] Whether Tu's interpretation is correct may be open to question. Even if the proverb means what it literally means, it can only be taken as one of the various views in a wide range, not *the* view of Confucian filial morality. Furthermore, this view cannot be the "orthodox" view, for Confucius himself talked about the case when parents are in the wrong.[49] According to *The Classic of Filial Morality*, Confucius explicitly said that

> when [the father] is not right, the son can*not not* contend with (诤 *zheng*) the father.... Hence, if the son follows the father without contending with him when the father is not right, how can this be filial? (XV)

Mencius also defended Zhang Zi 章子, who offended his own father by asking his father to do the right thing.[50] Xun Zi 荀子 even went as far as to say that following the father is merely a small virtue, compared with the great virtue of following righteousness, which sometimes may require one not to follow one's father; he gave specific reasons for occasions when the son must not follow the wish of the parents.[51]

According to Fung Yu-lan, on the spiritual side filial morality consists in:

> conforming ourselves to [our parents'] wishes, and giving them not only physical care and nourishment, but also nourishing their wills; while should they fall into error, it consists in reproving them and leading them back to what is right. After the death of our parents, furthermore, one aspect of it consists in offering sacrifices to them and thinking about them, so as to keep their memory fresh in our minds.[52]

In this chapter I follow this mainstream view on filial morality, and focus particularly on filiality as supporting and honoring one's parents.

It should be noted that the Confucians would agree with Raymond Belliotti in thinking that parental care and nurture are reasons for filial obligation of the child, and would agree with Jan Narveson and Christina Sommers in thinking that the child should not abandon his parents after they have devoted ("invested") so much in nurturing him. As a matter of fact, the concept of reciprocity is of extreme importance in Confucian culture, and in Chinese culture in general.[53] For the Confucians, however, there is a lot more to it.

What kind of reasons do the Confucians have for justification of filial morality? Although filial morality is a cardinal virtue in Confucianism and there are numerous discussions of it by classical Confucian writers, one can hardly find a well-formed systematic justification by them. This is so perhaps because in the old days there was an overwhelming feeling for filial morality and it did not need philosophically argumentative justifications. The Chinese did not distinguish reason from feeling. For them the *xin* 心, which guides one's behavior, is both the heart and the mind; namely, the heart/mind. Mencius, for example, directly appealed to human feelings for justification of moral virtues. When there was already a strong feeling for a moral belief, philosophical justification was hardly needed in order to convince people of it. For our purpose, however, appealing to feelings is not enough. We need to explore philosophical justifications.

Regarding justification, I agree with John Rawls when he states:

> What justifies a conception of justice is not its being true to an order antecedent to and given to us, but its congruence with our deeper understanding of ourselves and our aspirations, and our realization that, given our history and the traditions embedded in our public life, it is the most reasonable doctrine.[54]

The issue of filial morality may be seen as part of the larger issue of justice. To see how the Confucians justify the doctrine of filial morality, we need to see how this doctrine is congruent with their deeper understanding of themselves, and we need to understand this doctrine as one deeply embedded in their tradition. Specifically, we need to look into the central concept in Confucianism, the concept of *jen*, and its place in Confucian ethics. Now I will look at filial morality in relation to *jen*, then examine this concept in two important aspects of Confucianism, self-realization and duty ethics.[55]

First, let us look at filial morality as a requirement for *jen*. As discussed in chapter 4, the central concept of *jen* in Confucian philosophy requires a person to love people, but to love them with gradations. Confucius and Mencius believed that a person practicing *jen* should start with his or her parents and siblings and then extend it to other people. Confucius said that "filial morality and brotherly respect are the root of *jen*."[56]

This view is deeply rooted in the Confucian understanding of the self, of personal identity. The Confucian self is embedded in a nexus of human relationships. The self is seen as the focus of many concentric circles, starting from the family as the closest to the center, and extending to the community, to the country, and then to the whole world.[57] Thus, a person's identity has many layers. For example, when one watches a competition played by one's home team with another team, one naturally sides with the home team. This is a way of identifying oneself and developing an awareness of one's identity. What the home team is, however, depends on circumstances. It may be a game played by one's high school against another high school from the same city, or by one's city team against another city, or by one's state team against another state, or, at the Olympics, by one's national team against another nation. Here there is an order of expanding one's self to broader and broader domains. Our identification of ourselves at different levels is more evident during wartime. In a civil war one tends to identify oneself as either a Northerner or Southerner (in the U.S. Civil War), or either a Nationalist or Communist (in the Chinese civil war); in an international war, people's awareness of their national identity becomes paramount (e.g., in the Sino-Japanese war during World War II).

Most times, however, one lives close to home. For the Chinese, the element of the family is constant in their awareness of their identity. The family is the foundation and the starting point of the expanding awareness of one's identity. Ethically speaking, self-identity is not merely a matter of mental awareness. It is a moral awareness that requires moral actions. The moral awareness of one's identity at each level requires one's moral contribution as a member of the human community to one's fellow human beings at each level. In this way, expanding one's moral community is the process of self-cultivation and self-realization.

Why must a person of *jen* start with loving one's parents? The Confucians observe the following line of reasoning. From childhood

a person must begin one's moral education. The first social environment a person finds oneself in is the family. The first people one is
acquainted with are, naturally, one's parents. Therefore, in order for
one to become *jen*, she must first learn to be *jen* with her parents;
and the *jen* in that aspect is filial morality.

Confucius compared the way to the virtuous person to what takes
place in traveling. We must first traverse the space that is near in
order to go to a distance.[58] *The Book of Rites* states,

As the people are taught filial morality and brotherly love at
home, with reverence toward the elder and diligent care for the
aged in the community, they constitute the way of a great king;
and it is along this line that states as well as families will
become peaceful. (10:45)

The great king is a moral role model for the people. The way of the
great king is also the way of a moral person. In order to be a moral
person, one must fulfill his or her filial duty.

Confucius put the way of the good person in the following order:
filial when at home, respectful to their elders when away from home,
becoming earnest and faithful, loving all extensively, and being
close to people of *jen*.[59] Similarly, Mencius believed that if one loves
her parents she will by extension be *jen* to people in general; and if
she is *jen* to people in general, she will be caring to everything in the
world.[60] If one does not learn to be *jen* at home, namely to be filial to
her parents while she is young, she would be asocial later in life and
it would be difficult for her to be *jen* to others after she grows up.
Therefore, *The Classic of Filial Morality* states that filial morality
forms the root of all virtues, and with it, all enlightening studies
come into existence (I). Filial morality is the fountainhead of *jen* and
the morality of *jen* first of all demands filial morality.

Second, filial morality is also a requirement for self-realization.
As indicated in chapter 4, the Confucian self has a temporal as well
as spatial existence. In addition to the synchronical dimension,
there is also the diachronical dimension, in which the self is a
process of realization and transformation. One important way to
understand the Confucian notion of filial morality is through understanding this diachronical dimension of the Confucian self.

In Confucianism, the self is not a ready-made soul or entity. It is
a process of realizing one's Heaven-endowed potential. All of us were

born with the potential to be fully human, but it takes lifelong efforts to realize this potential. For the Confucian, the realization of this potential is one's Heaven-imposed duty and the ultimate goal. In this view, the life process is not merely a biological growing-up and becoming older; it is most importantly a process of moral improvement and development. It is a process of unfolding our Heaven-endowed nature. Our ultimate destiny is to become *jen* or acquire full humanity. We can only reach this destiny through self-cultivation and self-transformation. We cultivate ourselves through reinforcing and expanding our human-relatedness.[61] Our human-relatedness starts with our relationship with our parents. Therefore, becoming a filial son or daughter is a necessary step for a person to move toward humanity.

In this sense, one endeavors to develop both physically and morally for the sake of one's own self (为己 *wei ji*). In urging their children to study, Chinese parents often remind the children of this notion by asking: "Are you learning (primarily) for others?" The answer is of course "no." One learns and grows for the sake of oneself. This also extends to filial morality.

Mencius maintained that human nature is good.[62] He believed that it belongs to our original heart to love our parents and that developing this original heart will directly lead to filial morality. Whether human nature is good, bad, or neutral is subject to dispute today as well as in Mencius's time. Confucians in general hold a person-making, not rule-following, ethics. In order to become a good person, one must develop a good character. It is hard to imagine someone who treats his or her parents badly to be a good person (with a good character). If self-realization is the way to develop into a good person as the Confucians believe, then filial morality is a requirement for our self-realization. Since filial morality is a step in our self-realization, being filial is not only for the sake of our parents; it is also for our own sake.

Speaking of our relationship with our fathers, Tu Wei-ming writes:

For their own sake as well as ours, we must appeal to our Heaven-endowed nature, our conscience, for guidance. After all, it is for the ultimate purpose of self-realization that we honor our fathers as the source of the meaningful life that we have been pursuing.[63]

According to Tu, we can never realize ourselves as isolated individuals. We must recognize our personal locus as a starting point of self-realization with reference to our parents among other relationships. Therefore, we must honor and respect our parents, not because they dominate us or because we dare not disobey them; in a strong sense, we honor and respect them for our own sake, namely for our self-cultivation, self-realization, and self-fulfillment.

Lin Yutang 林语堂 writes: "The greatest regret a Chinese gentleman could have was the eternally lost opportunity of serving his old parents with medicine and soup on their deathbed, or not to be present when they died."[64] In a person's life there are many things that one must be able to do in order to live a fulfilled life. Serving one's aged parents is one of them. Without such an experience there is an irremediable lacking in one's life, which is a cause for lifelong regretting. This is so because, for the Confucians, filial morality is a main way to become *jen* and a requirement for self-realization. The loss of the opportunity of being the filial son or daughter is at the same time a loss of opportunity for living a wholesome life, a loss of opportunity for making progress in achieving the goal of *jen* and in developing into a fully cultivated human.

Therefore, for the Confucians filial morality is an essential link in our self-realization and self-transformation to be fully human. From this perspective, one's filial duty is by no means supererogatory. It is even not merely a duty for the benefit of other people (i.e., one's parents). It is in a deeper sense a duty one owes to oneself for the sake of oneself, because it is instrumental to one's self-development in becoming fully human, which is one's ultimate destiny and therefore one's highest self-interest, including one's own morality.

Finally, filial morality is also a requirement for Confucian duty ethics. Those who believe in the existence of filial obligations usually draw on the fact that parents do sacrifice significantly in raising children. The Confucians share this view. Can they then counter Blustein's argument that parental non-supererogatory sacrifices are merely discharging their duties? The answer lies in another dimension of the Confucian understanding of the self.

In the eyes of the Confucians, in society each of us occupies certain social roles, and our being is realized in these roles, as a son or daughter, a brother or sister, a father or mother, and so on. The relationships in which one finds oneself constitute the field in which the self is located as the focus. In this view, these roles are not something into which we as atomistic individuals accidently fell. They define who we are and what we are, what duty we have, and consequently what behavior we ought to carry out. In such a duty ethics the primary concern is one's duties and responsibilities, not individual rights as in the case of rights ethics.

The Confucian ideal is to build the society after the model of the family. In the family, members see each other as part of their own selves and they nurture and care for each other without negotiating reciprocity as a precondition. To view society as an extended family is to view it as, in Tu Wei-ming's words, "not an adversary system consisting of pressure groups but a fiduciary community based on mutual trust."[65] In such a human community the primary relationship between its members is that of benefactors and beneficiaries. This relationship is not on a contractual basis. According to this view, as descendants from the same ancestors living together on earth, all of us are, some of the time and in some way, benefactors and beneficiaries.[66]

In Confucian duty ethics the morality of *jen* demands that, within such a fiduciary community, those who have resources, spiritual as well as material, ought to be the benefactors, and those who are in need are entitled to be beneficiaries. One may receive benefits if one is entitled to them. From this fact, however, it does not follow that we will not be obligated to benefit our former benefactors when they later are in need and we in turn have the resources to be beneficial. The Chinese phrase "striving to get rich while failing to be *jen*" (为富不仁 *wei fu bu ren*) condemns those with resources who fail to be benefactors to those in need.[67] In a sense, possessing resources implies social responsibilities. In this century, some people have seen this simply as the "Chinese jealousy," which is an obstacle to modernization. This view may be simple-minded because it overlooks the deep moral principle beneath it.

In the Chinese culture people in need are usually unwilling to ask for favors; it is up to those who are capable of offering favors to come forward to do so, if they have a good sense of *jen*. In other words, it is the moral requirement of *jen* that compels the capable to offer benefits or favors to those in need. The person being offered a favor would show reluctance to accept it and decline out of modesty; unless he is sure that the offering party is sincerely willing to do so, he would not accept the offer. For the Chinese, a request has little to do with the generation of favors. If Jane English were right in believing that a request is a necessary condition for a favor, she would have to rule a great proportion of favors in the Chinese culture as nonfavors.

An often-cited Chinese proverb says that, "an earlier generation plants trees under whose shade later generations rest 前人栽树, 后人乘凉." This short sentence has rather profound significance. Traditionally, Chinese farmers would rest under a shade tree while they worked in the fields under the burning midsummer sun. When people doing things beneficial for future generations cite this proverb they mean that, if nobody had planted the trees, future generations would not be able to rest in the shade; therefore in order for their descendants to enjoy some benefits, they need to do things such as planting trees, even though they themselves cannot benefit from them. When the future generations receive the benefits "planted" by their forefathers, they will cite the proverb, meaning that they appreciate their forefathers' efforts in "planting" the seed for later beneficiaries. There is also this proverb, "While you drink the water you must not forget those who dug the well for you 喝水不忘掘井人." In such a culture, the relationship of benefactors and beneficiaries is not expressed in terms of rights, but in terms of duties and benefits we owe each other.

Based on this duty ethics, there is a mutual duty between parents and children. When the children are little, the parents have a duty to take care of the children; in turn, when the children have grown up and the parents are in need, the children have a duty to take care of the parents. In this duty ethics, from the premise that when a person is little her parents have a duty to benefit her, it does not follow that when her parents grow old and are in need she would not have a duty to be beneficial to them.

Confucius's teaching of "*shu* 恕," that is, extending one's own mind to others, enforces the duty ethic in filial morality. Confucius himself specifically applied the concept of *shu* to filial morality by including in the gentleman's code "To serve my father as I would expect my son to serve me."[68] Would every one of us wish that our children would accompany us when we are senile and lonely? Would every one of us wish that our children would serve us at our bedside when we are infirm and sick? If so, Confucius would say, then we ourselves must start serving our own parents.

A Confucian Response

What can be learned from the Confucian account of filial morality? Confucianism states that we humans are not atomistic, self-serving, rights-laden individuals coming to construct a society out of self-interest. We are defined by the social roles that we occupy and these social roles define our humanity. Humanity or *jen* morality demands filial morality. In such a human society, each of us is benefited some of the time and in some way, and we should feel grateful and show our gratitude for the benefits that we receive. This includes our relationship with our parents. It is here assumed that a normal person appreciates the fact that he has a life, and that a normal person appreciates the fact that his parents have endured hardships and sacrifices to bring him up. It is also assumed that between being born and not being born, a normal person would strongly prefer the former, and between being well cared for and not being well cared for when he was little, a normal person would strongly prefer the former. Then the person "owes" his parents a great favor for giving him life and bringing him up, even though he did not request either. Such a person is under moral obligation to reciprocate the favor he has received. When his parents are senile and need assistance, he is obliged to help. Although how much help he can offer depends on circumstances (just as how much benefit his parents could offer depended on circumstances), his moral obligation to help his aged parents is greater than his general duty to help other people in need. This, then, is a Confucian response to such writers as Jane English.

Gratitude, however, is not the sole ground for filial morality. The morality of *jen* demands people with resources within the fiduciary community to benefit others with graded love. When a person is little, his parents have the duty to benefit him. From that it does not follow that when his parents become senile and are in need he would not have a duty to be beneficial to them. Therefore, even though Jeffrey Blustein is right that parents do have a duty to care for their children, it does not follow that this would not result in children's obligations in the stronger sense, when grown up, to care for their aged and probably infirm parents. This, then, is a Confucian response to writers with Blustein's view.

Religion

Multiple Participation versus Exclusionism

I n my discussion of Confucian filial morality in chapter 5, I have briefly touched the religious dimension of Confucianism. Religion, defined in a broad sense, is important in all societies and occupies a crucial place in all cultures. Studying a cultural philosophy such as Confucianism without enquiring into the religious dimension would be inadequate. In this chapter I will focus on the religious dimension of Confucianism and its relationship with two other Chinese ethicoreligious systems, Taoism and Buddhism. I will show a fundamental difference between the Chinese and the Western practice of religion. I hope such a study will pave our way to chapter 7 on the relationship between Confucianism and democracy.

For many people in the West, a person's religious affiliation is a matter of total commitment; choosing one religion implies one's being excluded from other religions. A religious person is either affiliated with religion A or religion non-A, not both. One is either a Christian or a non-Christian, for example, a Judaist. Within the Christian tradition, one is either Catholic or Protestant. If a person of one affiliation wants to be affiliated with another, he or she must be converted to the latter, leaving the former behind. Although there are ecumenical conferences and organizations, few people are ecumenical or interfaithful across different religions. People in the West may think this characteristic is one of being religious itself.

Can a person integrate two or more distinct religions into one's life? Our exploration into multicultural coexistence must answer this question. The issue is not whether one can integrate or combine elements of various religions together to make up a new religion, which is certainly possible and has been done.[1] It is rather a matter of subscribing to different religions by the same individual without being converted from one religion to another. The renowned theologian Hans Küng called this question that of "dual citizenship in faith,"[2] or more appropriately, as I will discuss in this chapter, it is rather "multicitizenship in faith."

In recent years, along with the multiculturalism movement there has been debate among Western theologians about religious pluralism and religious diversity. For example, in support of his position of religious pluralism, John Hick, one of the most prominent contemporary Western theologians, recently quoted from the *Tao Te Ching* and embraced the idea that "the Tao that can be expressed is not the eternal Tao."[3] For him, this means that the Ultimate Reality or Truth can never be adequately expressed and grasped by humans. Hick proposes that a distinction be made between, on the one hand, the transcendent Ultimate and, on the other, a plurality of masks or faces or manifestations of this Ultimate "as Jahweh, as God the Father, as the Qur'anic Allah, as Brahman, as the dharmakaya, and so on."[4] The transcendent Ultimate cannot be directly expressed or grasped in any particular religion. For Hick this distinction is analogous to the one "between the [Kantian] noumenal Transcendent or Real or Ultimate, and its plurality of phenomenal manifestations within human consciousness."[5] Accordingly, every one of the (major) religious traditions can be true, yet none has the ultimate truth. While this understanding appears to open a door for multiple religious participation, Hick indicates a distaste:

We have to ask concerning these primary affirmations whether they conflict with each other. They conflict in the sense that they are different and one can only centre one's religious life wholeheartedly and unambiguously upon one of them . . . but not more than one at once.[6]

While wholehearted devotion to a single religion has been considered a virtue in the West, it is not clear why Hick would hold such a position, given his belief that no single religion has the whole truth. Hick's distaste for multiple religious participation is, of course, not untypical among Western theologians. Hans Küng maintains that one can hold multicitizenship culturally and ethically, but not religiously. He claims that "even with every cultural and ethical possibility for integration, the truth of every religion extends to a depth that ultimately challenges every person to a yes or no, to an either-or." Therefore, "a religious dual citizenship in the deepest, strictest sense of faith should be excluded—by all the great religions."[7]

One may be able to find support for this kind of exclusionism from the scriptures. In the Bible, for instance, the first of the Ten Commandments is "You must have no other god besides me":

> God spoke all these words: I am the Lord your God who brought you out of Egypt, out of the land of slavery. You must have no other god besides me. You must not make a carved image for yourself, nor the likeness of anything in the heavens above, or on the earth below, or in the waters under the earth. You must not bow down to them in worship; for I, the Lord your God, am a jealous God, punishing the children for the sins of the parents to the third and fourth generation of those who reject me.[8] (Exodus 20)

This passage clearly demands a total devotion to one single god from the worshippers. If a worshipper of this god is to follow these words, he or she cannot but reject all other gods. Of course, for such a person, this god is not just *a* god; it is *the* god, or simply, God.

Therefore, it is no surprise that the idea of multiple religious participation has been rejected almost entirely in Western religious communities. As John H. Berthrong observed, "For most Christians, that people can belong to more than one community of faith seems at best confusing and at worst, damning."[9]

However, exclusionism certainly is not characteristic of religion per se. A recent article on Buddhism in *USA Today* specifically points out that "Buddhists can be involved in other religions."[10] As a matter of fact, as I will show, "multicitizenship" in religion for the Chinese is nothing new but a part of everyday life.

My purpose here is to enhance mutual understanding between the West and the East on this matter by showing how the Chinese practice of religion is different from that of most Westerners. For this purpose, my task is not merely to point out a fact or to present a historical example in this matter, rather it is to help Westerners make at least some sense of the Chinese practice of multiple religious participation. I will show that in the Chinese culture there is a fairly harmonious interplay between the three major religions— Confucianism, Taoism, and Buddhism. This interplay is not only in society as a whole, but in individuals as well.

The question I attempt to answer here, then, is, how multicitizenship across these religions is possible: How can a person be a Taoist-Confucian? How can a person be a Buddhist-Confucian? How can a person be a Taoist-Buddhist? or even, How can a person be a Taoist-Buddhist-Confucian? Here I do not differentiate between being a Taoist-Confucian and being a Confucian-Taoist, and so forth, even though there might be some differences. My concern is rather how the two or three can come together in one person. For the sake of simplicity, I will discuss these questions under one title: "How can a person be a Taoist-Buddhist-Confucian?"

The Religiousness of Chinese Religions

Even though without a god in the strict sense, the religiousness of Buddhism has seldom been questioned, and therefore I see no need to argue for its religiousness. The term "Taoism" has two different but closely related denotations. It refers both to an organized religion and a religio-philosophic tradition that can be traced back to the *Tao Te Ching*. Whereas the latter is characterized by the ideal way of life as *wu-wei* (无为 noncontention, nonstriving), the former puts paramount value on longevity and immortality through *wu-wei* and other means.[11] The two are closely connected, though. Taoism as a religio-philosophy is the theologic source of religious Taoism. Lao Zi, the author of *Tao Te Ching*, is also believed to be the founder of religious Taoism. *Tao Te Ching* has a religious dimension not only because it is used by religious Taoism as its scripture; the book is itself religious. Ann-Marie Hsiung finds in the *Tao Te Ching*

> that the person who attains comprehension of Tao embodies the features of religious experiences. Such experiences can be

a mystic feeling of the finite individual facing the uncomprehensible cosmos that embraces chaos and this involves the participation of one with the anarchic ongoing whole. Personal experience [of] this wholeness relates to a process of self-actualization through physical and spiritual cultivation to reach harmony, which is a state of oneness that presents no separation or division.[12]

Philosophical Taoism is also value-laden. It prescribes a way of life in harmony with the cosmos, in which a person becomes one with infinity. For the sake of simplicity, in this chapter I treat Taoism—the organized religion and the religio-philosophic tradition—as a single value system.

There has been much discussion of and debate on the religiousness of Confucianism. Confucianism in many ways appears too secular to be a religion. It does not have a god, nor an organized way of worshipping in the way in which many other religions do. Nevertheless, today a majority of scholars have accepted Confucianism as a religion. Then, what is its religiousness?

Tu Wei-ming writes: "We can define the Confucian way of being religious as *ultimate self-transformation as communal act and as a faithful dialogical response to the transcendent.*"[13] According to Tu, being religious, for the Confucian, means being engaged in the process of learning to be fully human. Tu's definition is in accord with John Hick's belief that the function of religion is to provide contexts for salvation/liberation, which consists in various forms of the transformation of human existence from self-centeredness to Reality-centeredness.[14] Religion bears a fundamental concern for the ultimate in life. It is this ultimate, which is transcendent, that defines value in life and provides directions for one's striving in life, which in turn makes life meaningful.

Specifically, I think the religiousness of Confucianism can be seen in two ways. First, Confucianism, like any other religion in the world, establishes the ultimate through a leap of faith. Confucianism as an ethical system provides guidelines for a moral life. The foundation of Confucian ethics is the belief in the Tao (Way) and Heaven. *The Doctrine of the Mean* begins by stating:

What Heaven imparts to humankind is called human nature. To follow our nature is called the Tao. Cultivating the Tao is called education. (I)

Human nature, or the destiny of human life, is given here without a demonstration of any form. The Confucian would argue that human nature requires that one be moral, or that one endeavor to transform oneself in accordance with the Tao. The moral path is the only way to be true to one's self (see chapter 2). Why not something other than the Tao? The Confucian does not offer a further argument or demonstration.[15] The Tao is both an "is" (i.e., a given from Heaven in unfixed form) and an "ought" (i.e., a moral prescription or decree by Heaven). No rational argumentation is offered in this regard, and this is not surprising. As Kierkegaard has persuasively argued, in religion (he meant specifically Christianity), such a rational "proof" is impossible. There one can always ask the unanswerable question "But why God (or why Tao)?" The only thing to which we can appeal here is "a leap of faith." Confucianism is no exception in this regard. The Tao is taken as a given in the first place and the rest is ordered accordingly. This leap of faith puts Confucianism into the same category with many other world religions.

Second, a primary function of religion is to give meaning to people's lives and Confucianism provides an answer to the question of the meaning of life. It points to a relationship between the ultimate and the individual. Unlike believers in many religions, Confucians do not believe that the meaning of life lies in another world. Confucius himself refused to speculate about an afterlife and gods. His concern was exclusively with this life. Confucians in general are very this-worldly and believe that a this-worldly life alone can be meaningful. The meaning of life, according to the Confucian, lies in one's self-transformation through building human relationships with one's fellow human beings. Among these relations, one can be a good son or daughter, a good brother or sister, a good father or mother, a good friend, a good partner, and so on. Confucius once defined his central idea *jen* or humanity as "*ai*" or as caring about people.[16] The value of human life lies in the creation of a community in which one cares about, and is cared about by, other people. Being cared about by fellow human beings is a source, if not the only source, of the meaning of life. Life cannot be meaningful without this kind of care. Since this kind of care is most likely found in the family, the Confucian takes the family life to be the most basic and meaningful way of life. Through one's self-transformation into being fully human, one earns love in the family and in the enlarged family—the community.[17] When one dies, one will be remembered with love by others. In the family as in the community, one takes over the heritage that the ancestors have passed down, carries it on, and then passes it down to later generations. By doing this one joins one's own life, which is finite and temporary, into the stream of the (hopefully) infinite and eternal.

That which gives a person's life meaning may not be necessarily religious. The Confucian meaningful life has an important dimension that extends into religiousness. Common people by nature have an unconscious wish for immortality and in immortality we find life meaningful. In some religions this wish is expressed in the form of an eternal afterlife. One may say that in Confucianism the wish for immortality is expressed in the family and communal life. In this sense, one can understand the Confucian religiousness by following Herbert Fingarette in characterizing it as "the secular as sacred."[18] That is, taking one's daily secular experience such as family life and social dealings as religious experience. One can equally understand it by putting it the other way around: "the sacred as the secular." For if the meaning of life is a sacred matter, the Confucians find it only in the secular everyday life, not in a church or an eternal afterlife. Because the Confucians can find the sacred in the secular, they can, following their master, afford to not talk about afterlife and immortality. Like Blaise Pascal, the Confucians may wager on this issue, but in the opposite way: If there is no afterlife, this life is the only life we have. If there is afterlife, this life would be an extra bonus if we take it seriously. So, either way we must take this life very seriously.

Some people may still question the religiousness or spirituality of the Confucian life. Being religious, they may think, consists of holding some belief in a certain deity or deities, the belief that such a deity must indeed exist somewhere in the world, or for that matter, beyond the world. This understanding of religion, I contend, is too narrow. Religion has primarily to do with fundamental principles of life or ways of life. These principles may not be ultimately justified anywhere other than a transcendent belief system. In other words, even though one can justify some general principles in life, the ultimate principle itself is not justifiable by other principles. It has to land in a transcendent realm. In this way, religion is a belief system that connects us to the transcendent realm, though the transcendent does not have to be a deity. Understood this way, Confucianism, as well as Taoism and Buddhism, is indeed religious.[19]

The Difference between Three Religions

Needless to say, the idea of multiple religious participation presupposes the existence of different religions. That Taoism, Buddhism, and Confucianism are three different religions and hence different value systems can be seen in their different attitudes toward life.

The Confucian model of personhood is the "*jun zi*" (君子 *chün tzu*, "gentleman" or "gentle woman"). A *jun zi* is a person of *jen*, who is conscientious and considerate. Such a person is devoted to her person-making commitment and holds a persevering determination toward her goal. She takes every step in her life seriously and works very hard to make steady progress in order to make her wish come true. Such a person is seldom relaxed; she is cautious and watchful over herself even when she is alone.[20] She is also considerate of other people. She does not do to others what she does not want others to do unto her,[21] and she thinks about and bears in mind what others would like when she is pursuing her own advancement.[22] She takes rituals seriously and insists on them. While she likes good people, she overtly expresses her disapproval of bad actions and bad people.[23] In this way, a Confucian will be able to make good progress in her endeavors and achieve success through hard work. She may get along well with other people because she is considerate. Devoted to her goal, she evaluates her life almost solely on the progress she has made toward her goal. She feels happiness in sharing her success with her family and friends. At an extreme, she might prefer death to a fruitless life.

In the eyes of the Taoist, the Confucian is too desire-driven. The religious Taoist would focus on longevity by practicing *neitan* 內丹 and *waitan* 外丹,[24] staying away from worldly affairs. *Neitan*, or inner elixir, is the refining of one's spiritual essence in order to liberate it. *Waitan*, or outer elixir, is the searching for a formula of immortality or longevity. The philosophical Taoist would feel that one should follow the flow of nature. He follows the notion of "noncontention." His attitude toward things in the world is one of "either-way" (兩行 *liang xing*, "following two courses").[25] His life philosophy is being "waterlike." Water, being soft and shapeless, can fit itself into and put up with almost any environment. More important, he can have things accomplished this way. In Zhuang Zi's Taoist narrative, Cook Ding can preserve his knife like new after cutting up thousands of oxen because he follows the natural way by only inserting his knife at the joints.[26] Cook Ding would laugh at the Confucian when she cuts up the ox by hacking harder. For the Taoist, tactics are more important than strength. To put it in a different way, real strength can only result from good tactics. Like Zhuang Zi, the Taoist would not take personal goals so seriously as the Confucian does. After all, we can never be so sure about the goals we choose. If the Taoist has a goal, it would be a realistic one, one that takes into consideration his particular circumstances. The ideal of "noncontention" always reminds him to take one step back in a situation, and by doing so he is able to find ample room to maneuver. He would never push hard, but in achieving his goal he would always view opposite forces as complementary and would adapt himself to his environment.

However, in focusing on this way, a less than mature Taoist may not establish himself on solid ground. The idea of noncontention may cause him to miss opportunities in life; believing tactics is all that matters, he may not work hard enough to acquire positive knowledge. He may waste his youth and end up accomplishing nothing. Hence, he may not find such a life as fulfilling as he would wish. Seeing all others as being misled, a Taoist from the religious group may concentrate on longevity. By doing so he may not be as productive in life as the Confucian.

The Buddhist would stick to his conviction that the world is empty (无 *wu*). In his eyes, even the Taoist is too this-worldly. After all, there is not anything in the world that is substantial enough for us to fight for. Because of the empty nature of the world, we have no reason to feel joy or sorrow for things in our daily life. All we should have is peace of mind. In the mind, the Buddhist finds everything he needs. He may have a good sense of humor, which typical Confucians usually lack. While the self-disciplined Confucian is working hard, and the Taoist is speculating on tactics or contemplating the usefulness of the useless,[27] the Buddhist would be achieving contentment by reducing his desires to the minimum. His slogan would be "Less desires, less striving, more contentment." In real life, however, a common person can hardly maintain a Buddhist mind all the time.

People often feel the need to be happy and they obtain happiness through fruitful hard work or intelligent and successful business dealings. Unless a person has a very broad (open) mind, he cannot find the good life in Buddhism.

The above three are idealized stereotypes, of course. In real life few people are exclusively Confucian, Taoist, or Buddhist in such a typical way. The point is that the three religions exemplify three clearly different attitudes toward life. Even Laurence Thompson, who opposes attempts to understand religion in China as several systems of doctrine, has to treat the three traditions in three separate chapters in his now classic *Chinese Religion* under subtitles of "Taoist tradition," "Literati Tradition," and "Buddhist Tradition." He also points out that the ultimate transformation in China led, in the Taoist Way, to immortal transcendency; in the Buddhist Way, to enlightenment; and in the Confucian Way, to sainthood.[28] We may use "Chinese religion" instead of "Chinese religions" to emphasize that these traditions are all a manifestation of Chinese culture. It is undeniable, however, that they have different goals and different ways of practice. They are different religions.

Tension and Complementarity

As different religions coexisting in the same land, the relationships between them are twofold: conflicting and complementing. Conflicts can be seen mainly between Confucianism and Taoism and between Confucianism and Buddhism, probably because Confucianism has usually been the dominant view among the three and most closely associated with the state. As early as the pre-Qin era (before 221 B.C.E.), conflicts between Confucianism and Taoism were already evident. As philosophies, Confucianism values "being" (有　*you*) whereas Taoism values "nothingness" or "nonbeing" (无　*wu*). This difference has resulted in a direct conflict in their political philosophies. While Confucianism advocated positive moral construction in society by stressing the concepts of *jen* and *yi* (righteousness), Taoism opposed this kind of moral construction. The *Tao Te Ching* states:

When Tao is abandoned, there is [talk about] *jen* and *yi*. When cleverness and intelligence [are valued], there is much hypocrisy. When family relations no longer harmonize, there is [talk about] filiality and paternal kindness. When the country falls into disorder, there is [talk about] loyalty and allegiance. (chap. 18)

The Taoist believed that the Confucian's advocacy for *jen* and *yi* indicated that these virtues were already lost in society, and the talk about these virtues merely made them hypocritical labels. Contrary to Confucianism, the Taoist's solution is to return to simplicity:

Abandon sagehood and abandon cunning, the people will benefit a hundredfold! Abolish *jen* and abandon *yi*, the people will return to filiality and paternal kindness. Abolish cleverness and abandon profit mentality, thieves and robbers will no longer exist.[29]

The direct conflict between Confucianism and Taoism in this regard is whether the solution for an allegedly demoralized society is to enforce moral rules or is to turn people back to simplicity through laissez-faire governance. The Confucian was for the former, whereas the Taoist was for the latter.

After Buddhism was introduced into China, there was a prolonged battle between Confucianism and Buddhism. The battle was primarily centered on three issues:

1. Whether monks living in a monastery away from home, hence away from their parents, violated the traditional (Confucian) belief in filial morality.

2. Whether monks should kowtow to the emperor. In the Confucian tradition the emperor symbolized the highest power on earth and kowtowing to him was the necessary ritual to recognize this symbolism. The monk as a religious symbol was supposed to stand for a religious power that is supposedly higher than the secular, including the emperor.

3. Whether the human spirit survives physical death of the body. Confucius himself declined to talk about spirit or soul after death. Confucian scholars such as Wang Chong (王充 Wang Chung, 27–100 C.E.) explicitly rejected the idea that the spirit could survive physical death, while

the Buddhist, particularly of the Pure Land school, relied substantially on the idea of human spirit surviving death.

These conflicts clearly indicate the difference between Buddhism and Confucianism. Religious differences mixed with political and economical factors have caused major conflicts and persecutions in the history of China. In 845, Emperor Wu 武宗 issued a decree for the destruction and confiscation of Buddhist monasteries.[30]

On the other hand, these three religions also complemented one another. In the pre-Qin era there was the so-called Confucianism-Taoism complementarity (儒道互补 *ru dao hu bu*), for while Confucianism provided an active and positive attitude toward life, Taoism provided a largely passive and even perhaps negative attitude. Because of this difference, a person could retreat from the former to the latter. One may follow the ideal of "In office a Confucian, in retirement a Taoist."[31] That is, as a participating citizen, one should contribute one's part to the country and be conscientious with one's social duties. Once retired, one should not keep worrying about official business; instead one should follow and enjoy nature.

The complementarity between Confucianism and Buddhism is evident: whereas Confucianism encourages a person's success in life, both economical and intellectual, Buddhism encourages a life that values neither but pursues internal peace. Also, whereas Confucianism offers little help or consolation for the human desire for an afterlife, Chinese Buddhism does. As Herrlee G. Creel observed, "traditional Chinese thought had been almost silent on life after death. Buddhism offered at least a hope."[32] In fact, the complementarity between Buddhism, Confucianism, and Taoism partly explains why Buddhism, a foreign religion to start with, has found roots in the largely foreign-resistant Chinese culture. It is this kind of complementarity between Confucianism, Buddhism, and Taoism that provides a foundation for their harmonious coexistence in China.

In practice, efforts were made to reconciliate different faiths, particularly by Buddhists during the Tang dynasty (618–907 C.E.) when Buddhism flourished. The efforts were to show the commonalities and common ground between the three religions. For example, the Buddhist Zong-mi (宗密 Tsung-mi, 780–841 C.E.) stated that:

Confucius, Lao Zi, and Śākyamuni all attained Sainthood. They preached the teaching in different ways in accordance with their time and place. However, they mutually helped and benefitted the people by their teachings.[33]

Qi Chong (契嵩 Chi-chung), another Buddhist, stated:

All of three teachings are good. All the ways taught by saints are right—the good and right teaching is not only Buddhism, not only Confucianism, not only this, not only that. Buddhism and Confucianism are only offshoots of the original truth.[34]

While these remarks about reconciliation sound similar to John Hick's idea of "one Ultimate with many manifestations," contrary to Hick, the Chinese view has led directly to multiple religious participation.

The coexistence of Confucianism, Taoism, and Buddhism is not merely an existence side by side in the same land, they also coexist in the same mind. That is, the same individual may subscribe to all three value systems at the same time. The Taoist Ge Hong (葛洪 Ko Hung, 283–363 C.E.), in his classic work *Bao-pu Zi* (抱朴子 *Pao-pu Tzu*), advocated the idea that while Confucianism is to be used for social affairs, the Taoist method of body maintenance should be used for personal internal needs. The emperor Xiao Zong 孝宗 of the Southern Song (1163–1189 C.E.), proposed that one should use "Buddhism for the mind, Taoism for the body, and Confucianism for organizing society."[35] As a symbol of this integration, today there are at least seven temples in Taiwan where incense is offered to Confucius, Lao Zi, and the Buddha.[36]

It should be noted that "multiple religious participation" must not be confused with syncretism. "Syncretism" may be defined as "a tendency or effort to reconcile and unite various systems of philosophy or religious opinions on the basis of tenets common to all and against a common opponent."[37] There certainly has been syncretism in China as in any other major tradition. Multiple religious participation, however, is different from syncretism. People of multiple religious participation practice more than one religion with a recognition that these are different religions. They do it without making an effort to integrate them into one single religion on the basis of some common tenets. John Berthrong is right when he writes:

[In China] a person can be a Taoist, Confucian and Buddhist more or less at the same time. But this is a question slightly different from syncretism per se. It is more properly the question of dual or multiple membership.[38]

Here Berthrong, of course, is using "membership" metaphorically, for none of the three religions in China is strictly a membership religion. Let us now turn to this Chinese multiple "membership" way of being religious.

Being Taoist-Buddhist-Confucian

Now, how can the same person be a Taoist-Buddhist-Confucian? The question here is not merely whether the same individual can pay tribute to a Taoist temple today and participate in a Buddhist ceremony tomorrow. It is rather how the same individual can subscribe to three different value systems in a persistent and sensible way.

We can understand this practice in two ways: (1) multiple religious participation based on a person's multiple dimensions of existence, and (2) dialectical coexistence within the same dimension of one's existence.

First, as discussed earlier, the three religions occupy different dimensions of a person's life and perform different functions. Since a person has more than one dimension in life, one can incorporate different religions. By Xiao Zong's model, a person can have the peace of mind of a Buddhist, take good care of his physical well-being like a Taoist, and be a good citizen as a Confucian. A person may go on pilgrimage to the mercy goddess Guanyin 观音 at a Buddhist monastery in order to have an heir, invite a Taoist master to help get evil spirits out of his home, and ask Confucius to bless his loved one or to help his daughter get into a top university.

The renowned Chinese historian Chen Yinke 陈寅恪 (1890–1969) observed that, "those who outwardly observe Confucian norms may inwardly follow the principles of Buddhism or cultivate themselves according to the way of Taoism; there is no conflict between them."[39] A contemporary exemplar of the "Buddhist-Confucian" was Liang Shu-ming 梁漱溟 (1893–1988). Liang was a major Confucian in this century, spending most of his life practicing and reviving Confucianism, but he himself also claimed that his whole life belonged to

Buddhism.[40] In Liang's final years he maintained that he was still a Buddhist while he also accepted the title "the Last Confucian."[41] Many people have been perplexed by this apparent discrepancy. How is this possible? Liang was after two different issues in his life. One was the ideal of life, a question of personal existence; the other was the problem of China's future, which demands a social solution to its modern predicaments. These two problems were intertwined in Liang and he was so troubled that he attempted suicide at the age of nineteen.[42] As an individual, he found meaning of life in Buddhism; as a citizen he found that the only solution to China's modern predicaments was Confucianism.[43]

The way of multiple religious participation in the multiple dimensions of one's existence is not all there is to multiple religious practice. Different religions operate in the same dimension of one's life and thus create tension between one another. I suggest that, in the second way, there is a dialectical tension/complementary relation between these religions that is far more important in understanding the complementarity of Taoism, Buddhism, and Confucianism.

A Confucian scholar has said that Buddhism is like floating on the water, drifting wherever the current takes you, and Confucianism is like having a rudder in the boat to guide it in a certain direction.[44] This simile was meant to show the advantage or superiority of Confucianism over Buddhism. But if we read it from a different perspective with an open mind, we can find new meanings. Is it always so bad drifting along with the current? Perhaps it is better to drift for a while before using the rudder again. Sometimes it may be better to follow both ways alternately. Reading the simile this way may help us understand how one can employ both Confucianism and Buddhism.

How can Taoism fit into this scenario? Taoism may be best understood in this picture as using the force of the current to determine and follow the desired direction. For the Taoist, it would be foolish to fight the current head-on. He would make the current work to his advantage; in this case, moving him towards his destiny.

Even though it is not a simple matter for a person to act like a Taoist, a Buddhist, and a Confucian simultaneously at every moment, the three can work in the same person. One example is the famous Chinese poet Tao Qian 陶潜 (陶渊明 Tao Yuanming, 365–427 C.E.). Tao Qian was a Confucian, but his Taoist conviction made it possible for him to quit the post of the magistrate of Pengze county for a simple life close to nature and to write the poetry that few of his contemporaries could really appreciate. As Donald Holzman points out, Tao Qian's great achievement describes a complex but original attitude toward life and toward the world in general; this attitude "enabled him to remain faithful to traditional values of loyalty and respect for the social order while realizing . . . a new kind of fulfillment of his ambitions in retirement."[45] The traditional values of loyalty and respect for social order were undoubtedly Confucian values, while the Taoist attitude in him made it possible for Tao Qian to fulfill life away from society. Zhang Longxi comments:

> Confucianism, Taoism, and Buddhism . . . are not incompatible with one another in Chinese culture, and it would be pointless to argue that Tao Qian's thinking is exclusively Confucian or Taoist. He never had to choose between those different schools of thought but was able to incorporate, as so many Chinese intellectuals have done throughout the centuries, the various elements into a healthy eclectic outlook. In that very eclecticism the Chinese mind is able to keep itself open to the different possibilities of thinking.[46]

Without entering Tao Qian's mind or having his personal account, it may be difficult for some people to see how Confucianism and Taoism were incorporated in him. I will offer another way, more familiar to Westerners. Suppose you are the coach of a basketball team. Your Confucian mind will take the job of coaching seriously. You want to win. You inspire your players to be confident of winning and give them a strong motivation or desire to win. You make your players practice hard. But that is not enough. You need to study not only the strength of your team, but, perhaps more important, the weaknesses of your opponents. By applying the Taoist idea of *wu-wei*, you may be able to turn their strength into a weakness and make it work to your advantage. You may also want to give individual players more room for their own growth, let them find their unique place in following the flow of the world. After the game is over, either win or lose, your Buddhist mind (and perhaps Taoist mind as well) will remind you that you should not make a big deal of it. If you lose, you should not feel too bad about it. If you win, it is not a big deal either. After all, it is only a game.

However, this is not to say that as long as a person uses alternately the three life attitudes she must be a Taoist-Buddhist-Confucian. It is not so simple. Whether a person practices a way of life religiously does not depend on individual actions. It depends on the larger picture in which a person lives her life. It depends on the significance a person attaches to her actions. Specifically, it depends on the connections she makes between her chosen attitudes and actions on the one hand and the fundamental values in life within the culture on the other. Just as one can eat bread and drink wine without being a Christian communicant, one can do things in ways similar to the Taoist without being a Taoist, similar to the Buddhist without being a Buddhist, and similar to the Confucian without being a Confucian. However, if one makes the fundamental connections and thereby consciously makes one's actions a religious practice, one is being religious. If one consciously chooses to follow the Taoist, the Buddhist, and the Confucian ways of life alternately or even simultaneously, one is a Taoist-Buddhist-Confucian.

I am not suggesting this is the only way for the three to come together. They can function in various ways in the everyday world. On the one hand, one needs to take things seriously and work hard, that is, to be conscientious. On the other, it is important not to go against the current. It is also important to relax and enjoy peace of mind. In my opinion, when a person is growing up, she should probably practice more Confucianism. It will give her the motivation and driving force to learn and develop her potential fully. After she is ready for and enters real life in society, she should practice more Taoism. Together with the skills and knowledge learned in her early years, Taoist strategies will enhance her career. After she becomes old, she should practice more Buddhism. In order to have a good later life, she should not be overburdened by the success or failure of her early years. With a mind of emptiness, she will be able to be at peace with herself.

A good combination of all three is most desirable. Of course, all three cannot interplay in a harmonious and beneficial way unless one masters some kind of practical wisdom (*phronēsis*), to borrow Aristotle's terminology, unless one knows when and how to choose between and among them. The issue of practical wisdom, however, is beyond the present scope of my discussion.

Some Philosophical Considerations

One may think that the Chinese can practice more than one religion because their religions are not comprehensive. Obviously, each of the three religions covers some aspects of life more than other aspects; therefore they need to complement one another. In comparison, one may think that a religion like Christianity is comprehensive; it includes all that a person needs for a fulfilling religious life. However, this observation has only limited truth and it does not do enough justice to the real issue.

While different religions share substantial common values, each has its own configuration in assigning value to various aspects of human life. To assign a value to an aspect of life is to emphasize and hence to give some kind of priority to that aspect of life. It is logically as well as practically impossible to give priority to all aspects. In this sense, no particular religion can claim absolute comprehensiveness and every religion has its limitations. The Confucian may find that Christianity fails to give adequate emphasis to reverence to one's ancestors and parents, while the Christian may think that he has already given enough and there is no need for more reverence, not that he is missing something important. On the other hand, the Christian may find Confucianism wanting in regard to the afterlife, while the Confucian would think that there is just no need and no legitimate ground for that. The typical Christian may find Christianity providing comprehensive guidance to a meaningful life; a Confucian Christian (one who embraces both) would appeal to Confucianism to make up what she feels is missing with respect to reverence to her ancestors and parents.

The real issue is not one of comprehensiveness, but one of value; different people have different values at the same time, and the same people may have different values at different times. That is the real reason for the Chinese multiple religious practice.

What, then, is the philosophical foundation for Chinese multiple religious participation? I think the foundation can be found in all three traditions. One psychological obstacle for multiple religious participation is a strong holding to a fixed self, which is lacking in all three religions. The Buddhist believes that the self is unreal and insubstantial. The Taoist advocates a "waterlike" attitude. Lao Zi said "the sage does not have a fixed mind."[47] The Buddhist and Taoist would see no problem mingling with other religions.

Among the three religions, Confucianism has appeared to be the least open to multiple religious participation. On the one hand, Confucianism enjoyed a predominant status because of its affiliation with the state during most of its history, and it did not want to give that up. On the other hand, some Confucian doctrines value unity rather than plurality.[48] Nevertheless, there have been elements within Confucianism in favor of flexibility and plurality. For example, Confucius said that "the gentleman is not an implement (器 *qi/chi*)."[49] An implement is something fixed, unchanging, and inflexible. The idea of not being an implement leaves room for flexibility to incorporate other things, including Taoism and Buddhism. Confucius even said that he held an attitude of *"wu ke wu buke"* (无可无不可 "It's okay if okay, and it's okay if not okay"), toward various ways of life.[50] For the Chinese people who like multiple religious participation, these ideas were good enough for them to justify their practice.

Human psychology is not a unitary process. It may need different things and take different courses under different circumstances and at different times. This characteristic of the Chinese mind is well illustrated in Archie J. Bahm's comparison of the Western, Indian, and Chinese attitudes toward activity and passivity. Bahm observes that while Europeans encourage activity, Hindus encourage passivity, Chinese accept the need for both activity and passivity, each in turn. He explicates:

> Why accept both activity and passivity, each in turn? Observe everyday experience. There is a time to arise and a time to go to bed, a time to work and a time to rest. The sun rises, and the sun sets. Initiation of activity is symbolized by *yang*. Completion of activity or rather achieving of passivity is symbolized by *yin*. Every being (*tao*) consists of both *yang* and *yin*. . . . Being and doing are equally important, equally natural, equally good.[51]

The Chinese have a tendency to strive for a balance by harmonizing different aspects of things. They tend to let each aspect have its turn and thus, instead of mixing them together, let them alternately work together. In the Chinese mind, since different religions have different strengths and weaknesses, they may play different roles in the same person's life.[52]

Conceptually and philosophically, both Confucianism and Taoism believe in the Way as the *Tai Ji* (太极 Great Ultimate), which literally means the highest or greatest utmost. The highest utmost cannot be exhausted by a single teaching. Therefore, the Taoists believe in following two or more courses at the same time. *Zhuang Zi* suggested that the Tao may be found in all philosophical schools.[53] The Confucian classic *The Doctrine of the Mean* states that several courses can be pursued without conflict.[54] Confucius believed that different paths may lead to the same destination.[55] When Buddhism was first introduced to China, it was put in the language familiar and congenial to Confucianism and Taoism.[56] Therefore, regardless of the apparent discrepancies between the three religious doctrines, scholars could incorporate all three into the Way with relatively little difficulty. After all, no one can claim to have exhausted the Way.

Now, one may want to ask: How can one believe in different things? What about truth? The point here seems to be that, if *A* is true, then non-*A* has to be false. If you believe in *A*, you cannot at the same time rationally believe in non-*A*. If you and I disagree, we cannot both be right. As has been discussed in chapter 2, here perhaps lies one of the greatest differences between the Chinese and the Western mind. The Chinese do not regard semantic truth as highly as Westerners. As Chad Hansen puts it, Chinese moral theories have "the requirement that our utterance be appropriate as opposed to being [semantically] true."[57] As a matter of fact, the requirement for appropriateness is not limited to language; it is a requirement for human behavior in general, including religious practice. Even in religion, the Chinese have never assigned an unconditional value to semantic truth as has been done in the West. Therefore, they did not need a Nietzsche to ask the question astonishing to most Westerners, "What is the good/value of [semantic] truth?"

The message from the Chinese is similar to the one R. C. Zaehner has read from Hinduism. It is worthwhile to quote in full what Zaehner writes at the end of his remarkable book *Hinduism*:

What, then, is the message of Hinduism? If it has a message at all, it would seem to be this: to live out your *dharma* which is embedded in the conscience, to do what instinctively you know to be right, and thereby to live in harmony with the *dharma* of all things, so that in the end you may see all things in yourself and yourself in all things and thereby enter into the eternal and timeless peace which is the *dharma* of *moksha*, the "law" of "freedom" that has its being outside space and time yet comprises and hallows both.[58]

If one can see all things (including people) in oneself and oneself in all things, then one has become one with the Dharma or Tao. All distinctions are distinctions within one's being, not without. This, then, is the truth of life.

Therefore, unlike Aristotle, a Chinese philosopher would not say, "Although I love my teacher, I love truth more than I love my teacher."[59] For the Chinese, the most important thing is to participate in creating a better world for everyone, not to find out some objective truth. So in responding to questions like "Who is smarter, Lao Zi or Confucius?" while the typical Western mind would tend to choose one or the other, the Chinese may answer "They are both very smart." Is that not enough? Does it really matter that much if we have an either-or answer? Not at all. This nonobsession with [semantic] truth partly explains why the Chinese have no problem accepting Taoism, Buddhism, and Confucianism together.

Another reason for embracing different religions is that "breadth 宽" has been a traditional Chinese virtue. Breadth is not merely tolerance. To be tolerant means to be able to put up with different things. Breadth requires more than tolerance. It means being tolerant with a genuine understanding. Therefore, with this attitude, even if one finds discrepancies between different religions one may simply put them aside and concentrate on what is important in these ways of life. In Chinese this is called "seeking common ground while reserving differences (求同存异 *qiu tong cun yi*)." It is an important aspect of Chinese wisdom.

Finally, one most important Chinese value is harmony (和 *he / ho*). The Chinese believe that harmony is a value in itself and is preferable to conflict. In the Chinese view of dialectic harmonization, the Tao or Way is a process of harmonizing differences of things. The

Tao is one and is the source of all polarities. It has two complementary elements or aspects, *yang* and *yin*. A harmonious interplay of *yang* and *yin* is most desirable. The world is full of polarities. But polarities are not necessarily contradictions. As Cheng Chung-ying puts it, when we find ourselves at one of the polarities and at the edge of a conflict, we can and should, through understanding and re-understanding of reality and ourselves, "project ourselves into a situation where conflict and antagonism will disappear through an overall process of adjustment of ourselves to the world."[60] For instance, Ming Tai Zu (明太祖 Tai-tsu), the first emperor (1368–1398?) of the Ming dynasty, attempted to harmonize the three religions by saying that while Confucianism is the Way of *yang* or manifest virtue, Taoism and Buddhism are *yin* or hidden virtue. For him, the *yang* virtue is the culmination of this-worldly doctrine and can be relied upon for countless generations, and the *yin* virtues are secret aids of the kingly Way; together the two comprise the Way of Heaven.[61] Chinese pragmatic minds do not tend to take principles, particularly theoretical principles, rigidly. Between the option of "harmonizing differences" and "fighting it out" they tend to choose harmonization. This is perhaps the ultimate reason for Chinese embracing multiple religious participation.

While the Buddhists' willingness to participate in the process of harmonizing differences has helped Buddhism become very successful in China, the unwillingness to harmonize has been detrimental to the development of Christianity in China. For example, in 1704, the papal authority issued a decree to ban Chinese Christians' participation in traditional Chinese rites. The pope stated in the decree that "One name and one only God for Chinese, T'ien-chu or the Heavenly Lord. . . . Ritual acts in honor of Confucius also had to stop." In 1706 the Chinese emperor Kang Xi 康熙 responded by expelling from the country all Christian missionaries who refused to abide by the rule that allowed Chinese Christians to observe the traditional rites.[62]

Then, what lessons can be drawn from all this? Today we live in an increasingly smaller world with people of different cultural backgrounds. In order for different cultures to coexist, we need first of all to tolerate different religious beliefs and practices. We also need to look beyond tolerance. We cannot live well with our neighbors of different religions unless we have a genuine understanding of them. We cannot have a genuine understanding of them unless we understand their religions. One way to understand religions different from our own is to try to practice different religions. A Chinese Christian with a strong Confucian background may understand both Confucianism and Christianity better than a mere Confucian or a mere Christian. She may be better equipped for promoting both cultures and living across the two cultures. Some people may think she is being incoherent. But what is wrong with such an "incoherence"? The Chinese example indicates that as long as we keep an attitude of breadth, we will be able to accommodate different religions.

John Hick and others have explored, in theory, the possibility of coexisting religions that are valid respectively on their own account. This theory can be used to support the idea of multiple religious participation. If no single religion has the ultimate truth and each only reflects a facet of the Ultimate as Hick maintains, then no religion is absolute or perfect. If religion expresses the human drive for perfection, then one ought to embrace different religions in order to make one's spiritual life as perfect and fulfilling as possible within human limitations. Of course there is a provision to it—there must be a productive way to put them all to work. The Chinese case provides a practical illustration of how some religions, even though seemingly contradictory, can be integrated into an individual's life.

Although my thesis here can be prescriptive, it is first of all descriptive. It describes the way in which countless Chinese have lived their lives. So, the question here is not whether multiple citizenship in faith (multiple religious participation) is possible, but whether it is desirable. I do not claim that multiple religious participation is the only way to a fulfilling religious life. But it is one way. And very likely a good way.

The jacket of this book shows a Chinese painting in which three old men are exploring the Way, a Confucian, a Taoist, and a Buddhist. For the Chinese, all three are great teachers. If a fourth person were to join them, would he be welcome? Now, let us turn to the relation between Confucianism and democracy in the final chapter of the book.

Justice

Confucian Values and Democratic Values

The relationship between democracy and Confucianism has been an important issue for people interested in Chinese culture. One noteworthy position on this issue has been presented by Samuel P. Huntington. He asserted that the world is now entering an age of "the clash of civilizations."[1] Specifically, the clash is between democratic Western civilization and undemocratic civilizations in the rest of the world, Confucian and Islamic civilizations in particular. Huntington suggests that, in order for democracy to take root in a Confucian society, undemocratic elements in Confucianism must be superseded by democratic elements. If this is the way to the future, what does this kind of democracy mean to a Confucian society like China? What does it imply for the Confucian tradition itself?

The tension between democracy and Confucianism had been felt long before Huntington's remark, of course. Ever since the idea and ideal of democracy came to China, responses to it have been made in a variety of directions. Some people say that Confucianism is already democratic and what is needed, instead of importing Western democracy, is to improve Confucian democracy. Some say Confucianism is essentially antidemocratic and has to give way to democracy. Others claim a Confucian society such as China needs a kind of democracy radically different from Western democracy and Western democracy will have to stay out of China. Still others assert that, while traditional Confucianism is not democratic, both are good and should be integrated, therefore China must democratize Confucianism or confucianize Western democracy.

The philosopher's task, of course, is not to predict what actually will happen in China. It is to analyze the issue conceptually and point out, among many other things, what *ought* to be. Philosophers, as philosophers, can meaningfully say what ought to happen only as a corollary of conceptual analysis. I hope my investigations in previous chapters have now established or demonstrated some of the patterns and peculiarities of the Chinese tradition, on the basis of which, particularly the harmony model, the issue of the relation between Confucianism and democracy can be resolved.

Before we move further into the issue, let us be aware of some of the ramifications and problems. On the one hand, because our concern is democracy in China and the Chinese tradition involves more than Confucianism, our consideration should not be limited to Confucianism alone. On the other hand, because Confucianism is the predominant value system in China, our discussion will focus more on Confucianism than other views. I will look into a number of interrelated issues: first, whether there has been a democratic tendency in traditional Chinese values; second, whether democracy as a social value can be incorporated into traditionally predominant Chinese value systems; and third, based on conceptual analysis, what the future should hold for democracy in China.

I will show, first, that democracy has not been a significant value in traditional Chinese culture; second, that democracy and Confucianism have essentially conflicting values and therefore cannot be integrated into a single value system without substantially compromising both; finally, contrary to Samuel Huntington, I will demonstrate that democracy ought to and is most likely to find a home in China as an independent value system among other traditional Chinese value systems, and will do so without significantly jeopardizing Confucianism.

Democracy and China's Need

Needless to say, the word "democracy" has been used in so many ways that people today often disagree about exactly what it means.

Many controversies about democracy focus on whether it is merely a procedural method for political decisions or whether it has value contents.[2] Joseph Schumpeter in his pathbreaking work *Capitalism, Socialism, and Democracy*, for example, proposes a minimal definition of democracy. According to Schumpeter,

> the democratic method is that institutional arrangement for arriving at political decisions in which individuals acquire the power to decide by means of a competitive struggle for the people's vote.[3]

Schumpeter's use of "democratic method" instead of "democracy" indicates that he views democracy primarily as a procedural form or an institutional arrangement.

Is democracy merely an institutional arrangement? Francis Fukuyama recently argued that the consolidation of democracy must occur on four levels:

1. Ideology, "the level of normative beliefs about the rightness or wrongness of democratic institutions and their supporting market structures."

2. Institutions, which include "constitutions, legal systems, party systems, market structures, and the like."

3. Civil society, "the realm of spontaneously created social structures separate from the state that underlie democratic political institutions."

4. Culture, including "phenomena such as family structure, religion, moral values, ethnic consciousness, 'civilness,' and particularistic historical traditions."[4]

He regards culture as the "deepest level" of democracy.

Many people would agree with Fukuyama that democracy penetrates culture and is therefore value-laden. Jürgen Domes, for instance, also defines democracy primarily as a value-laden political system. In addition to its formal dimension, Domes defines democracy specifically as characterized by three principles:

1. Liberty: guaranteed and institutionalized human rights for all inhabitants of a given country and guaranteed and institutionalized civil rights for all adult citizens of a given country;

2. Equality: having the goal of securing equal life chances for all citizens of a given country and making constant efforts to develop the political and social reality toward a state that is as close to that goal as possible;

3. Pluralism: the guaranteed existence and operation of competing organizations that articulate and aggregate the different political, economic, social, and cultural interests that exist in a given country, and the consideration of such different and divergent interests as legitimate.[5]

The concepts of liberty and equality, I maintain, are at the core of liberal democracy. "Liberty" here implies that the people have an inborn right to freely choose the way they are to be governed; a government is legitimate only if the people choose to be governed by it. Without liberty, people would not be able to choose. Therefore, without liberty there can be no democracy. Also, the bearer of the rights to liberty is the individual. Only through individuals can liberty be exercised. Therefore, liberty must be understood first of all as individual liberty.

Equality may be seen as a condition under which liberty is practiced. As Alexis de Tocqueville observed, "The principle of equality, which makes men independent of each other, . . . tends to make them look upon all authority with a jealous eye and speedily suggests to them the notion and the love of political freedom."[6] Democracy implies that people have an equal say in decisions that affect their lives. Unless they are equals, their say cannot carry equal weight. When it comes to elections or referenda, equality means that one person has one vote. No one has more or less a vote than anyone else. This is the idea that an individual has a sovereignty over himself or herself. The sovereignty of each is the same as anyone else's. If people are not equal, there will be no basis for democracy. The affinity between liberty and equality has not gone unnoticed. John Locke, for example, understood liberty to mean political equality. For him, equality means "equal right that every man hath to his natural freedom, without being subjected to the will or authority of any other man."[7]

Pluralism can be seen as a presupposition for democracy. For if individual liberty and equality are to be valued and promoted, there must be room for a variety of voices and preferences. Without such a diversified environment, democracy cannot be fully exercised. Pluralism does not only mean that diversity is to be tolerated, it also means that diversity ought to be valued.

Clearly Domes's definition is heavily value-laden, in sharp contrast to Schumpeter's. Their definitions of democracy represent the two ends of a spectrum. Whereas Schumpeter's is a minimal definition, Domes's is moving toward the other end. Without a context, it makes little sense to ask whose definition is right. For, after all, they may be talking about different things with the same word. The question we should ask here is, what kind of democracy does China need? I believe the answer is democracy with the values of individual liberty, equality, and pluralism.

Without these values, democracy as a mere procedure is an abstract form. The form of democracy has been and is still used or misused in China. Unless we make explicit the values found in democracy, the misuse is likely to continue. For example, within the Chinese Communist Party (CCP), democracy as a form of voting has been practiced. Missing, however, is the value of individual liberty. Within the CCP, members can vote, but the party leadership demands absolute loyalty. The value of loyalty takes the place of individual liberty in the current mainland Chinese version of democracy. Even when the voting procedure is carried through, the outcome has almost always been a unanimous decision. This is in sharp contrast to the practice in the U.S. Congress where representatives often do not vote with their party platform. Their vote may be based on their own judgment, not their party's.

In *Democracy in America* Alexis de Tocqueville wrote:

If a democratic republic, similar to that of the United States, were ever founded in a country where the power of a man had previously established a centralized administration and had sunk it deep into the habits and the laws of the people, I do not hesitate to assert that in such a republic a more insufferable despotism would prevail than in any of the absolute monarchies of Europe; or, indeed, than any that could be found on this side of Asia.[8]

When democracy is used merely as a voting procedure, it can be counterproductive in countries like China where people have formed the habit of following a centralized administration, either a dynasty or a party, which they may have mistakenly identified as representing their own interest and to which they habitually render unconditional loyalty. Unless individual liberty is valued, voters will not realize that they ought to feel free in choosing their representatives; and unless voters can freely choose to vote for their representatives, there cannot be true democracy. Here "free choice" does not merely mean choice without external coercion. It also means choosing candidates on the basis of individual liberty. Imagine a people in whom loyalty to their leader is such an overwhelming value that no matter what happens they will always cast their votes for their leader. Such a so-called democracy would be no better than a tyranny. This form of government is not worth fighting for, except perhaps as a mere preliminary step from totalitarianism to real democracy.

Also we are considering democracy in a country where Confucianism would continue to exist. The characteristics of Confucianism, as I shall argue below, call for a democracy embedded with the values of individual liberty, equality, and pluralism.

Furthermore, when we speak of the possibility of the clash of civilizations, we have to talk about values in different civilizations. When we discuss Confucianism throughout the past, present, and future, we do not mean by it a definite type of political system or social institution. Rather we have in mind a value system, even though it once assumed a social institutional form in Chinese history (e.g., in the Han dynasty). Institutional Confucianism, defined by Ambrose Y. C. King as a system "in which Confucianism was the ideological and institutional infrastructure,"[9] no longer exists in China and probably will not exist in the future. Therefore there is little chance for a clash between Confucianism and democracy as social institutions in the future. To be sure, democracy of any kind must have its social, institutional form and has to be practiced through a procedural form. Democracy carries with it also a body of values. In order to meaningfully compare and discuss Confucianism and democracy together, we must stay within the same dimension; we must look at their value contents.

Therefore, while acknowledging that democracy has institutional forms, in this chapter I focus on democracy on a cultural level and consider it mainly as a value system that advocates "government by the people." This value system is centered on the rights of individuals to liberty and equality. In this value system, pluralism is also an important element.[10]

While this formulation is not intended to be a final definition in an extensive exploration of democracy in general, it should be sufficient for our purpose here to highlight that the kind of democracy discussed here is value-laden, and to identify the values it contains. If we recognize that democracy is value-laden, then no matter how we think about democracy and Confucianism, we have to think about how values from both sides interact.

Whether There Has Been Democracy in Traditional Chinese Culture

If we begin with the above understanding of democracy, it should be clear that there have not been democratic values in mainstream Chinese culture. However, although many scholars in the field today do not seem to believe that Confucianism or other Chinese philosophies are democratic, some disagree. They claim that Confucianism has contained democratic values all along. For instance, elaborating on his version of "Confucian philosophy of democracy," Leonard Shihlien Hsü saw such values as "public opinion," "government by the consent of the governed," even "liberty" and "equality" in Confucianism.[11] Is Confucianism really democratic? In order to make my thesis relevant I must make this point clear before moving on any further.

Among influential Chinese philosophers Mencius is probably the closest to the idea of democracy and is most cited by those looking for democratic elements in traditional Chinese thought.[12] Mencius said,

[In a state] the people are the most important; the spirits of the land and grain [guardians of territory] are the next; the ruler is of slight importance.[13]

This thought is often called the thought of "民本 *min-ben*," or people-as-the-foundation. Some people think this is Chinese democracy. For example, Dr. Sun Yat-sen 孙逸仙 (1866–1925) said that Confucius and Mencius more than two thousand years ago already advocated democracy because they advocated the common good and emphasized the importance of the people.[14]

However, Mencius's thought is not democracy as defined by individual liberty and equality. First of all, Mencius's thought does not exclude having a king as the sole decision-maker for social affairs. Rather, as Shu-hsien Liu properly pointed out, Mencius's idea of people-as-the-foundation and the idea of having a good king mutually rely on each other.[15] This is so because it is the notion that when the king makes a decision, he should consider the well-being of the people first. It would be unreasonable if we were to look for a form of government without a king in Mencius. The point here is that Mencius's form of government is what Lin Yutang has called "parental government."[16] It requires that "the king treat his people as he treats his children (爱民如子 *ai min ru zi*)." Nevertheless, even though he has the children's well-being in mind, it is the father who is the sole decision-maker, not the children. The decision-making power of the father does not come from the children, and the king's power comes from Heaven, not from the people. In this picture there is no room for individual liberty and equality, which are essential to democracy. This kind of government is at most "for the people." It is highly questionable whether it is "of the people." It is clearly not "by the people."

Mencius believed that when the king lost the "Mandate of Heaven," then people's rebellion was justified. Some people think this implies that Mencius believed that the people have a right to rebel. But as Joseph Levenson rightly remarked,

> the famous "right to rebel" was a contradiction in terms. People rebelled not because they had any theoretical legal right, but because actual legal arrangements left little scope to their lives. Until they succeeded, rebels had no right, and the people's will, if they claimed to express it, had to wait on Heaven's choosing.[17]

Of course, Heaven's choosing in reality solely depended on the success or failure of the rebellion. As the old Chinese saying goes "success makes [the rebels] kings and nobles, failure makes [them] bandits (成则王侯败则贼 *cheng ze wanghou bai ze zei*)." The point is that, even though one can give moral approval of a rebellion, a right to rebel as an accepted social arrangement is entirely out of the question.

Secondly, the question of whose well-being should be put first has little to do with democracy. A dictator might put his people's well-being first. Yet it is not democracy. Just as the fact that gold is treated by someone as most precious does not mean that gold is given the right of liberty and equality, whether the people are treated as most important has little to do with whether the people have the rights of liberty and equality. The Confucian concept of government is "government by gentlemen" and "governance by moral force." However, the gentlemen may be mistaken in believing that they have made a decision for the best interest of the people, or they may really represent the best interest of the people, but the people, due to lack of knowledge or wisdom, do not like it. In relation to the first case, democracy would prove advantageous if the people, through a democratic political procedure, avoid decisions against their interest. The second case exposes some disadvantage in democracy if the people, against the advice from the wise, make wrong decisions. Neither case, however, would indicate that the Confucian form of government is democratic.

There may be practical and expedient reasons for Confucians in today's world to make Confucianism look democratic. However, the claim that Confucianism is democratic is seriously flawed and, as I will show later, this move is misdirected. In a way, it can be said that the attempt to prove Confucianism to be democratic is no more reasonable than an attempt by a Chinese Christian, who is convinced of the holiness of Christianity yet does not want to abandon Confucianism, to prove Confucianism to be Christian in nature.

It may be true that Confucian intellectuals such as Yan Fu 严复 (1853–1921), Kang Yuwei 康有为 (1858–1927), Liang Qichao 梁启超 (1873–1929), Zhang Binglin 章炳麟 (1868–1936), and Liu Shipei 刘师培 (1884–1927) first welcomed the idea of democracy in China. This does not show that Confucianism has an intrinsic affinity for democracy. First, in a country like nineteenth-century China, only intellectuals had the opportunity and political sensitivity to be exposed to the Western idea of democracy. In a Buddhist or Islamic country it is likely for Buddhist or Islamic intellectuals to be among the first to be exposed to and perhaps welcome democracy, and this does not necessarily indicate that Buddhism or Islam has an intrinsic affinity for democracy (though it may have). Let us not forget that it was also true that some Confucian intellectuals were staunchly opposed to democracy. Second, when these Confucian intellectuals were first exposed to democracy, they primarily understood it as merely a form of government, that is, a multiparty system, a parliamentary system, or the like. They certainly did not understand that a true democracy could mean a person's freedom to choose to be disloyal to the Qing dynasty or a future dynasty of the Han people. That is, they failed to see the central value or values that come with the form of democracy.

If Mencius's idea is not that of real democracy, we can conclude that democracy is not a value in traditional Chinese thought. As a matter of fact, when democracy was introduced to China early in this century, "Mr. Democracy," as it was called then, was seen as diametrically opposed to traditional Chinese value systems, particularly to Confucianism. The slogans "Welcome Mr. Democracy!" and "Down with Confucianism!" were uttered in the same breath. While this position against Confucianism may have been too extreme, the opposition itself did not occur by accident. It at least indicates some essential tension between democracy and Confucianism. Contrary to the political philosopher Hsü Fu-kuan 徐复观, who believed that the real spirit of Confucianism leads to democracy,[18] I will show next that the spirit of Confucianism and that of democracy, as defined earlier, contradict each other in essential ways.

Whether Confucianism and Democracy Are Compatible

If democracy has not been at the heart of traditional Chinese culture, and the two are inevitably going to face each other in China, then are democracy and traditional Chinese culture, Confucianism in particular, compatible?

Philosophers, including prominent Chinese philosophers of this century, are widely divided on this issue.

Liang Shu-ming, for example, thought that there is no room in Chinese culture for democracy. He wrote that, because of the peculiarity of Chinese culture, "it is not that China has not entered democracy, it is rather that China cannot enter democracy."[19] He believed that traditional Chinese value systems alone provide a solid foundation for a good civil society. Mou Tsung-san, a prominent contemporary New-Confucian, sees the inadequacy of traditional Confucianism and believes that, through a transformation of the Confucian moral subjectivity into a cognitive subjectivity (subjectivity of understanding), Confucianism will provide an adequate foundation for democracy. It is not clear how such a transformation can actually take place, though.[20] Mou includes liberty, equality, and human rights in democracy.[21] It is doubtful that these values can be integrated into Confucianism. Shu-hsien Liu, in contrast, sees many difficulties in grafting democracy onto Confucianism and maintains that, unless politics is separated from morals, democracy will not find itself at home in China.[22] Liu is certainly right in thinking that democracy must have the form of a social institution. What about the value contents of democracy? If democratic values are to enter the ethical realm, then the question about the relationship between these values and Confucian values cannot be avoided.

Let us take a closer look at the relation between democracy and the Chinese traditions.

In chapter 3 of his *Cultures and Philosophies of the West and East* Liang Shu-ming observed:

Chinese thought is [characterized by] accepting and staying within whatever one's role defines (安分 *an fen*), contentment, continence, and maintaining good health. It by no means advocates the pursuit for material enjoyment. The Chinese, no matter under what circumstances, can find satisfaction and demonstrate endurance. He does not necessarily want to change the environment. Eastern culture seeks not conquest of nature but harmony with nature.[23]

Here Liang presented a picture of mixed attitudes toward a life of Confucianism ("accepting and staying within whatever one's role defines"), Buddhism (denouncing material enjoyment, emphasizing endurance), and Taoism ("maintaining good health," "seeking not conquest of nature but harmony with nature"). These are the three major value systems in Chinese culture. Obviously, in the way in which they are presented, there is nothing democratic.

Among the three, Buddhism stands aloof from worldly affairs. It renounces the world.[24] Therefore it has little to do with issues related to democracy, which is a very worldly matter. While it is not impossible for democracy and Buddhism to be grafted together, the two parts would occupy very different dimensions and there would be little organic connection between them. The Taoist advocates a concept of freedom or liberty that is negative in nature. Instead of overcoming obstacles to satisfy our desires, the Taoist thinks that one should eliminate one's own desires in order not to feel oppressed by external constraints. This notion of liberty, though it has merits in itself, is in direct opposition to the concept of liberty in democracy.[25] Unless this opposition can be resolved, Taoism and democracy cannot be integrated into a single value system. Given the vital importance of the notion of liberty in each system and the nature of each system here, such a resolution is highly unlikely.

Confucianism and democracy do have fundamentally conflicting values. First, democracy, as we have seen, presupposes the concept of individual rights. A democratic society is one in which individuals' rights are recognized and respected. Following this way of thinking, in order for democracy to prevail, the concept of rights must be introduced and established. It requires the recognition that some basic rights of individuals are inalienable. Confucianism, at least in the traditional form, has no place for the concept of rights.[26] It is, however, a serious mistake to think that Confucius left out the concept of rights by negligence. In the ideal society that Confucius envisioned, there is supposed to be no need for rights.

On the issue of whether human nature is good or bad, rights-based theories typically lean toward the view that human nature is bad or flawed. Rights are viewed as the basis for individuals to stand up for themselves. When others impose on someone, this person can stand on a right. The Confucian social ideal is that of *jen*. If all people embody *jen* as Confucius wished, everyone in the society would be taken care of. The Confucians view civil society as the family. In the family everyone ought to look after others. Ideally there is no need for anyone to stand up for oneself against family members. The very idea of rights and the suggestion of the need for rights already imply the failure of *jen*.

A Chinese intellectual once made the following remark on the difference between the West and China:

The notion of rights can be said the only element in the European-American political thought—this notion is even applied to relations between father and son and between husband and wife, the most immediate and intimate relations of all. For the Chinese mind, this is simply unintelligible. How can you talk about rights between father and son and between husband and wife?[27]

From the viewpoint of the rights-theorist, of course one can, and indeed must, talk about rights between father and son and between husband and wife. Today some brides and grooms even sign a prenuptial contract to protect their own rights. In the Confucians' eyes, this talk itself presupposes the failure of the ideal of the family, the foundation of Confucian society. For the Confucians, being a good husband implies treating his wife well, and being a good wife implies treating her husband well. What more can be, and needs to be, required morally than requiring the husband to be a good husband and the wife, a good wife? The husband and wife are meant to be one, not two separate lives. Therefore, for the Confucians it is meaningless or even destructive to talk about their rights against each other.[28]

In a way, the Confucian ideal world is much like the place called "Nowheresville" by Joel Feinberg. This place is full of "benevolence, compassion, sympathy, ... men helping one another from compassionate motives merely."[29] However, contrary to Feinberg's own conviction that such a world is intrinsically defective for the lack of rights, if such an ideal world were to be fully actualized, there would be no need for rights. (Are there rights in the Christian Heaven? What for?) The real problem is that such a world is never even close to being actualized. In reality, things are far less pretty. Nevertheless, the Confucian ideal is to build such a world, and in such a world there is no need, and hence by design no room is left, for rights. One perhaps could make room and "add" rights onto Confucianism. That would severely change the internal structure of Confucianism, which is primarily based on *jen*.

Second, in Confucianism the primary concern for individuals has to do with duty, not liberty. The Confucian dictum is "To return to propriety through self-control constitutes *jen*."[30] Controlling oneself implies suppressing one's desires and self-interest, including the desire for individual liberty. For the Confucians the first order of a person's social life concerns the family life. In the family, liberty is typically not a primary concern.[31] In a family model of society, people are defined by their social roles and these roles come with responsibilities. One's responsibilities usually override one's liberty. For example, in an unhappy marriage a woman often stays married because she feels she has responsibilities as a mother to her children and as a daughter-in-law to her parents-in-law.[32] Even though not bluntly against divorce, the Confucian is, compared with a liberal-minded Western democrat, likely to place more weight on one's responsibilities than on one's liberty.

Closely connected to duty is the Confucian notion of loyalty (忠 *zhong*). A. C. Graham translated *"zhong"* as "doing-one's-best-for-others" and noted that it "is used especially of devoted loyalty to a ruler, but also of wholeheartedness on behalf of inferiors."[33] When Duke Ding 定公 asked how the ruler should employ his ministers and how the ministers should serve their ruler, Confucius replied, "A ruler should employ his ministers according to the principles of propriety, and the ministers should serve their ruler with loyalty."[34] However, loyalty is not only a virtue between the ruler and subject. In Confucianism loyalty is also a virtue among people in general.[35] Replying to Fan Chi's 樊迟 question on the meaning of *jen*, Confucius said, "In private life, courteous, in public life, diligent, in relationships, loyal."[36] In a broad sense, children's filiality to parents and trust between friends are also loyalty.

Loyalty implies being bound to others. Individual liberty presupposes one's autonomy. A bound person is not really fully autonomous. Therefore, as long as people have to be loyal to others, they are not really entirely free in the liberal sense. There is an essential tension between loyalty and liberty. Of course someone can freely *choose* to be loyal. That does not mean that liberty and loyalty as primary virtues point in the same direction. One could freely choose to be a slave, too.

Confucian loyalty becomes even more binding when it is coupled with another cardinal Confucian value, *yi* 义. Usually rendered in English as "righteousness," *yi* has more than one meaning.[37] In a primary sense, *yi* requires that we do not abandon friends when they are in trouble or in need of our help, and that we do not let friends down even under extreme circumstances. This Confucian emphasis on loyalty with *yi* as a central Confucian virtue can be seen throughout history. For instance, in 1948 after Chiang Kai-shek 蒋介石 (1887–1975) was forced to resign from the presidency of the Republic of China, he still had almost full control of the government. The acting president, Li Zongren (李宗仁 Li Tsung-jen 1890–1969), formally in the post, was simply unable to perform the duties of the presidency without having real power. A main reason for this was that people in the government had an overwhelmingly strong loyalty to Chiang. This kind of loyalty is almost incomprehensible to many Westerners. In contrast, a democratic society such as the United States is characterized by a lack of loyalty. Voters are willing to withdraw their support from a leader and turn to someone else at almost any time. Elected officials simply cannot count on loyalty from the voters. Lack of loyalty is intrinsic to the dynamics of democratic politics. While principles of democracy tend to make a society more dynamic, Confucianism tends to strive to stabilize society through well-defined relationships. The two are not moving in the same direction.

Third, as we have seen, a fundamental value for democracy is equality, whereas in Confucianism people are essentially unequal because of their social roles. For example, besides holding that the son should be filial to his father, Mencius also believed that the primary human relationships are duty between ruler and subject, distinction between husband and wife, and precedence of the old over the young.[38]

To be sure, in a certain sense the Confucian also has a notion of equality. Donald Munro characterizes this equality as "descriptive," "natural" equality, in contrast to the "evaluative" equality in early Christianity. The descriptive notion of equality, Munro maintains, is that humans are born with common attributes or characteristics; but it does not mean that "men are of similar 'worth' or deserve similar treatment," as understood in early Christianity.[39] Wm. Theodore de Bary also points out that a distinctive feature of Confucianism is its emphasis on equity rather than equality:

> Confucians accepted social distinctions as an inevitable fact of life and believed that differences in age, sex, social status, and political position had to be taken into account if equity were to be achieved in relations among unequals.[40]

Confucians believe that we are what we make ourselves to be. While everyone has the potential to make oneself a sage or a gentleman (*jun zi*), in practice because people are at different stages of this process, they are not on the same footing. Therefore they are not equal.[41] To add the notion of "evaluative" equality into Confucianism would inevitably undermine the Confucian ideal of "*jun zi*" that is at its core.

Confucianism is characteristically paternalistic. Paternalism may be seen as an inevitable consequence of the lack of equality within the tradition, a natural extension from the concept of *jen*, and a corollary of the Confucian ideal of meritocracy. For Confucius, the character of the morally superior person is like wind, that of the inferior person is like grass. The grass always bends in whatever direction the wind blows.[42] Mencius advocated that those who use their minds should rule those who use their muscles.[43] A cardinal Confucian virtue for the able and wise is to direct and take care of the less able and less wise. For example, it is the inescapable duty of the Confucian intellectual to speak on behalf of the masses.

In contrast, in democracy the concepts of liberty and individual rights assure that an individual is entitled to make choices for himself or herself even if they are wrong or unwise.[44] For that, Confucianism leaves little room. In Confucianism, under the name of common good, paternalism prevails over individual liberty and individual autonomy.

As far as pluralism is concerned, Confucianism appears to have been sending out conflicting messages. On the one hand, as I have indicated in chapters 1 and 6, it accords with Zhuang Zi's idea of following two courses at the same time; on the other hand it strongly advocates unity. Particularly as it has been presented by Mencius, Xun Zi (Hsün Tzu), Zhu Xi (Chu Hsi), and numerous later Confucians, Confucianism places an emphasis on unity (大一统 *da yitong*). On the whole, unity is valued above plurality in Confucianism.

Unity here means not only political unity and territorial unification, but also unity of thought and ideology. Confucius placed paramount importance on following the way of the Zhou dynasty[45] and thereby excluded other options. While Mencius believed that the only way to settle the empire was through unity, that is, oneness,[46] Xun Zi advocated the idea of using a unitary principle in deciding world affairs.[47] *The Doctrine of the Mean* states that "Today throughout the empire all carts have wheels with the same gauge; all writing is with the same characters; all conduct follows the same norms." (XXVIII). This is stated evidently with enthusiastic approval. The Gong Yang (公羊 Kung-Yang) school of Confucianism virtually took unity to be the sole manifestation of Tao/Way.

Pluralism, while giving individuals more free choice in life, does not itself reinforce the value of unity. Democracy as a whole gives paramount respect to an individual's will. From a democratic point of view, unity is good only if the majority willingly choose unity. In contrast, in Confucianism, unity itself is a value that must be upheld. It can be argued that the Confucian emphasis on unity should be given credit for the long history of unity of the Chinese people.

Today, forces for reunification of the mainland and Taiwan still appeal to this Confucian value for inspiration.

From the above discussion we can see that the central values in Confucianism point in the opposite direction from democratic values. Let me make it clear that I am not asserting that one cannot find words or bits of thought in Confucian works of over two thousand years that are in accord with democracy or its related ideas. However, I believe that, even if found, they are too marginal to be significant in Confucianism. The real spirit of Confucianism, as has been demonstrated above, is not in these words or bits of thought.

Nor do I mean, as some readers might suspect at this point, that democratic values simply cannot be inserted into Confucianism. The question is rather, as I will discuss below, how to preserve the integrity of Confucianism. I believe that, because of the essential tension between democratic values and some undemocratic Confucian values, they are not compatible within one integrated system. In other words, the two cannot be integrated into a single value system without substantially sacrificing either democratic or Confucian values.

Now we have shown the essential tensions between Confucian and democratic values. What is the problem in this picture? The problem is that both sets of values are worthwhile. On the one hand, such democratic values as liberty, equality, and pluralism are desirable; on the other hand, so are Confucian values like the family, duty, loyalty, unity, and so forth. The problem, I believe, as many contemporary Confucians do, is that these Confucian values are as cherishable as democratic values. I believe, as strongly as many New-Confucians do, that traditional Confucian virtues such as loyalty, filial morality, paternalism, and unity are good values and ought to be retained.

Just because the Confucian virtues are in conflict with some democratic values, it does not mean that they are less good or less valuable. As a matter of fact, I believe that the real strength of Confucianism is not in being or becoming democratic, but in those traditional virtues that are not democratic. It is a simple-minded inference that, since democracy is good, anything that is undemocratic must be bad. An argument can be made that in the United States and throughout the democratic West, healthy society has been threatened precisely by the diminishing of traditional values similar to these undemocratic Confucian values. Prominent scholars like Samuel Huntington have made much the same mistake by thinking that, because democratic values are good, undemocratic or nondemocratic Confucian values must be abandoned or superseded.

Democracy as an Independent Value System in China

At this historically critical and conceptually perplexing point, where ought China to go? Or what ought Chinese intellectuals to advocate?

China needs both democratic and Confucian values. Because democratic values and some undemocratic Confucian values, while both desirable, are not compatible in a single integrated system, the only way out has to be for democracy to exist in China independently of Confucianism. As I will show, the ideal here is *not* a single integrated system of values.

As indicated earlier, the Confucian ideal sets a very high standard for human morality, and if the Confucian ideal of society were to be fully realized, it would be a perfect society. Unfortunately, it has never been fully realized, nor does it seem likely to ever be fully realized. While fully geared toward the best human relations, Confucianism is not well equipped for the situation when the dark side of human capacities takes over. We may compare the idea to the case of sharing a pie with a number of people. Everyone is supposed to have sufficient love for everyone else so nobody will be left without a fair share. What if someone takes another's share? The typical Confucian answer is that *jen* demands that no one take more than one's share. While this approach may work, it does not sound as strong as the rights approach. With rights, one can stand up to claim one's entitlement more forcefully. Similar cases can be made in other areas where a tension exists between Confucianism and democracy. I call this weakness of Confucianism the "practical weakness." It calls for a complementary value system. Hence there is a need for democratic values in China.

Among the three major value systems in China, Confucianism, Taoism, and Buddhism, none can play the role of democracy. We have shown that Confucianism cannot. Taoism emphasizes *wu-wei* (noncontention). It advocates a character of flexible will and of following the current. It is fundamentally at odds with the democratic value of striving for individual rights and interests. Buddhism, on the other hand, believes in renouncing the world. The Buddhist is supposed to stand aloof from worldly affairs. As in Confucianism, forbearance is heavily valued in Buddhism. One should be able to put up with whatever situation one finds oneself in. In none of these value systems is the idea of standing up for one's self-interest valued. For all these reasons, democratic values are needed in China.

Since Confucianism is the predominant value system in China and is not compatible with democracy in one integrated value system, will the two clash with one another as democracy enters China? There are four possible answers to this question.

1. Confucianism and democracy will inevitably clash. Given the strong roots of Confucianism in the Chinese mind and its "forever-surviving" history in the past, we have reasons to believe that Confucianism will survive and, as a result, China will go its own way toward prosperity and will not embrace democracy.

2. Confucianism and democracy will inevitably clash. Given the world we have today, Confucianism will give way to democracy and only democracy will prevail.

3. Democracy will exist in a Confucian society with a substantially revised version of Confucianism in which elements favorable to democracy supersede undemocratic elements.

4. Perhaps Confucianism and democracy are incompatible only in the sense that they cannot be conceptually integrated into one value system, but they may coexist in the way in which Confucianism and Buddhism, though incompatible within one value system, coexist.

Among those who choose the first possibility is Liang Shu-ming, who maintained that, because of lack of individualism, China has not had the kind of democracy as in the West, and will not have it in the future either.[48] In addition to authors who outrightly reject democracy, I also include in this group those who would want China to have minimal democracy, namely democracy without rights of individual liberty and equality. Recently such Western scholars as Henry Rosemont Jr. have appeared to favor this first alternative.[49]

However, most Chinese, particularly scholars in the field, seem to hold that an undemocratic China in the future is unacceptable. Furthermore, many Chinese people in recent history have been fighting for democracy and it has gained ground on both sides of the Taiwan Straits. This fact at least indicates the likelihood for democracy to take root in (mainland) China.

On the other hand, since the May Fourth Movement of 1919 some people have favored the second possibility. They are for complete Westernization in China. Chen Xu-jing 陈序经 (1903–1967), for example, wrote:

> The issue we have to resolve today is not whether China should Westernize itself, but whether China can hurry up to be completely Westernized. We can say that the method of going back to the old culture and the method of compromising between the two cultures are matters of the past both in theory and in fact; it is no longer an issue and there is no value to discuss it anymore. We can say that theoretically complete Westernization is now necessary. The real issue is whether we can do in a short time or a very long time; whether we do it ourselves or we are forced by others to do it.[50]

For Chen, the current Western culture is not Western in nature; it represents the future of humankind. He believes that culture is a whole and its parts—whether political, economic, or religious—cannot be separated. If China wants to learn from the West, it has to accept everything and become entirely Westernized.

This view has received tremendous resistance ever since it was voiced. Needless to say, in theory China could remain Chinese without Confucianism. However, given past experience in some predominantly Confucian-influenced regions such as Singapore, Japan, South Korea, and Taiwan, and given the deep roots of Confucianism in China, it does not seem likely to happen in China in the near future. If it were to happen, it would indeed be a serious loss for Chinese culture.

Samuel Huntington embraces the third possibility. Pointing out what he sees as the impending clash between democracy and some traditional cultures in various parts of the world, Huntington writes:

> Great historic cultural traditions, such as Islam and Confucianism, are highly complex bodies of ideas, beliefs, doctrines,

assumptions, writings, and behavior patterns. Any major culture, including even Confucianism, has some elements that are
compatible with democracy, just as Protestantism and
Catholicism have elements that are clearly undemocratic. Confucian democracy may be a contradiction in terms, but democracy in a Confucian society need not be. The question is: What
elements in Islam and Confucianism are favorable to democracy, and how and under what circumstances can these supersede the undemocratic elements in those cultural traditions?[51]

Huntington is evidently applying a hierarchical model of thinking
here. For him, Confucianism can survive democratization by superseding or abandoning its undemocratic values. Admittedly, this
option is not entirely impossible. The question is, is that too great a
price for Confucianism to pay? Can Confucianism do better than
that?

To be sure, as a value system Confucianism is not unchangeable.
It has changed in many ways since Confucius's time, and needs to
change further in many aspects. To some extent the vitality of
Confucianism lies in its potentialities for and perhaps willingness to
change. However, it does have some elements that are so crucial
to Confucianism that it cannot survive substantially without
them. Features such as its emphasis on the family, filial morality,
and self-cultivation, are an indispensable part of Confucianism.
Because these emphases lead in different directions from individual
liberty and equality, if the emphasis were to shift to the latter,
one cannot help asking: How Confucian would this new system
be?

Can Confucianism survive without values such as emphasis on
the family, filial morality, loyalty, and respecting the old? If so, how
much Confucianism would be left? Is a much watered-down "Confucianism" worth preserving? If not, how can these values be superseded by democratic values? If it only means that in the "democratic
Confucianism" these traditional values should not be carried to
extremes, don't we already have that in Confucianism?[52] How are
values like filial morality and respecting the old supposed to work
within a "democratic Confucianism"? The attempt to democratize
Confucianism by superseding its traditional values will inevitably
jeopardize the integrity of Confucianism and the result will be a loss
of the real value and spirit of Confucianism.

In addressing the future of Confucianism, Alasdair MacIntyre comments:

Confucianism appears to face a recurrent type of dilemma: *either* it retains its highly specific and concrete character, thus tying itself to particular Chinese forms of social relationships of a traditional kind and, while not necessarily exempting the concrete embodiments of these forms altogether from moral criticism, rendering its moral standpoint inseparable from loyalty to these now often radically changing forms, *or* it makes itself relevant to types of social order in which these forms of social relationships do not or no longer exist, but in so doing it empties itself of specific moral content and so diminishes its doctrine of the virtues by specifying them only in barren generalities.[53]

MacIntyre may have overstated the point by suggesting that in today's China forms of social relationships for which Confucianism was suited may no longer exist. He is certainly right in indicating the danger that attempts to make a value system universally valid or applicable will reduce it to barren generalities.

Unfortunately it appears that today some New-Confucians are doing just that. The attempt to make Confucianism "democratic" will only make it nondescript, make it "neither fish nor fowl." It is time to give up the attempt to mix together everything that is good separately, in order to produce the perfect ideology. In logic this is called "the fallacy of composition." It cannot succeed and should be abandoned. The New-Confucians' attempt to democratize Confucianism also shows that these people may not have sufficient confidence in Confucianism. In fact, those who have been trying to prove Confucianism to be democratic or to democratize Confucianism may have overvalued democracy and undervalued Confucianism. I am convinced that they are both valuable and should be upheld respectively, to a certain extent.

I therefore believe that the most desirable and realistic likelihood lies in the last of the four alternatives. According to this alternative, democracy and Confucianism will coexist in China. To be sure, this kind of coexistence cannot be that of institutional Confucianism with democracy as a social institution. The future social institution in China must be democratic. This coexistence cannot be merely a matter of a democratic social institution with Confucian moral value; there must be room for democratic values as well. Perhaps we can say that it is a matter of democratic social institutions with democratic values *and* Confucian values. As value systems, democracy and Confucianism may influence each other. Nevertheless, they are two different, largely independent value systems. While there is no deductive way to show exclusively what will actually happen in the future, we can present reasons to show how this possibility is more likely than others.

Shu-hsien Liu acknowledges that "the cornerstone of democracy is the notion of rights and pluralism, but the Chinese tradition emphasizes the notion of duty and the ideal of unity (大一統 *da yitong*)."[54] The Chinese tradition that emphasizes the notion of duty and the ideal of unity is mainly Confucian tradition. Liu sees that the task to liberate ourselves from the tradition is "almost like thoroughly remoulding ourselves (脫胎換骨 *tuotai huangu*)."[55] As a starting point to make Confucianism democratic, Liu proposes to reinterpret the Neo-Confucian idea of "one principle and many manifestations (理一分殊 *li yi fen shu*)."[56] According to this interpretation, even though there is only one ultimate value, *jen* or the Tao, its manifestations can be various. If we combine both the one and the many, there will be both unity and plurality; then there will be room within Confucianism for democracy.

Pluralism and unity are only one of several opposite pairs that exist between democracy and Confucianism. But it is a good starting point for Confucianism to be adjusted in order to work with democracy. And I believe Confucianism does need to shift more toward pluralism before it can coexist well with the democratic value system.

However, Liu's approach is different from mine. Expanding the pluralistic tendency within Confucianism, Liu is moving toward an "internal opening" approach, namely, introducing the values of liberty and equality onto Confucianism. My approach may be characterized as an "external opening," namely, opening to the prospect of coexistence with a democratic value system. In other words, Liu's approach would make liberty and equality Confucian values by granting them full membership in the Confucian value system, while mine would make them "next-door neighbors," hopefully good neighbors. If we follow Liu's lead and introduce liberty and equality into Confucianism, then the end result of Liu's approach would not be different from Huntington's.

As value systems, Confucianism and democracy may coexist in two ways. First, some people are more Confucian than democratic—endorsing Confucian values more than democratic values such as individual liberty and equality, while others are more democratic than Confucian—endorsing individual liberty and equality more than Confucian values. Second, and perhaps more important, the values of Confucianism and democracy may coexist in the same individual, that is, the same individual may subscribe to values of both democracy and Confucianism, but be under some circumstances more democratic, and under other circumstances more Confucian. I believe that various values that are not consistent with one another may all be worth pursuing. Where that is the case, we need to achieve a delicate balance between them. The question now is how this is possible.

I have shown in chapter 6 that the three major value systems in China, Confucianism, Taoism, and Buddhism, have coexisted. Their coexistence is not merely an existence side by side in the same land, they also have coexisted within individuals. That is, the same individual subscribes to more than one value system at the same time. Human psychology is not a linear process that always follows a consistent single pattern, as some people believe. We have different values, desires, and needs. One can, and probably ought to, pursue these values and desires alternately.

In a similar way, democracy will enter this picture. In my model, the large picture will be like this. The Confucian, the Taoist, and the Buddhist, who have been engaged in a dialogue for an extended period of time, may invite another participant, "Mr. Democracy," to join them and continue their dialogue.[57] Then we will see the four different value systems sitting side by side. The primary characteristic of this dialogue will not be to seek domination, but to harmonize. When there is too much voice from one party, it is time for those in dialogue to shift attention to another voice. For instance, the concept of rights should be voiced when there is too much emphasis on paternalism and the paternalistic practice has become oppressive; Confucianism, Taoism, and perhaps Buddhism should be voiced when the rights talk has aroused too much individualism. Thus, even though there inevitably will be tension between Confucianism and democracy, similar to the tension between Buddhism and Confucianism, the four systems can nevertheless keep themselves in balance and harmony.

One may still think that to put democracy side by side with Buddhism and Taoism sounds odd because, after all, democracy is not a religion. I am not presenting democracy as a religion. I view it as a value system, as I do Buddhism and Taoism. Perhaps it would help if one tried to think of the picture of democracy and Confucianism coexisting as independent value systems similar to the picture of Confucianism and Mohism coexisting as independent value systems. Confucianism could not have been made better by being made Mohistic then, nor will it be made better by being made democratic now.

Thus the four separate value systems will not only compete with one another, but also complement one another in the same land. Again, this does not simply mean that in China there will be four groups of people, the Confucians, the Taoists, the Buddhists, and the Democrats competing with one another. The same individual can subscribe to and incorporate more than one value system. It may sound paradoxical but is nevertheless true that with Confucianism, Taoism, and Buddhism already in place, China is perhaps more suitable for democracy than many countries in the world.

Beneath the surface of democracy prevailing in the world today, there is a crisis. In the United States, for instance, the prevalence of democracy came along with a diminishing of traditional (Christian) values. One cannot say that some of the regrettable situations in the United States today, such as the problem of the national debt, of skyrocketing crime rates, of the homeless, of teenage pregnancy, have nothing to do with the way democracy has been practiced. What has happened seems to be that, while Christians stress the common ground between Christianity and democracy, they have failed to recognize the difference and tension between the two value systems. When Americans adopted the French revolutionary slogan "Liberty, Equality, and Fraternity!" they arranged these values in exactly that order, but overvalued liberty at the expense of fraternity. Had it been seen as a value independent of the other two, fraternity perhaps would have fared better and society would be better off today. Or, if people recognized that Christianity and democracy are two independent value systems, Christians might have a better chance of preserving their heritage. Unfortunately that is not what has happened. Perhaps democracy would do better if there were a balancing force such as Confucianism to complement it. For instance, given that democracy emphasizes individual liberty, the Confucian emphasis on the family would help to make a better society.

Upon entering into Chinese culture, democracy may find support from some aspects of existing Chinese value systems. Through the interpretations of early Chinese Buddhists and other sympathizers, Buddhism found some support from Taoism and Confucianism upon its arrival in China.[58] The same thing can happen with democracy. As a matter of fact, many democratic supporters have been doing this in seeking to interpret Confucianism as being democratic. However, just as people have later found out that Buddhism is not Taoism or Confucianism, they will find out that democracy as a value system is not Confucianim. This matter will become clearer after democracy finds its own home in Chinese society.

Thus, in my model democracy and Confucianism will coexist but only as independent value systems. Here "independent" is used in a weak sense, in the sense we say that Buddhism and Confucianism are independent value systems. It is fundamentally different from the New-Confucian model, in which Confucianism will be democratized and thereby democratic values such as individual liberty and equality will be added to Confucianism.

Now, one may ask, what difference does it really make? In my model, Confucianism has to acknowledge (once again?) that it is not *the* value system but only one of several value systems in China, even though it may be able to retain its predominant status in society. By distinguishing democracy from itself, Confucianism will be able to retain its unique characteristics without losing itself in a "melting pot" of various values.

In a society where Confucianism and democracy exist as independent value systems, a person who subscribes to both Confucianism and democracy will hear these two voices. Sometimes they are very different, even opposite, voices. For example, in politics, should a person owe loyalty to a leader or put individual liberty first? Within the party, should someone emphasize unity or individual liberty? In family life, should someone put filiality or equality first? In these cases it would seem that the Confucian would favor the first of the alternatives, whereas the democrat the second. There is no question that a wise person should balance the two sides, but the tension therein is obvious. Then how should we accommodate the tension? In my model the tension here is an external tension between Confucian values and democratic values. In the New-Confucian model, there would be two possibilities: (1) there would be no such tension within democratized Confucianism because such values as loyalty and filiality are undemocratic and hence have been superseded. In such a case I contend there is no more Confucianism. (2) there would be a tension between two values within the "new (democratized) Confucianism," and therefore neither side of the tension is more Confucian than the other. I do not see the merit of this model. I prefer the model in which Confucianism is Confucianism and democracy is democracy, and between the two, tension is tension and complementing is complementing.

If my argument is cogent, then what is the historic mission for Confucianism today? It is certainly not to "democratize" itself, as some New-Confucians have been advocating. It is rather to uphold its own traditional characteristics, to demonstrate its peculiar strength that other value systems lack. This is the only way in which Confucianism can secure its place in the world of the future.

Concluding Remarks

In this book I have argued that the general characteristics of Chinese philosophy in its ontological, epistemological, ethical, and religious aspects all directly or indirectly support Confucianism and democracy as two coexisting independent value systems, capable of complementing one another.

The harmony model is at the core of the Chinese culture. Following two or more courses at the same time is a practice in virtually all Chinese philosophical schools. Most Chinese follow a multiple approach to life. For the Chinese, ontologically the identity or reality of an entity may be viewed in more than one way. Truth is not a matter of simply fitting into a particular given mold of being, but rather a process of Way-making, which can be accomplished in many forms. The Confucian understanding of the self, morality, and the good life follows a way of thinking that is radically different from mainstream Western thinking. Chinese multiple religious participation, as a practical demonstration of the harmony ideal, has provided a good model for democracy in China.

I believe that the core values of democracy, such as individual liberty and equality, are not only missing in Confucianism but they are also in fundamental tension or conflict with Confucianism. Nevertheless, democracy is not the only value that is worth pursuing in the world. I believe both of these value systems have their own merits and thus are valuable on their own account. I believe that the attempt to integrate Confucianism with democracy is fundamentally misdirected and should be given up.

I believe China needs democracy, and China will have it. Thus, between the two currently prevailing, contesting alternatives—that China should retain Confucianism without democracy and that Confucianism should become democratized—I propose a third way out—democracy as a value system independent of Confucianism in China. And I believe that this is the only way for Confucianism to survive and hopefully to flourish in its homeland, and for democracy to become more socially responsive and responsible.

Notes

Introduction

1. Levenson (1968).

2. Fukuyama (1989).

3. Tu (1986).

4. Tu (1993c), 221.

5. Cf. A. C. Graham's *Disputers of the Tao* (1989), 13, and Arthur F. Wright (1959), 79.

6. Hall and Ames (1987), 331.

7. See Held (1995), particularly Alison M. Jaggar's and Sara Ruddick's articles in chapters 10 and 11.

8. Lakoff and Johnson (1980), 143.

1. Being

1. Eddington (1958), xi–xv.

2. Dong Zhongshu (1985), *Chun Qiu Fan Lu: Wu Xing Xiang Sheng.*

3. For example, in Zhou Dunyi's *Tai Ji Tu Shuo.*

4. For an exposition of *qi* and energy, see Zukav (1979).

5. As has been pointed out by numerous scholars, "substance" is a misleading translation for *ousia*. See Owens (1963), 139. "Primary being" seems to have some advantages over "substance," but because "substance" has become the conventional rendering (and translation) of Aristotle's *ousia*, it is sometimes more convenient to use than "primary being." In any case, I use both interchangeably in this chapter. But we have to bear in

193

mind that in Aristotle *ousia* does not mean substratum, which "substance" may imply.

6. *Metaphysics*, 1028a10–17. See Apostle (1966), 108.

7. Although the phrase is commonly translated as "essence," J. Owens thinks it is best translated as "the What-IS-being." See Owens (1963), 180–89.

8. *Metaphysics*, 1028b4. See Apostle (1966), 109.

9. See Halper (1989), 4.

10. While many commentators believe that in Aristotle form and essence are the same, Loux disagrees. But there should be no question that in Aristotle at least form and essence are closely linked. For these different views, see Frede and Patzig (1988), and Loux (1991).

11. Loux (1991), 7.

12. Ibid., 33.

13. Aristotle used the example of the ox in *Categories*, 2b22–28. See Ackrill (1963), 7.

14. Mair (1994), 26–27.

15. *Metaphysics*, 1030a22–23. See Apostle (1966), 122.

16. *Metaphysics*, 1035a2–5. Sometimes Aristotle seems to believe that natural objects have an ontology different from artificial objects (e.g., 1043b19–23). But when he talks about the relation between an individual, its form, and its matter, he does not keep the distinction so clear. The statue, bronze, and the shape are his favorite examples in investigating *ousia*. I also use similar examples, though my argument does not depend on them.

17. According to Loux's interpretation, Aristotle holds that, in addition to being an ox, a pack of flesh and bones also has an essence; it is also a primary *ousia*. This interpretation would bring Aristotle much closer to Zhuang Zi. But it seems that many Aristotle commentators would disagree with Loux in this regard. See Loux (1991), chapter 7, "The Completed Hierarchy of Essences and Two Problems."

18. *Zhuang Zi*, chapter 2, my translation. Cf. Mair (1991), 15.

19. "This" (是 *shi*) and "that" (彼 *bi*) stand for two sides of a thing. But it does not exclude the possibility of a third or fourth; just as in English we use "on the one hand . . . on the other," which does not necessarily mean that there are only two aspects and no more.

20. *Zhuang Zi*, chapter 2.

21. *Metaphysics*, 1045b17–21. See Apostle (1966), 145.

22. *Metaphysics*, 1033a6–23. See Apostle (1966), 118.

23. For instance, in Heller (1990).

24. I do not intend to launch a full-fledged argument against the "four-dimensional worm" theory. The theory, after all, is not Aristotle's.

25. *Metaphysics*, 1030a23–24. See Apostle (1966), 112.

26. *Zhuang Zi*, chapter 6.

27. Mair (1991), 16.

28. Cf. Chen Ku-ying (1983), 62–63, note 1.

29. Feng and English (1974), 30.

30. My translation, based on Graham (1981), 57, and Mair (1994), 19.

31. See Chen Ku-ying (1983), 75.

32. Graham (1981), 54, with slight revisions by me. Wing-tsit Chan translated the last sentence as "This is called following two courses at the same time." Chan (1963), 184.

33. Graham (1981), 58, with my revisions. *"Fan ran yao luan* 樊然殽乱*"* which means formless, orderless, or chaotic, Graham translated as "inextricably confused," which, though literally correct, may convey a negative sense. But Zhuang Zi is by no means bothered by the formless or chaotic character of reality. Since Wang Ni presumably represents Zhuang Zi, I use "formless" instead.

34. *Metaphysics*, 1030a12–13. See Apostle (1966), 112.

35. Wiggins (1980), 146.

36. Graham (1981), 61, with my revisions. The last sentence Graham translated as "Between Chou and the butterfly there was necessarily a dividing." The use of the word "necessarily" gives the sentence a strong sense of metaphysical necessity that Zhuang Zi would not accept. The original is *"ze bi you fen yi* 则必有分矣*"* Chen Ku-ying interprets it as *"bi ding shi you suo fen bie de* 必定是有所分别的*"* I translate it as "there must be some difference."

37. See Chen Ku-ying (1983), 92.

38. Walter Benesch (1997) has referred to it as "aspect/perspective logic," 177.

39. *The Book of Change*, Appended Remarks, part 5. Zhou (1991), 261.

40. Chan (1963), 268.

41. To what extent the Confucians applied this metaphysical commitment to social tolerance, however, is debatable. See my discussion of the Confucian notion of unity in chapter 7.

42. Zaehner (1968), 86.

43. Radhakrishnan and Moore (1957), 74.

44. Ibid., 83.

45. Ibid., 79–80.

46. Hegel (1929), section 115.

47. Heidegger (1962), 67/42. The first number is the page number in Macquarrie and Robinson's English translation (1962), and the second number is the page number of the German original as indicated in the English translation.

48. Ibid., 263/220.

49. Ibid., 261/218.

50. Ibid., 260/218.

51. Ibid., 182/142.

2. Truth

1. Hansen (1985), 492.

2. Smith (1980), 427.

3. Ibid., 430. "*Jun zi* (君子)" is usually rendered as "the superior man." This rendering is artificial. The English word "gentleman" means "a well-mannered and considerate man with high standards of proper behavior" (*The American Heritage College Dictionary*, 3rd ed. [Boston: Houghton Mifflin Company, 1993], 569). Although it is not an exact match, it does catch the basic meaning of "*jun zi*." The Chinese term has been mainly used to refer to men, even though it is not gender-specific. The female gender indicator "nü 女" is usually attached to "*jun zi*" when referring to a woman (gentlewoman).

4. See Parkes (1987).

5. Heidegger uses three different words for truth: unveiling (*Enthüllen*), uncovering (*Entdeckung*), and disclosing (*Erschliessen*). He explains the difference between them as follows: "We shall call the unveil-

ing of an extant being—for example, nature in the broadest sense—*uncovering*. The unveiling of the being that we ourselves are, the Dasein, and that has existence as its mode of being, we shall call not uncovering but *disclosure, opening up*." Heidegger (1982), 215.

6. Heidegger (1962), 258–59/216.

7. Ibid., 261/218–19.

8. "On the Essence of Truth," Heidegger, *Basic Writings* (1977), 123.

9. Heidegger (1962), 261/218.

10. Ibid., 263/220.

11. Ibid., 263/220.

12. Ibid., 255/212.

13. Ibid., 263/221.

14. Ibid., 267/225.

15. Ibid., 105/75.

16. Ibid., 119/86.

17. Ibid., 343/297.

18. For some key articles in this political-philosophical movement, see *Chinese Studies in Philosophy* 25.2 (Winter 1993–94), especially the editor's introduction.

19. For instance, Hu Fuming, Zhang Cheng, and *Guangming Daily*'s Special Commentator (1993–94).

20. Chang (1989b), 230.

21. R. B. Blakney translated these two sentences as "In it are essences, subtle but real, embedded in truth" and "Cultivate the Way yourself, and your virtue will be genuine," in Blakney (1955), 73, 107.

22. *Zhuang Zi*, chapter 2.

23. Ibid., chapter 6.

24. John Dewey holds that "the adverb 'truly' is more fundamental than either the adjective, true, or the noun, truth. An adverb expresses a way, a mode of acting." Dewey (1953), 128.

25. *Zhuang Zi*, chapter 31.

26. Chang (1989b), 230. Roetz also believes that "*ch'eng* [*cheng*] is a kind of Confucian counterpart to the Taoist *chen* [*zhen*]," Roetz (1993), 92.

27. See Tu (1989), chapter 1.

28. For interpretations of *The Doctrine of the Mean*, I rely largely on Tu (1989).

29. See Chan (1963), 97, note 6.

30. See Tung Fang-suo (1994), 63–73.

31. The Confucian notion of "tian 天," which is often rendered in English as "Heaven," refers to a cosmological moral principle or a divine power, not a place to live an afterlife.

32. Quotations from *The Doctrine of the Mean* are from Chan (1963), with minor revisions by this author when appropriate.

33. *Mencius*, Lau (1970), 123.

34. Tu (1989), 72–73.

35. *Mencius*, 7A:1.

36. Fung (1993), 322.

37. Heidegger (1962), 262/219.

38. Heidegger (1982), 221.

39. Liu (1992), 541.

40. Such as Caputo (1971), 127–38, and Richardson (1967), 286–307.

41. Caputo (1989), 178.

42. Caputo (1993), 2.

43. Hatab (1995), 404.

44. Elliston (1978), 68.

45. Vogel (1994).

46. Sartre (1946), 410–11.

47. Vogel (1994), 49–50.

48. Heidegger (1962), 344/297.

49. Heidegger (1982), 165.

50. Heidegger (1962), 344/298.

51. Vogel, 68.

52. *Analects*, 12:2.

53. Ibid., 6:28.

54. Cf. Gray (1965), 543.

55. *The Doctrine of the Mean*, XXI.

56. Cf. *The Doctrine of the Mean*, XX, and *Mencius*, 4A:12.

57. *Analects*, 3:3.

58. This relation is reflected in Tu Wei-ming's discussion of the relation between *jen* and *li* in Tu (1968).

59. Zhou Dunyi, *Tong Shu* 通书 (*T'ung Shu* or *General Principles of the Book of Change*); quoted from Chang (1989), 101.

60. *Mencius*, 7A:4.

61. Heidegger (1962), 265/223.

62. Ibid., 228/183.

63. Dreyfus (1991), 239.

64. See chapter 4.

65. Heidegger (1962), 322/277.

66. Ibid., 323/278.

67. Ibid., 264/222.

68. Ibid., 314/270.

69. For an additional sense of authenticity in Heidegger, see Ciaffa (1987).

70. Interview in *Listening* 6 (1971): 35. Directly quoted from Allen (1993), 82.

71. Versenyi (1965), 181.

72. Tu (1989), 77–78.

73. Heidegger (1962), 264/221.

74. Ibid., 265/222.

75. Ibid., 155/118.

76. Ibid., 167/129.

77. Ibid., 167/129.

78. *The Doctrine of the Mean*, I.

79. Heidegger (1962), 331/285.

80. Heidegger (1977), 125.

81. Ibid., 125.

82. Ibid., 127.

83. Ibid., 129.

84. Ibid., 140.

85. Deng (1993), 497–99.

86. *Analects*, 2:4. The ideal of sagehood, however, may not be practical for ordinary people. See *"Jen* and Caring with Gradations" in chapter 4.

87. Heidegger (1962), 237/193.

88. Hansen (1985), 493.

89. Ibid.

90. Heidegger (1977), 271.

91. Heidegger (1962), 259/216.

92. Tu (1989), 19.

93. Hall and Ames (1987), 55.

94. *Zhuang Zi*, chapter 6.

95. Wang Yang-ming (1970), *Instructions for Practical Learning*, 3.

96. Cf. Tu Wei-ming, "A Confucian Perspective on Learning to Be Human," in Tu (1985), 51–66.

97. *Analects*, 15:33.

98. See Fang (1990), 688.

3. Language

1. *Analects*, 13:3.

2. Fung (1952), 60.

3. This interpretation may be traced back to Dong Zhongshu's *Luxuriant Gems of the Spring and Autumn Annuals* 春秋繁露, chapter 10.

4. *Analects*, 12:11.

5. *Mencius*, 7A:45.

6. *Analects*, 12:11.

7. See Wang Li (1981), 262.

8. *Analects*, 8:14.

9. Cheng Chung-ying (1991), 224.

10. *Analects*, 6:23.

11. *Mencius*, 1B:8.

12. Chan (1963), 41.

13. *Xun Zi*, chapter 22.

14. Ibid.

15. Chan (1963), 125, note 33.

16. Ibid., 126.

17. *Xun Zi*, chapter 22.

18. Ibid.

19. Ibid.

20. Even in the West, the use of a person's first (personal) name and last (family) name indicates relationships involved.

21. *Xun Zi*, chapter 22.

22. See Locke (1905), book III, chapter III.

23. Ibid., book III, chapter VI.

24. *Über Sinn und Bedeutung* (1892). In Martinich (1985).

25. Russell (1919), 213–19.

26. *London Review of Books*, quoted from the backcover of Kripke (1980).

27. Kripke holds that some definite descriptions are rigid designators. Ibid., 60.

28. Ibid., 30.

29. Ibid., 122, 136.

30. Ibid., 122.

31. Ibid., 127.

32. Goldberg (1971), Quine (1977), Dupré (1981), and Kitcher (1984).

33. Quine (1977), 159.

34. Hennig (1979), 9.

35. See Wilson (1982), and Field (1973), 462–81.

36. Putnam (1973), 702.

37. Pine (1989), 74, 18.

38. Putnam (1973).

39. Chen Chi-yun (1992).

4. Ethics

1. For instance, Wolf (1994).

2. Chisholm (1976), 23.

3. Ibid., 36.

4. Nelson (1990), 277–78.

5. Jaggar (1983), 28–29.

6. Gilligan (1982), 74. As scholars have noted, Gilligan's model should not be construed as saying that all women are alike and all men are alike in moral thinking.

7. Noddings (1984), 49.

8. Tu Wei-ming, "Embodying the Universe: A Note on Confucian Self-Realization," in R. Ames with W. Dissanayake and T. Kasulis (1994), 177.

9. *Analects*, 2:4.

10. This may *partly* explain why abortion has become acceptable in China, which had been influenced heavily by the Confucian value that the more children one has the better. Under the Confucian notion of selfhood as an earned status, the fetus is not really yet human. Therefore, it has not earned the dignity and "rights" that a full human person has. While this does not necessarily make abortion morally permissible (e.g., there may be other considerations), it does make it relatively easier to accept abortion.

11. Ames (1994).

12. Tu (1985), 57–58.

13. Chisholm (1976), 24.

14. This conception of ruler-subject relation is subject to abuse, of course. See chapter 7.

15. Held (1987), 114–15.

16. Some feminist philosophers, however, have criticized this mother-child model of human relationship. See Hoagland (1991).

17. Gilligan (1982), 21.

18. Ibid., 21.

19. I will come back to this issue in chapter 7.

20. Boodberg (1953), 328.

21. Teruo (1965).

22. Tu (1981).

23. *Analects*, 12:22.

24. Ibid., 7:29.

25. *Mencius*, 2A:6.

26. Ibid., 7B:31.

27. *Analects*, 17:6.

28. Ibid., 17:22.

29. *Mencius*, 2A:6.

30. Ibid., 1A:5.

31. Tong (1973).

32. *The Doctrine of the Mean*, XX.

33. *Analects*, 12:1.

34. Gilligan (1982), 125.

35. Noddings (1984), 5.

36. *Analects*, 6:28.

37. Gilligan (1982), 139.

38. Ibid., 62.

39. *Analects*, 3:3.

40. Ibid., 4:15.

41. Noddings (1984), 14, 61.

42. Ibid., 25.

43. Noddings (1984), 55.

44. Ibid., 54.

45. Ibid., 109. Some feminists such as Virginia Held have been critical of Noddings in this regard. See Held (1987).

46. Tronto (1987), 658.

47. *Analects*, 13:18.

48. Ibid., 4:18.

49. de Bary (1991), 34–35.

50. *Mencius*, 6B:6.

51. Ibid., 4B:11. "Right" here is a translation/interpretation of "*yi* 义," which can also be understood as "appropriate." *The Doctrine of the Mean* states, "*yi* means setting things right and proper (义者宜也, *yi zhe yi ye*)" (XX). For a discussion of Confucian *yi*, see Cheng Chung-ying (1991).

52. *Mencius*, 4A:19.

53. Noddings (1984), 56–57.

54. For a good discussion of care- and principle-orientation, see Blum (1988).

55. *Analects*, 6:28.

56. For a discussion of the difference between *jen* and sagehood, see Chang (1989a), chapter 11. Later Confucians, such as Ch'eng Hao 程颢 ("a person of *jen* forms one body with all things without any differentiation") and Han Yu 韩愈 ("universal love is called *jen*"), elevated *jen* to the level of sagehood, which is evidently not Confucius's belief.

57. *Mo Tzu*, 4:2, in *Twenty-Two Masters*, 236.

58. *Mencius*, 3B:9.

59. Ibid., 7A:46.

60. *Analects*, 1:6.

61. *The Doctrine of the Mean*, XX.

62. *Analects*, 1:2.

63. *Mencius*, 1A:7.

64. Ibid., 7A:45.

65. *Mo Tzu*, 4:2, in *Twenty-Two Masters*, 235.

66. Noddings (1984), 83.

67. Ibid., 54.

68. Ibid., 16.

69. Ibid., 29. For a different view, see Benhabib (1987), 154–77.

70. Noddings (1984), 51.

71. Ibid., 86.

72. Some feminists, like Neo-Confucians, believe in universal love without gradations. This is not the place, nor is it the author's intention to develop a full-fledged defense of graded love. If the argument for graded love presented here seems inadequate or unconvincing, I am content if I have shown that some feminists share the Confucian view in this regard. For a recent defense of the Confucian graded love, see Lai (1991).

73. See Fung (1953), 44.

74. This is the saying of the Song Neo-Confucian Cheng Yi-chuan (程颐 *Cheng Yi*, 1033–1107), *Yi-Shu* 遗书, chapter 22. Ho Lin 贺麟 comments that Cheng's saying was right in principle that one must not lose integrity; the mistake made by Cheng was to consider a widow's remarrying a matter of losing integrity. The idea that one's moral integrity is more important than one's life is in line with Mencius (*Mencius*, 6A:10). See Ho (1988), 192–97.

75. According to Chang (1989a, chapter 8), it was not developed to such an extreme until the Southern Song dynasty (1127–1279).

76. *Analects*, 6:26.

77. Ibid., 17:25.

78. *Mencius*, 3B:2.

79. Fung (1953), 9.

80. Liu (1992), 223.

81. Ibid., 225.

82. Sarah Queen recently argued that some of the yin-yang chapters were written by Dong's disciples, not by Dong himself (Queen 1996, 101). There should be no doubt, however, that Dong was largely responsible for the basic doctrines.

83. Dong Zhongshu, *Luxuriant Gems of the Spring and Autumn Annals*, chapter 53, quoted in Fung (1953), 42–43.

84. For a good discussion of yin-yang and women in China, see Tao (1987), 501–12.

85. See Chang (1989a), 152.

86. In the *Analects*, we are told a story that Confucius's stable was burned down when he was out. Upon his return Confucius asked, "Have any people been hurt?" He did not ask about the horse (10:12).

87. It is questionable that there was Confucianism before the Han Confucians. It is, however, safe to say that the basic doctrines of Confucianism already existed in the works of Confucius and Mencius.

5. Family

1. Obenchain (1994), 154.

2. Russell (1922), 40.

3. In addition to English (1979), some of these views can be found in, for example, Simmons (1979), and Slote (1979), 319–25.

4. English (1979).

5. Ibid., 353.

6. Ibid., 352.

7. Ibid.

8. Ibid.

9. Ibid.

10. In a recent article, Nicholas Dixon attempts to rescue Jane English from the criticism that English requires no filial obligation of the grown children after they no longer have friendship with their parents. Dixon suggests that these grown children are still under obligations to their parents on the basis of "residual duties of friendship." This kind of "obligation," however, is too weak to serve our purpose for filial obligations. See Dixon (1995).

11. Belliotti (1986), 152.

12. Ibid., 152.

13. Narveson (1987).

14. Ibid., 66.

15. Ibid., 74.

16. Belliotti (1988), 288.

17. Narveson, 72.

18. Ibid., 73.

19. Belliotti (1988), 288.

20. Ibid., 289.

21. There are always exceptions. Some people will choose not to have children. But so far whether one should have children or not has not become a moral problem.

22. Sommers (1986).

23. Ibid., 74.

24. See Whalen Lai (1991).

25. Sommers (1986), 75.

26. Blustein (1982).

27. Ibid., 176.

28. Ibid., 177.

29. Ibid., 176.

30. Ibid., 183.

31. Ibid., 182.

32. Ibid., 164.

33. Ibid., 183.

34. Nancy Jecker argued along a similar line that parents deserve gratitude for supererogatory actions and for duty-meeting actions that satisfy certain constraints, in Jecker (1989).

35. Both quoted from Liang Shu-ming's "The Elements of Chinese Culture 中国文化要义," in Liang (1990), 28; Chien's originally appeared in his "Weekly Article" in *Da Gong Bao* 大公报, Chong Qing, November 1942, and Hsieh's is from his *Filiality and Chinese Culture* 孝与中国文化, Young Army's Publisher.

36. *The People's Daily* (Chinese overseas edition), Beijing, August 25, 1993, 3.

37. For instance, in the Marriage Law, Section 3, Article 15, "Children have a duty to support and assist their parents. . . . When children fail in such duty, parents who cannot work or have difficulty with their living

have a right to demand alimony from their children." Also the Senior Citizen Protection Act (1996), Article 2, Section 11.

38. See Huang (1992), 10. Some think *The Classic of Filial Morality* was compiled by Han Confucians. Huang argues that the fact that *The Spring and Autumn Annuals of Master Lü* (compiled in the third century B.C.E.) quoted it, indicates that it was before Han dynasty. See Huang (1992), 4–5.

39. See Lo (1993).

40. *Analects*, 2:7.

41. *Mencius*, 5A:4.

42. Ibid., 4A:26.

43. See note 31 in chapter 2.

44. Tang (1953), 322.

45. It follows that, not having children would be an inadequacy for a well-rounded life and one would probably do something to compensate for the missing piece in life. Traditionally this has been done through adoption.

46. This is also one of the Ten Commandments in the Bible.

47. See Tu (1985), 113–30. Also Tu (1989), 42.

48. Tu (1985), 117.

49. *Analects*, 4:18.

50. *Mencius*, 4B:30.

51. *Xun Zi*, XXIX.

52. Fung (1952/3), 359.

53. See Yang (1958).

54. Rawls (1980), 519.

55. For the relation of filial morality to the Chinese society as a whole, see Hsieh (1986), 167–87.

56. *Analects*, 1:2.

57. Cf. Tu (1993c), 144.

58. *The Doctrine of the Mean*, XV.

59. *Analects*, 1:6.

60. *Mencius*, 7A:45.

61. This leads to the "synchronical" dimension of the Confucian self, which we will discuss subsequently.

62. *Mencius*, 6A:6.

63. Tu (1985), 127.

64. Lin (1931), 751–57.

65. Tu (1989), 48.

66. Cf. Rosemont (1988, 1991).

67. *Mencius*, 3A:3.

68. *The Doctrine of the Mean*, XIII.

6. Religion

1. For instance, Theosophy brought together elements from Hinduism, Buddhism, Christianity, Spiritualism, Egyptian Hermeticism, perhaps something from Jewish Kabbalism, and occultism generally. Braden (1949), 243.

2. Küng and Ching (1989), 273–83.

3. Hick (1993).

4. Ibid., 25–26. Also Hick (1973).

5. Ibid., 27.

6. Hick (1989), 373.

7. Küng and Ching (1989), 281–82.

8. Quoted from Suggs, Sakenfeld, and Mueller (1992), 82.

9. Berthrong (1994), 27. For a discussion of this rejection, see Berthrong's introduction.

10. della Cava (1994).

11. For more discussion on the difference between Taoism as a philosophy and as a religion, see Ren (1992).

12. Hsiung (1995), 64.

13. Tu (1989), 94.

14. Hick (1989), 14.

15. In this regard, Mencius's effort in *Mencius* (2A:6, 6A:1–6) is more an illustration than an argument. In contrast, one can say that Xun Zi's case that human nature is evil is just as forceful or forceless as Mencius's.

16. *Analects*, 17:22. See discussion in chapters 4 and 5 of this book.

17. In traditional China, people usually lived in the same village for generations, and for them, all people with the same family name in the same village were of the same family. In this sense, the enlarged family was a community.

18. The title of Herbert Fingarette's little but influential book is "Confucius—The Secular as Sacred," Fingarette (1972).

19. For a detailed account of the religiousness of Confucianism, see Taylor (1990).

20. *The Great Learning*, chapter 6.

21. *Analects*, 12:2.

22. Ibid., 6:28.

23. E.g., ibid., 4:3.

24. Thompson (1996), 83.

25. *Zhuang Zi*, chapter 2.

26. See discussion in chapter 1 of this book.

27. The Taoist believes that everything can be useful, depending on how you look at it. See *Zhuang Zi*, chapter 1, section 2.

28. Thompson (1996), 80.

29. *Tao Te Ching*, chapter 19.

30. These persecutions were mainly driven by political and economic reasons. For one thing, the large number of Buddhist monasteries that pulled able-bodied men away from production and owned large tax-exempt land was considered a threat to the state. See Chan (1968), 118.

31. Welch (1966), 158.

32. Creel (1953), 197.

33. Zong Mi, *Yuan Ren Lun*, quoted from Nakamura (1960), 288.

34. Nakamura (1960), 288–89.

35. Xiao Zong, *Treating All Three Doctrines Fairly* (San Jiao Ping Xin Lun), book A, quoting from *Taoism and Traditional Culture*, Editorial Board of *Cultural Knowledge* (1992), 39.

36. Cheng Chih-ming (1988), chapter 13. Also in Ching (1993), 218.

37. *Funk & Wagnalls Standard Dictionary*, Comprehensive International Edition (1970), 1272.

38. Berthrong (1994), 178.

39. Chen Yinke (1980), 196, quoting from Zhang (1992), 121.

40. Liang (1989), 528.

41. Alitto (1986), 337–38.

42. Jiang (1993).

43. For some insightful discussion, see Zheng (1995), 187–245.

44. This simile is attributed to Chang Shih, a colleague of Master Zhu Xi (Chu Hsi, 1130–1200). See de Bary (1988b), 306.

45. Holzman (1988), 244–50.

46. Zhang (1992), 123–24.

47. *Tao Te Ching*, 49.

48. See more discussion in chapter 7.

49. *Analects*, 2:12.

50. *Analects*, 18:8.

51. Bahm (1977), 54.

52. Cf. Chan (1963), 184–85.

53. *Zhuang Zi*, chapter 33.

54. *The Doctrine of the Mean*, XXX.

55. *The Book of Change*, Appended Remarks, 2:5. Zhuo (1991), 261.

56. For instance, Hajime Nakamura gave some very detailed examples of how sinified Buddhism was made in the process of being translated into Chinese. See Nakamura (1960), "Part III: The Ways of Thinking of the Chinese."

57. Hansen (1985), 492.

58. Zaehner (1968), 192.

59. While what Aristotle meant by "truth" may be debatable, when this saying is cited, people often mean by it the factual truth.

60. Cheng Chung-ying (1991), 194–95.

61. Berling (1980), 46–47.

62. Chiu (1984), 36, 371.

7. Justice

1. Huntington (1993), 49.

2. For different versions of democracy, see Macpherson (1972), where Macpherson writes, "Democracy has become an ambiguous thing, with different meanings—even apparently opposite meanings—for different people" (2).

3. Schumpeter (1947), 269.

4. Fukuyama (1995a), 7–14.

5. Domes (1989), 203. As a type of political system, Domes also includes in his definition of democracy "three basic rules," that is, people's sovereignty, division of powers, competitive elections. For the purpose in this book, I will focus on liberty, equality, and pluralism.

6. de Tocqueville (1954), 304.

7. Locke (1952), section 54.

8. de Tocqueville (1954), 282.

9. See King (1993), 110ff.

10. Let me say that, even though democracy can be understood in other ways, the issue of whether and how the value system characterized by individual liberty and equality exists in China still needs to be addressed.

11. Hsü (1975), 174–97. For a recent similar claim, see Huang and Wu (1994), 69–87, and Zhou (1984), 268.

12. Another Chinese philosopher who has been considered "democratic" was Huang Tsung-hsi (Huang Zongxi 黄宗羲, 1610–95). Huang's thought, however, was much closer to Mencius's "*min-pen*" than to democracy as defined here, and being a "deviation" from the traditional Confucianism, Huang did not have much influence in the society. See de Bary (1983).

13. *Mencius*, 7B:14.

14. Sun (1984), 70.

15. Liu (1992), 19.

16. Lin (1939), 206.

17. Levenson (1964), 12.

18. Hsü (1981), 412–13.

19. Liang (1990), 48.

20. Mou (1992), 128–32.

21. Ibid., 15.

22. Liu (1992), 17–40.

23. Quoted from Cui (1992), 562. My translation.

24. There are different branches and hence different attitudes in Buddhism. For the sake of brevity, I will confine my discussion to mainstream Buddhism.

25. For a lucid discussion of this issue, see Ni (1996).

26. Rosemont (1988).

27. Liang Rengong, *History of Pre-Qin Political Thoughts*, 147; original publication date and place are not available; quoted from Liang (1990), 248.

28. The correlate of this is that Confucian, and most Chinese, couples do not praise each other in front of others, no matter how happy they are with each other. On the contrary, they would speak of each other in front of people in a humble way. Westerners would probably see this as discourteous and disrespectful. If the couple is one and humility is a virtue as the Confucians believe, their way makes good sense. After all, one should only praise others, not oneself; and the spouse is not the *other*.

29. Feinberg (1970), 243–57.

30. *Analects*, 12:1.

31. Cf. Fung Yu-lan, *China's Road to Freedom* (新事论, *Xin Shi Lun*), chapter 4: On The Family and State, in Huang and Wu (1993), 270–80. Also Liang (1990), 19–24.

32. Today few Westerners will appreciate this kind of sacrifice, and in many regards this kind of sacrifice even appears no longer defensible. Nevertheless, facing a difficult situation like divorce, the Confucian husband and wife would be more likely to first ask the question "What about the children?" not "What about me?"

33. Graham (1989), 21.

34. *Analects*, 3:19.

35. For a discussion on this matter, see Chang (1989a), 142–49.

36. *Analects*, 13:19.

37. For a discussion of *yi*, see Cheng Chung-ying, "On *Yi* as a Universal Principle of Specific Application in Confucian Morality," Cheng (1991), 233–45.

38. *Mencius*, 3A:4. See Lau (1970), 102.

39. Munro (1969), 2.

40. de Bary (1988), 186.

41. For the lack of equality in Confucianism, also see Lin (1939), 186–89, under the title "Privilege and Equality."

42. *Analects*, 12:19.

43. *Mencius*, 3A:4.

44. Walzer (1981) made this point: "It is not only the case that the people have a procedural right to make the laws. On the democratic view, it is right that they make the laws—even if they make them wrongly" (386). In this article the tension Walzer drew between philosophy (the endeavor after the truth) and democracy (the principle of majority rule) is rather similar to the kind of tension I see between Confucianism and democracy: The Confucian believes in a right way—*the* right way—of doing things; and nobody, not even the majority, is entitled to do wrongly.

45. *Analects*, 3:14.

46. *Mencius*, 1A:6.

47. *Xun Zi*, chapters 6 and 7.

48. Liang (1990), 251, 242, 256.

49. Rosement (1991).

50. Chen Xu-jing (1995), 194.

51. Huntington (1991), 310.

52. For instance, Tu Wei-ming argues that in Confucianism values like filial piety should not be interpreted to the extreme. See Tu (1985).

53. MacIntyre (1991), 120.

54. Liu (1992), 259.

55. Ibid.

56. Ibid., 522–53.

57. In a recent article, Francis Fukuyama suggests that Confucianism is not so much resistant to democracy coming to China. But given the tension between democratic values and Confucian values, it is hard to imagine that Confucianism would readily welcome democracy. Confucian persons, embodied with values that may not be exclusively Confucian, could welcome democracy; but that would be for reasons other than Confucianism. See Fukuyama (1995b), 20–33.

58. de Bary (1969), 125–38.

Bibliography

Ackrill, J. L., trans. (1963). *Aristotle's Categories and De Interpretatione.* Oxford: Oxford University Press.

Alitto, Guy (1986). *The Last Confucian: Liang Shuming and the Chinese Modernity.* Berkeley: University of California Press.

Allen, Barry (1993). *Truth in Philosophy.* Cambridge: Harvard University Press.

Ames, Roger (1994). "The Focus-Field Self in Classical Confucianism." In Ames with Dissanayake and Kasulis (1994), 187–212.

Ames, Roger, with Wimal Dissanayake and Thomas P. Kasulis, eds. (1994). *Self as Person in Asian Theory and Practice.* Albany: State University of New York Press.

Aristotle (1966). *Aristotle's Metaphysics,* trans. Hippocrates G. Apostle. Bloomington: Indiana University Press.

Bahm, Archie J. (1977). *Comparative Philosophy: Western, Indian and Chinese Philosophies Compared.* Albuquerque, N.M.: World Books.

Belliotti, Raymond A. (1986). "Honor Thy Father and Thy Mother and To Thine Own Self Be True." *The Southern Journal of Philosophy* 24.2.

——— (1988). "Parents and Children: A Reply to Narveson." *The Southern Journal of Philosophy* 26.2.

Benesch, Walter (1997). *An Introduction to Comparative Philosophy: A Travel Guide to Philosophical Space.* New York: St. Martin's Press.

Benhabib, Seyla (1987). "The Generalized and the Concrete Other: The Kohlberg-Gilligan Controversy and Moral Theory," In Kittay and Meyers (1987), 154–77.

Berling, Judith (1980). *The Syncretic Religion of Lin Chao-en.* New York: Columbia University Press.

Berthrong, John (1994). *All under Heaven: Transformation Paradigms in Confucian-Christian Dialogue.* Albany: State University of New York Press.

217

Blakney, R. B., trans. (1955). *The Way of Life—Lao Tzu*. New York: Penguin Books.

Blum, Lawrence A. (1988). "Gilligan and Kohlberg: Implications for Moral Theory." *Ethics* 98: 472–91.

Blustein, Jeffrey (1982). *Parents and Children: The Ethics of the Family*. New York: Oxford University Press.

Boodberg, Peter A. (1953). "The Semasiology of Some Primary Confucian Concepts." *Philosophy East and West* 2.4.

Braden, Charles (1949). *These Also Believe*. New York: Macmillan.

Caputo, John (1971). "Heidegger's Original Ethics." *New Scholasticism* 45.1: 127–38.

——— (1989). "Thinking, Poetry and Pain." *Southern Journal of Philosophy* 28, Supplement.

——— (1993). *Against Ethics: Contributions to a Poetics of Obligation with Constant Reference to Deconstruction*. Bloomington and Indianapolis: Indiana University Press.

Card, Claudia, ed. (1991). *Feminist Ethics*. Lawrence: University Press of Kansas.

Chan, Wing-tsit (1963). *A Source Book in Chinese Philosophy*. Princeton, N.J.: Princeton University Press.

——— (1968). "The Historic Chinese Contribution to Religious Pluralism." In Jurji (1968).

Chang Tainien 张岱年 (1989a). *Studies of Chinese Ethical Theories* 中国伦理思想研究. Shanghai, China: Shanghai People's Publishing House.

——— (1989b). *Concepts and Categories in Chinese Ancient Philosophy* 中国古代哲学概念范畴要论. Beijing: China Social Science Publisher.

Chen Chi-yun (1992). "Rectification of Names in *Analects* and Confucius' Notion of Truth and Philosophy of Language" 论语正名与孔子的真理观和语言哲学. In *Chinese Studies* 汉学研究 10.2: 27–51.

Chen Ku-ying 陈鼓应 (1983). *A Contemporary Exposition and Interpretation of Zhuang Zi* 庄子今注今译. Beijing: China Books.

Chen Xu-jing 陈序经 (1995). *Out of the Orient (Zou Chu DongFang* 走出东方, a collection of Chen's articles published in the 1930s), ed. Yang Shen 杨深. Beijing: Chinese Broadcasting and TV Publishing House.

Chen Yinke (1980). "The Relation between Tao Yuanming's Thought and 'Clear Talk'" 陶渊明之思想与清谈之关系. (Chen's Essays, First Series). Shanghai: Shanghai Guji Publisher.

Cheng Chih-ming (1988). *Chinese Morality Books and Religion* 中国善书与宗教. Taipei: Student Book Store.

Cheng, Chu-yuan, ed. (1989). *Sun Yat-Sen's Doctrine in the Modern World*. Boulder, Colo., and London: Westview Press.

Cheng Chung-ying (1991). *New Dimensions of Confucian and Neo-*

Confucian Philosophy. Albany: State University of New York Press.

Chien Mu 钱穆 (1942). "Weekly Article." In *Da Gong Bao* 大公报. Chong Qing, November 1942, quoted from Liang Shu-ming (1990).

Ching, Julia (1993). *Chinese Religions*. Maryknoll, N.Y.: Orbis Books.

Ching, Julia, and Hans Küng (1989). *Christianity and Chinese Religions*. New York: Doubleday.

Chisholm, R. (1976). *Person and Object*. La Salle, Ill.: Open Court.

Chiu, Milton M. (1984). *The Tao of Chinese Religion*. New York: University Press of America.

Ciaffa, Jay (1987). "Toward an Understanding of Heidegger's Conception of the Inter-relation between Authentic and Inauthentic Existence." *Journal of British Society for Phenomenology* 18.1: 49–59.

Confucius (551–479 B.C.E.). *Analects* 论语. In Xie 谢冰莹 et al. (1987).

Creel, Herrlee G. (1953). *Chinese Thought from Confucius to Mao Tse-tung*. Chicago: University of Chicago Press.

Cui Dahua 崔大华 (1992). *Zhuang Zi Studies* 庄学研究. Beijing: People's Publishing House.

de Bary, Wm. Theodore, ed. (1969). *The Buddhist Tradition in India, China and Japan*. New York: Vintage.

——— (1983). *The Liberal Tradition in China*. Hong Kong: The Chinese University of Hong Kong, and New York: Columbia University Press.

——— (1986). "Human Rites: An Essay on Confucianism and Human Rights." In Eber (1986).

——— (1988a). "Neo-Confucianism and Human Rights." In Rouner (1988), 183–98.

——— (1988b). "Neoconfucianism as Traditional and Modern." In Larson and Deutsch (1988).

——— (1991). *The Trouble with Confucianism*. Cambridge: Harvard University Press.

della Cava, Marco R. (1994). "Nirvana in the '90s: Buddha Beckons the Material World." *USA-Today*, August 10, 1994, 1D.

Deng, Qiubo 邓球柏 (1993). *Commentary and Interpretation of Yi Jing* 白话易经: 附注释讲解. Changsha, China: Yuelu Publishers.

Deutsch, Eliot, ed. (1991). *Culture and Modernity: East-West Philosophic Perspective*. Honolulu: University of Hawaii Press.

Dewey, John (1953). *Reconstruction in Philosophy*, New York: Mentor.

Dixon, Nicholas (1995). "The Friendship Model of Filial Obligations." *Journal of Applied Philosophy* 12.1: 77–87.

Doctrine of the Mean (*Zhong Yong* 中庸). In Xie et al. (1987).

Domes, Jürgen (1989). "China's Modernization and the Doctrine of Democracy." In Cheng (1989).

Dong Zhongshu 董仲舒 (179–104 B.C.E.). *Luxuriant Gems of the Spring and Autumn Annuals (Chun Qiu Fan Lu / Ch'un Ch'iu Fan Lu* 春秋繁露). In *Twenty-Two Masters* (1985), 768–810.

Dreyfus, Hubert L. (1991). *Being-in-the-World*. Cambridge: MIT Press.

Dupré, John (1981). "Natural Kinds and Biological Taxa." *Philosophical Review* 90.1: 66–90.

Eber, Irene, ed. (1986). *Confucianism: Dynamics of a Tradition*. New York: Macmillan.

Eddington, Arthur (1958). *The Nature of the Physical World*. Ann Arbor: University of Michigan Press.

Editorial Board of *Cultural Knowledge* 文史知识编辑部, eds. (1992). *Taoism and Traditional Culture* 道教与传统文化. Beijing: China Books Publishers.

Elliston, Frederick (1978). "Heidegger's Phenomenology of Social Existence." In *Heidegger's Existential Analytic*. ed. F. Elliston. New York: Mouton Publishers.

———, ed. (1978). *Heidegger's Existential Analytic*. New York: Mouton Publishers.

English, Jane (1979). "What Do Grown Children Owe Their Parents?" In O'Neill and Ruddick (1979), 351–56.

Fairbank, John, ed. (1958). *Chinese Thought and Institutions*. Chicago: University of Chicago Press.

Fang, Litian 方立天 (1990). *A Developmental History of Chinese Ancient Philosophical Problems* 中国古代哲学问题发展史. Beijing: China Books.

Feinberg, Joel (1970). "The Nature and Value of Rights." *Journal of Value Inquiry* 4: 243–57.

Feng, Gia-Fu, and Jane English, trans. (1974). *Chuang Tzu: Inner Chapters*. New York: Vintage Books.

Field, Hartry (1973). "Theory Change and the Indeterminacy of Reference." *Journal of Philosophy* 70.14: 462–81.

Fingarette, Herbert (1972). "Confucius—The Secular as Sacred." New York: Harper Torchbooks.

Frede, Michael, and Gunther Patzig (1988). *Aristotle's "Metaphysics Z."* 2 vols. Munich: Verlag C. H. Beck.

Fukuyama, Francis (1989). "The End of History?" *National Interest* 16: 3–18.

——— (1995a). "The Primacy of Culture." *Journal of Democracy* 6.1 (January): 7–14.

——— (1995b). "Confucianism and Democracy." *Journal of Democracy* 6.2 (April): 20–33.

Fung Yu-lan 冯友兰 (Feng Yu-Lan, 1952). *A History of Chinese Philosophy*, vol. 1, trans. Derk Bodde. Princeton, N.J.: Princeton University Press.

—— (1953). *A History of Chinese Philosophy*, vol. 2, trans. Derk Bodde. Princeton, N.J.: Princeton University Press.

—— (1993). *Collected Works of Feng Yu-lan* 冯友兰集, ed. Huang Kejian and Wu Xiaolong. Beijing: Qunyan Publishing House.

Gilligan, Carol (1982). *In a Different Voice*. Cambridge: Harvard University Press.

Goldberg, Bruce (1971). "The Linguistic Expression of Feeling." *Amercian Philosophical Quarterly* 8.1: 86–92.

Graham, A. C., trans. (1981). *Chuang Tzu: The Inner Chapters*. London: George Allen & Unwin.

—— (1989). *Disputers of the Tao*. La Salle, Ill.: Open Court.

Gray J. G. (1965). "Martin Heidegger: On Anticipating My Own Death." *Personalist* 46.

Great Learning 大学. In Xie et al. (1987).

Guangming Daily's Special Commentator (1993–94). "Practice Is the Sole Criterion of Truth." *Chinese Studies in Philosophy* 25.2 (Winter).

Hall, David, and R. Ames (1987). *Thinking through Confucius*. Albany: State University of New York Press.

—— (1995). *Anticipating China: Thinking through the Narratives of Chinese and Western Culture*. Albany: State University of New York Press.

—— (1998). *Thinking from the Han: Self, Truth, and Transcendence in Chinese and Western Culture*. Albany: State University of New York Press.

Halper, Edward (1989). *One and Many in Aristotle's Metaphysics: The Central Books*. Columbus: Ohio State University Press.

Hanen, Marsha, and Kai Nielson, eds. (1987). *Science, Morality, and Feminist Theory*. Calgary, Alberta: University of Calgary Press.

Hansen, Chad (1985). "Chinese Language, Chinese Philosophy, and 'Truth'." *Journal of Asian Studies* 44.3: 491–519.

Harding, Sandra (1987). "The Curious Coincidence of Feminine and African Moralities: Challenges for Feminist Theory." In Kitty and Meyers (1987), 296–316.

Harrell, Stevan, and Huang Chun-chieh, eds. (1994). *Cultural Change in Postwar Taiwan*. Boulder, Colo.: Westview Press.

Hatab, Lawrence (1995). "Ethics and Finitude: Heideggerian Contributions to Moral Philosophy." *International Philosophical Quarterly* 35.4.

Hegel, G. W. F. (1929). *System Der Philosophie. Erster Teil. Die Logik*. Stuttgart: Fr. Frommanns Verlag (H. Kurtz).

Heidegger, Martin (1962). *Being and Time*, trans. John Macquarrie and Edward Robinson. New York: Harper & Row.

―――― (1982). *The Basic Problems of Phenomenology*, trans. Albert Hofstadter. Bloomington: Indiana University Press.

―――― (1977). *Basic Writings*, ed. David Farrell Krell. New York: Harper & Row.

Held, Virginia (1987a). "Non-contractual Society: A Feminist View." In Hanen and Nielson (1987).

―――― (1987b). "Feminism and Moral Theory." In Kittay, Feder, and Meyers (1987), 111–28.

――――, ed. (1995). *Justice and Care: Essential Readings in Feminist Ethics*. Boulder, Colo.: Westview Press.

Heller, Mark (1990). *The Ontology of Physical Objects: Four-Dimensional Hunks of Matter*. New York: Cambridge University Press.

Hennig, Willi (1979). *Phylogenetic Systematics*, trans. D. Dwight Davis and Rainer Zangerl. Urbana: University of Illinois Press.

Hick, John (1973). *God and the Universe of Faiths*. London and Basingstoke: Macmillian.

―――― (1989). *An Interpretation of Religion: Human Responses to the Transcendent*. New Haven, Conn.: Yale University Press.

―――― (1993). "A Religious Understanding of Religion: a model of the Relationship between Traditions." In J. Kellenberger (1993).

Ho Lin 贺麟 (1988). *Culture and Life* 文化与人生. Beijing: Commercial Publisher.

Hoagland, Sarah Lucia (1991). "Some Thoughts about 'Caring.'" In Card (1991), 246–63.

Holzman, Donald (1988). "Book Review on *Six Dynasties Poetry* by Kang-i Sun Chang." *Harvard Journal of Asian Studies* 48: 244–50.

Hsieh Yu-wei (1986). "Filial Piety and Chinese Society." In Moore (1986), 167–87.

Hsiung, Ann-Marie (1995). "Religious Experience in Taoism." *Asian Culture Quarterly* 23.3: 63–66.

Hsü, Leonard Shihlien (1975). *The Political Philosophy of Confucianism*. New York: Harper & Row.

Hsü Fu-kuan 徐复观 (1981). *Collected Articles—Continued*. Taipei: Time Culture Publishing Company.

Hu Fuming 胡福明 (1993–94). "Practice is the Criterion of Truth." *Chinese Studies in Philosophy* 25.2 (Winter).

Huang Chun-chieh, and Wu Kuang-ming (1994). "Taiwan and the Confucian Aspiration: Toward the Twenty-First Century." In Harrell and Huang (1994).

Huang Junlang 黄俊郎 (1992). "Sketching on *the Classic of Filial Piety* 孝经略说." In Lai and Huang (1992).

Huntington, Samuel P. (1991). *The Third Wave: Democratization in the Late Twentieth Century.* Norman: University of Oklahoma Press.

———— (1993). "The Clash of Civilizations." *Foreign Affairs* 72.3 (Summer): 22–49.

Jaggar, Alison (1983). *Feminist Politics and Human Nature.* Totowa, N.J.: Rowman & Allenheld.

Jecker, Nancy (1989). "Are Filial Duties Unfounded?" *American Philosophical Quarterly* 26.1: 73–80.

Jiang Jin 姜进 (1993). "Liang Shuming and the Emergence of 20th-Century New Confucianism." *Chinese Historians* 6.2: 1–26.

Johnson, Mark, and G. Lakoff (1980). *Metaphors We Live By.* Chicago: University of Chicago Press.

Jurji, Edward J., ed. (1968). *Religious Pluralism and World Community.* Leiden, Netherlands: E. J. Brill.

Kellenberger, J., ed. (1993). *Inter-Religious Models and Criteria.* New York: St. Martin's Press.

King, Ambrose Y. C. 金耀基 (1993). *Chinese Society and Culture* 中国社会与文化. Hong Kong: Oxford University Press.

Kitcher, Philip (1984). "Species." *Philosophy of Science* 51: 308–33.

Kittay, Eva Feder, and Diana T. Meyers, eds. (1987). *Women and Moral Theory.* Totowa, N.J.: Rowman & Littlefield.

Kripke, Saul. (1980). *Naming and Necessity.* Cambridge: Harvard University Press.

Küng, Hans, and Julia Ching. (1989). *Christianity and Chinese Religions.* New York: Doubleday.

Lai, Whalen. (1991). "In Defence of Graded Love." *Asian Philosophy* 1.1: 51–60.

Lai Yanyuan 赖炎元, and Huang Junlang 黄俊郎. (1992). *Reading the Classic of Filial Piety: New Interpretation* 新译孝经读本. Taipei: Sanmin Books.

Lakoff, George, and M. Johnson. (1980). *Metaphors We Live By.* Chicago: University of Chicago Press.

Larson, G., and E. Deutsch, eds. (1988). *Interpreting Across Boundaries: New Essays in Comparative Philosophy.* Princeton, N.J.: Princeton University Press.

Lau, D. C., trans. (1970). *Mencius.* Baltimore: Penguin Books.

Lenk, Hans, and Gregor Paul, eds. (1993). *Epistemological Issues in Classical Chinese Philosophy.* Albany: State University of New York Press.

Levenson, Joseph R. (1965, 1964, 1968). *Confucian China and Its Modern Fate: A Trilogy.* 3 vols. Berkeley and Los Angeles: University of California Press.

Li Chenyang (1995). "Fung Yu-lan." In McGreal (1995), 148–52.

Liang Shu-ming 梁漱溟 (1989). *Collected Works of Liang Shu-ming* 梁漱溟全集. Vol. 1. Jinan, China: Shandong People's Publishing House.

——— (1990). *Collected Works of Liang Shu-ming* 梁漱溟全集. Vol. 3. Jinan, China: Shandong People's Publishing House.

Lin Yutang (1931). "On Growing Old Gracefully." In Sommers and Sommers (1993).

——— (1939). *My Country and My People.* New York: John Day.

Liu, Shu-hsien 刘述先 (1992). *Confucianism and Modernization* 儒家思想与现代化, ed. Jing Hai-Feng 景海峰. Beijing: Chinese Broadcasting and TV Publishing House.

——— (1995). "Reflections on World Peace through Peace among Religions—A Confucian Perspective." *Journal of Chinese Philosophy* 22: 193–213.

Lo Ping Cheung 罗秉祥 (1993). "Philosophical Reflections on Filial Morality 孝之哲学反省." *Legein Monthly* 鹅湖月刊 218: 38–41.

Locke, John (1905). *An Essay Concerning Human Understanding.* La Salle, Ill.: Open Court.

——— (1952). *The Second Treatise of Government.* New York: Liberal Arts Press.

London Review of Books (1980). Quoted from the backcover of S. Kripke's *Naming and Necessity.* Cambridge: Harvard University Press.

Loux, Michael (1991). *Primary Ousia: An Essay on Aristotle's Metaphysics Z and H.* Ithaca, N.Y.: Cornell University Press.

MacIntyre, Alasdair (1984). *After Virtue.* 2nd ed. Notre Dame, Ind.: University of Notre Dame Press.

——— (1991). "Incommensurability, Truth, and the Conversation between Confucians and Aristotelians about the Virtues." In Deutsch (1991).

Macpherson, C. B. (1972). *The Real World of Democracy.* New York: Oxford University Press.

Mair, Victor H., trans. (1994). *Wandering on the Way: Early Taoist Tales and Parables of Chuang Tzu.* New York: Bantam Books.

Martinich, A. P., ed. (1985). *The Philosophy of Language.* New York: Oxford University Press.

McGreal, Ian P., ed. (1995). *Great Thinkers of the Eastern World.* New York: HarperCollins.

Mencius (371–289 B.C.E.?). *Mencius* 孟子. In Xie 谢冰莹 et al. (1987).

Mo Zi 墨子 (fl. 479–438). *Mo Zi.* In *Twenty-Two Masters* (1985).

Moore, Charles, ed. (1986). *The Chinese Mind: Essentials of Chinese Philosophy and Culture.* Honolulu: University of Hawaii Press.

Mou Tsung-san 牟宗三 (1992). *Reconstruction of Moral Idealism* 道德理想主义的重建, ed. Zheng Jiadong 郑家栋. Beijing: China Broadcasting and TV Publishing House.

Munro, Donald J. (1969). *The Concept of Man in Early China.* Stanford, Calif.: Stanford University Press.

Nakamura, Hajime (1960). *The Ways of Thinking of Eastern Peoples.* Tokyo: Japanese National Commission for UNESCO.

Narveson, Jan (1987). "On Honoring Our Parents." *The Southern Journal of Philosophy* 25.1.

Nelson, Lynn Hankinson (1990). *Who Knows: From Quine to a Feminist Empiricism.* Philadelphia: Temple University Press.

Ni Peimin 倪培民 (1996). "The Taoist Concept of Freedom." In Shanahan and Wang (1996).

Noddings, Nel (1984). *Caring: A Feminine Approach to Ethics and Moral Education.* Berkeley and Los Angeles: University of California Press.

Obenchain, Diane B. (1994). "Spiritual Quests of Twentieth-Century Women: A Theory of Self-Discovery and a Japanese Case Study." In Ames with Dissanayake and Kasulis (1994).

O'Neill, Onora, and William Ruddick, eds. (1979). *Having Children.* New York: Oxford University Press.

Owens, Joseph (1963). *The Doctrine of Being in the Aristotelian "Metaphysics."* Toronto: Pontifical Institute of Medieval Studies.

Paper, Jordan (1995). *The Spirits Are Drunk: Comparative Approaches to Chinese Religion.* Albany: State University of New York Press.

Parkes, Graham, ed. (1987). *Heidegger and Asian Thought.* Honolulu: University of Hawaii Press.

People's Daily 人民日报 (Chinese overseas edition) (1993). Beijing, August 25.

Pine, Ronald C. (1989). *Science and the Human Prospect.* Belmont, Calif.: Wadsworth.

Putnam, Hilary (1973). "Meaning and Reference." *Journal of Philosophy* 70.19: 699–711.

Queen, Sarah A. (1996). *From Chronicle to Canon: The Hermeneutics of the "Spring and Autumn," According to Tung Chung-shu.* New York: Cambridge University Press.

Quine, W. V. (1977). "Natural Kinds." In Schwartz (1977), 155–75.

Radhakrishnan, S., and C. Moore, eds. (1957). *A Sourcebook in Indian Philosophy.* Princeton, N.J.: Princeton University Press.

Rawls, John (1980). "Kantian Constructivism in Moral Theory: The John Dewey Lectures 1980." *Journal of Philosophy* 77.

Ren Ji-yu 任继愈 (1992). "The Taoist and Taoist Religion" 道家与道教. In *Taoism and Traditional Culture,* ed. the Editorial Board of Cultural Knowledge. Beijing: China Books.

Richardson, William, S. J. (1967). "Heidegger and the Quest of Freedom." *Theological Studies* 28.

Roetz, Heifer (1993). "Validity in Chou Thought: On Chad Hansen and the Pragmatic Turn in Sinology." In Lenk and Paul (1993).

Rosemont, Henry Jr. (1988). "Why Take Rights Seriously: A Confucian Critique." In Rouner (1988), 167–82.

——— (1991). *A Chinese Mirror: Moral Reflections on Political Economy and Society.* La Salle, Ill.: Open Court.

Rouner, Leroy S., ed. (1988). *Human Rights and the World's Religions.* Notre Dame, Ind.: University of Notre Dame Press.

Russell, Bertrand (1919). "Descriptions." In Martinich (1985).

——— (1922). *The Problem of China.* London: George Allen & Unwin.

Sartre, Jean-Paul (1946). "Existentialism Is a Humanism." In Solomon (1992).

Schumpeter, Joseph A. (1947). *Capitalism, Socialism, and Democracy.* 2nd ed. New York: Harper.

Schwartz, S. P., ed. (1977). *Naming, Necessity, and Natural Kinds.* Ithaca, N.Y.: Cornell University Press.

Shanahan, Timothy, and Robin Wang (1996). *Reason and Insight: Western and Eastern Perspectives on the Pursuit of Moral Wisdom.* Belmont, Calif.: Wadsworth.

Sharma, Arvind, ed. (1993). *Our Religions.* New York: HarperCollins.

Simmons, A. John (1979). *Moral Principles and Political Obligations.* Princeton, N.J.: Princeton University Press.

Slote, Michael (1979). "Obedience and Illusion." In O'Neill and Ruddick (1979), 319–25.

Smith, Huston (1980). "Western and Comparative Perspectives on Truth." *Philosophy East and West* 30.4: 423–37.

Solomon, Robert C., ed. (1992). *Morality and the Good Life.* 2nd ed. New York: McGraw-Hill.

Sommers, Christina H. (1986). "Filial Morality." *The Journal of Philosophy* 83.8: 439–56. Reprinted in Kittay and Meyers (1987), 69–84.

Sommers, Christina, and Fred Sommers, eds. (1993). *Vice & Virtue in Everyday Life: Introductory Readings in Ethics.* 3rd ed. New York: Harcourt Bruce Jovanovich.

Suggs, M. Jack, K. D. Sakenfeld, and J. R. Mueller (1992). *The Oxford Study Bible: Revised English Bible with the Apocrypha.* New York: Oxford University Press.

Sun Yat-sen 孙逸仙 (1984). *The Teachings of the Nation-Founding Father* 国父遗教. Taiwan: Cultural Book.

Tang Chün-i 唐君毅 (1953). *The Spiritual Value of Chinese Culture* 中国文化之精神价值. Taipei: Zhongzheng Books.

Tao, Chia-lin Pao 鲍家麟 (1987). "The Idea of Yin-yang and Women's Status in China 阴阳学说与妇女地位." *Chinese Studies* 汉学研究. 5.2: 501–12.

Taylor, Rodney, L. (1990). *The Religious Dimensions of Confucianism.* Albany: State University of New York Press.

Teruo, Takeuchi (1965). "A Study of the Meaning of Jen Advocated by Confucius." *Acta Asiatic* 9: 57–77.

Thompson, Laurence G. (1996). *Chinese Religion: An Introduction,* 5th ed. Belmont, Calif.: Wadsworth.

Tocqueville, A. de (1954). *Democracy in America,* vol. 2. New York: Vintage Books.

Tong, Lik Kuen 唐力权 (1973). "Confucian Jen and Platonic Eros: A Comparative Study." *Chinese Culture* 中国文化 14.3: 1–8.

Tronto, Joan C. (1987). "Beyond Gender Difference to a Theory of Care." *Sign: Journal of Women in Culture and Society* 12.4: 644–63.

Tu Wei-ming (1968). "The Creative Tension between *Jen* and *Li,*" *Philosophy East and West* 18.1–2: 29–39.

—— (1981). "Jen as a Living Metaphor in the Confucian *Analects.*" *Philosophy East and West* 31.1: 45–54.

—— (1985). *Confucian Thought: Self As Creative Transformation.* Albany: State University of New York Press.

—— (1986). "Towards a Third Epoch of Confucian Humanism." In Tu (1993a), 141–59. Originally in Eber (1986).

—— (1989). *Centrality and Commonality: An Essay on Confucian Religiousness.* Albany: State University of New York Press.

—— (1993a). *Way, Learning, and Politics: Essays on the Confucian Intellectual.* Albany: State University of New York Press.

—— (1993b). "Embodying the Universe: A Note on Confucian Self-Realization." In Ames, with Dissanayake and Kasulis (1993).

—— (1993c). "Confucianism." In Arvind Sharma (1993).

Tung Fang-suo 东方朔 (1994). "The Meaning of the Word Truth 论诚的意义在先秦儒家思想中的生成与显发." *Journal of Confucius-Mencius Society* 孔孟学报 68.

Twenty-two Masters (1985). *Twenty-two Masters* 二十二子. Shanghai: Shanghai Classics Publisher 上海古籍出版社.

Versenyi, Laszlo (1965). *Heidegger, Being, and Truth.* New Haven and London: Yale University Press.

Vogel, Lawrence (1994). *The Fragile "We": Ethical Implications of Heidegger's "Being and Time".* Evanston, Ill.: Northwestern University Press.

Waley, Arthur (1989). *Analects of Confucius.* New York: Random House.

Walzer, Michael (1981). "Philosophy and Democracy." *Political Theory* 9.3 (August): 379–99.

Wang Li 王力, ed. (1981). *Ancient Chinese* 古代汉语. Rev. ed. Beijing: China Books 中华书局.

Wang, Xianqian 王先谦, ed. (1988). *Xun Zi Ji Jie* 荀子集解. Beijing: China Books 中华书局.

228 *Bibliography*

Wang, Yang-ming 王阳明 (1970). *Collected Works of Wang Yang-ming* 王阳明全集. Taipei: Wenyou Bookstore.
Welch, Holmes (1966). *Taoism: The Parting of the Way*. Boston: Beacon Press.
Wiggins, David (1980). *Sameness and Substance*. Cambridge: Harvard University Press.
Wilkerson, T. E. (1993). "Species, Essence, and the Names of Natural Kinds." *Philosophical Quarterly* 43: 170, 1–19.
Wilson, Mark (1982). "Predicate Meets Property." *Philosophical Review* 91.4: 549–89.
Wolf, Margery (1994). "Beyond the Patrilineal Self: Constructing Gender in China." In Ames with Dissanayake and Kasulis (1994), 251–70.
Wright, Arthur F. (1959). *Buddhism in Chinese History*. Stanford, Calif.: Stanford University Press.
Xie, Bingying 谢冰莹, et al. (1987). *Readings of the Four Books* 四书读本. Taipei: Sanmin Books.
Xun Zi 荀子. (fl. 298–238 B.C.). (1992). *Interpretations of the Collected Work of Xun Zi* 荀子集解, ed. Wang Xianqian 王先谦. Beijing: China Books.
Yang, Lien-sheng (1958). "The Concept of *Pao* as a Basis for Social Relations in China." In Fairbank (1958).
Zaehner, R. C. (1968). *Hinduism*. Oxford: Oxford University Press.
Zhang Cheng (1993–94). "There is Only One Criterion." *Chinese Studies in Philosophy* 25.2 (Winter).
Zhang Longxi (1992). *The Tao and the Logos: Literary Hermeneutics, East and West*. Durham, N.C.: Duke University Press.
Zheng Jiadong 郑家栋 (1995). "The Religiousness of Confucian Thought" 儒家思想的宗教性问题. In Zheng Jiadong and Ye Haiyan (1995), 187–245.
Zheng Jiadong and Ye Haiyan 叶海烟, eds. (1995). *New-Confucianism Forum* 新儒家评论. vol. 2. Beijing: China Broadcasting and TV Publishing House.
Zhou Yangshan 周阳山, ed. (1984). *Reconstructing the Traditional Culture* 文化传统的重建. Taipei: Shibao Publishing Co.
Zhou, Zhenfu 周振甫 (1991). *Interpreations and Commentary of the Yijing* 易经译注. Beijing: China Books 中华书局

Zukav, Gary (1979). *The Dancing Wu Li Masters: An Overview of the New Physics*. New York: Bantam Books.

Index

Abortion, 202 n. 10
Ames, Roger, 4, 60, 93
Analects, 41, 63, 65, 96, 100, 109–110, 127
Aretē, 51
Aristotle, 2, 5, 13–24, 26–27, 29–30, 33, 77, 155, 159
Atman, 31–33
Authenticity; authentic, 46–48, 51–53, 55–56, 100; authentic and inauthentic, 53

Bahm, Archie J., 157
Bao-pu Zi 抱朴子 (*Pao-pu Tzu*), 151
Being, 2, 11, 12, 13, 27, 29–31, 33, 41, 44–45, 51–52, 58–59, 91, 148; being as identity, 11–12; being *qua* being, 14
Belliotti, Raymond, 119–122, 130
Benesch, Walter, 195 n. 38
Berthrong, John, 141, 151–152
Bhagavad Gita, 31
Bible, 141, 208 n. 46
Blustein, Jeffrey, 124–126, 135, 138
Boodberg, Peter, 96
Book of Change 易经, 30, 55
Book of Rites 礼记, 72, 128, 133
Brahman, 31–32, 140
Buddhism; Buddhist, 5, 139, 141–142, 146–155, 157–160, 171, 173, 180–181, 186–187; Pure Land, 150

Caputo, John, 45
Care; caring, 4, 50, 56, 89–90, 92, 96, 98–101, 103–108, 144; caring about, 97–99, 102; caring for, 45, 97; ideal of, 96, 100; care perspective, 101; with gradations, 105, 108. *See also* ethics
Chan, Wing-tsit, x, 31, 70
Chang Tainien 张岱年, 41
Chen Chi-yun, 86
Chen Xu-jing 陈序经, 182
Chen Yinke 陈寅恪, 152
Cheng 诚, 41–44, 48–50, 52–55, 57, 60; as sincerity, 41, 43
Cheng Chung-ying, 67, 160
Chiang Kai-shek, 176
Chien Mu 钱穆, 127
Chisholm, Roderick, 90–91, 95
Christianity; Christian, 128, 139, 144, 155–156, 160–161, 171, 177, 187
Classic of Filial Morality 孝经, 127–128, 130, 133
Comparative philosophy, 5–6, 9; as bridge-building, 5–6; primary goal of, 5
Confucian(s), 31, 41–45, 47–50, 52–53, 56–62, 66–68, 72–76, 85–87, 89–90, 92–96, 99–102, 105, 107–108, 114, 123, 126–128, 130–136, 138, 142–150, 152–158, 161, 163, 171–181, 183, 185–188; Neo-